THE
RAILWAY
GAME

THE RAILWAY GAME

A STUDY IN SOCIO-
TECHNOLOGICAL OBSOLESCENCE

J. LUKASIEWICZ

McCLELLAND AND STEWART LIMITED

Cover art courtesy Canadian National

The Canadian Publishers
McCelland and Stewart Limited
25 Hollinger Raod
Toronto, Ontario

Printed and bound in Canada

Carleton

Contemporaries

A series of books designed to stimulate
informed discussion of current and
controversial issues in Canada, and to
improve the two-way flow of ideas
between people and government.

ISSUED UNDER THE EDITORIAL
SUPERVISION OF THE INSTITUTE OF
CANADIAN STUDIES, CARLETON
UNIVERSITY, OTTAWA.
DIRECTOR OF THE INSTITUTE
A.D. DUNTON

CONTENTS

LIST OF FIGURES

LIST OF TABLES

FOREWORD

. . . . blockaded and imprisoned by Ice and Apathy, we have at least ample time for reflection – and if there be comfort in Philosophy may we not profitably consider the PHILOSOPHY OF RAILROADS (Keefer, 1972, p. 3).*

The time has indeed been more than ample: over 125 years have elapsed since Thomas Coltrin Keefer (1821-1914) introduced his popular and influential 1849 essay in which he explained the significance of railway technology and advocated its development in Canada (Keefer, 1972). In the succeeding years a vast network of railways has been constructed, with more track per capita in Canada than in any other country (two miles per thousand people in 1970, twice as much as in the U.S. and over four times more than in West Germany). But understanding railway transportation and technology has not made such strides. Although between 1917 and 1961 four major investigations by Royal Commissions were completed,** railway transportation in Canada continues to be plagued with problems whose origins reach to the early years of railroading.

There has been, therefore, a strong incentive to look into the railway problem in Canada (and, more generally, in North America), to analyse it in specific terms and thus promote its appreciation. In broader perspective, such study has offered the opportunity to examine an interesting and significant case of society-technology interaction typical of industrialized societies, a phenomenon whose impact is difficult to predict and control. Coincidentally, the study of railways in North America has appeared timely for a number of reasons (as discussed more extensively in Chapter 16).

*Sources and references are listed alphabetically and chronologically by senior author and year under References, p. 283.

**The schedule of investigating transportation in Canada every 15 years (on the average, since 1917) has been maintained with the initiation, in 1974, by the Minister of Transport of a broad review of transportation policy (Transport Canada, 1975, 1975a, b, c).

First, over the next decade, it has been predicted that the volume of freight traffic will increase considerably, to the extent that – in Canada at least – the capacity of the existing railway network will become grossly inadequate. According to CN President Bandeen (1974), "The point has now been reached where we have just about extended capacity to the limit of the present plant, and what is needed now is a major building program almost as large in scope as the original building of the transcontinental railway." Railways will have to expand and modernize, and will need large amounts of capital; to provide it, new methods of railway financing will have to be developed.

Secondly, because of the diminishing availability of cheap oil, and general difficulties in meeting the energy demand, transportation in North America – now totally dependent on oil – will have to become more energy-efficient, and will have to switch to other energy sources such as electricity, which can be generated from any kind of fuel. On both counts, the shift of most of the intercity traffic to modern, electric railway provides the desirable alternative.

Another aspect of interest concerns the transfer of technology. Since World War II, the United States has been in the forefront of "high technology" innovation. And yet, surprisingly, modernization of some of the older technologies is being accomplished in Western Europe and Japan, with no U.S. participation, and imported to North America. This is true of both the small automobile and of the railways.

On the North American continent, there is little awareness of the vigorous renaissance the railways of Western Europe and Japan have been undergoing for the past ten or more years. In fact, Canada and the U.S. maintain today the most extensive, but also – in some respects – most highly obsolete and inefficient railway systems, which are not able to compete effectively with the newer transportation modes. The task that Keefer set for himself – "to disseminate popular information upon a too unpopular subject, and turn a portion of that earnest and eager covetousness of foreign prosperity back upon our own neglected resources" (Keefer, 1972, p. 4-5) – has yet to be accomplished.

The attitude of the North American public, the governments, the regulatory agencies, the railway companies, the politicians, the transportation specialists and the information media to-

wards railways tends to be either sentimental and naively optimistic, or conservative and negative;* it is divorced from the
technological and economic realities of modern railway transportation.

There are the diminishing ranks of train buffs and romantic
admirers of railways, for whom a curious mystique still sur-
rounds the locomotives, the trains and stations, and the traditional operations. The sights and sounds of a steam railroad, the
memories of relaxed or even luxurious travel, are all part of this
nostalgic image.

There are also those for whom the railways continue to sym-
bolize national pride and achievement. Such feelings and attitudes are very much evident in Berton's history of the CPR
(Berton, 1970, 1971a, 1974) and in his article "What We Once
Did We Can Do Again" (Berton, 1971b), written on the occasion of publication of *The Last Spike* (the second volume of
CPR's history by Berton). Another recent history of Canadian
railways by Legget (1973) ends on an equally proud note:
"[Railways'] great traditions and century-old record of fine service provide a firm basis for their further development as a vital
part of the transportation network of this second largest country
in the world."

But for a large number of people the railways have been a
source of continuing disappointment. To these people, the railways – chronically bankrupt and neglected, decrepit enterprises – represent monuments to corporate arrogance and bureaucratic ineptness, a technology with no development potential, best to be forgotten.

Occasionally, an overly optimistic note is sounded, as in an
editorial in *The Ottawa Journal* of June 7, 1973, which has thus
evaluated the performance of the "people's railway" in 1972:

> The CNR has come a long way since it used to be the butt
> of snide jokes about the inability of publicly-owned cor-
> porations to be anything but a drain on taxpayers' dollars.
> . . . In addition to contributing to rather than detracting
> from the national wealth, CN is to be congratulated for its
> imaginative efforts to keep rail passenger service alive and
> competitive with airlines and buses.

Actually, in 1972, CN received $40.7 million in government

* As discussed by Nelles (Keefer, 1972, p. ix et seq.)

subsidies (under the 1967 National Transportation Act), an increase of $9.7 million or 24% over the 1971 figure. The number of revenue passengers decreased by 10%, and the revenue passenger miles by 6%. On the prime Toronto-Montreal passenger run, only 72% of CN's trains arrived with less than 6 minutes delay (only 50% during the four winter months). Two-thirds of CN's transcontinental trains were late; in the worst two week period, the average delay was 12 hours. In 1972, the number of derailments in Canada was three times that in 1959, and nearly double that in 1969.

More surprisingly, there are even professionals who view Canadian railways, indeed transportation in general, in rosy colours. In the definitive study *Canadian Transportation Economics* (1967), A. W. Currie, while noting that "throughout our transportation history we have not been able to resolve the conflict between preserving private enterprise and using public funds to carry out national objectives" nevertheless states that "we have always been supplied with safe, efficient, and low cost service." One finds little support for this assertion in Currie's extensive text.

A 1973 assessment by the faculty of engineering of a prominent Ontario university provides another example of unwarranted – in the light of the information presented in this study – optimism.

> The rail industry . . . is viewed by many as ancient and archaic, but Canadian railways are rapidly introducing new equipment and new attitudes. The Canadian rail industry is rapidly gaining recognition throughout North America. They are making money! The effort devoted to research and development places them at the forefront of their technology. The tonnages moved are increasing rapidly. The industry is growing again after overcoming severe problems.

On the whole, the professional and bureaucratic view of the railway situation in Canada is characterized by deep conservatism, as demonstrated in the course of recent panel discussions on surface transportation (Khan, 1975). It was only the foreign speakers who discussed specific data and progress. The representatives of Canadian railways, government and regulatory agencies, all seemed to say that "the situation is not as bad as it seems, but in any event, it couldn't have been any different and cannot be changed significantly."

Regrettably, such emotional or unsubstantiated perceptions are irrelevant to the understanding of railways today. The existing literature on Canadian railways is of not much help either: it is neither very extensive, nor is it concerned, for the most part, with a critical appraisal. Most of the works, whether dealing with the history of railway development (e.g. Berton, 1970, 1971a, 1974; Currie, 1957; Glazebrook, 1938; Legget, 1973; Skelton, 1916; Stevens, 1960, 1962, 1973) or with the economic aspects (e.g. Currie, 1967; Innis, 1971) can be characterized as chronological narratives, sometimes rich in circumstantial detail but lacking in critical judgement, comparative evaluation, discussion of alternatives and specific data.* Typically, although much of the text is often devoted to the description of the growth of railway network, in no book (with one exception: Skelton, 1916) will one find accurate maps which would show – at a glance – how railway lines and traffic have been developing in Canada; in several books, (Innis, 1971; McDougall, 1968; Stevens, 1973; Thompson and Edgar, 1973) not a single map is included. What appears to be missing – but what is required to gain a realistic appreciation of railways in Canada today – is a rational analysis based on specific information and evaluation of railway technology and operations here and abroad – a task that this study attempts to broach.

Inevitably, such evaluation will appear critical of the numerous institutions and organizations involved. But the reader should keep in mind that the purpose of the analysis is not to lay the blame but to demonstrate the various deficiencies of the railway transportation system and thus enhance the reforms which are long overdue.

I trust that, when so viewed *The Railway Game* will emerge as a constructive study in the eyes of the readers, and especially of the actors of today's railway scene in Canada. Those actors – the regulatory and other agencies of the government, the rail-

---

*The work of an American, L. T. Fournier (1935), Professor of Economics at Princeton University, *Railway nationalization in Canada*, is an exception. It contains much critical evaluation and suggests remedies. To a lesser extent, this is also true of *Transport Competition and Public Policy in Canada* by H. L. Purdy (1972). Extensive information which does not go beyond the 1950s is to be found in the reports of several official investigations (Canada, 1917; 1932; 1951; 1961).

way companies, the labour unions, the industry – should not be held responsible for faithfully following the regulations and laws which have become grossly inadequate and obsolete.

Although this investigation should be of interest to the general public, I have not refrained from reinforcing the text with the "hard" data presented as graphs and tables. As noted in Chapter 25, we can no longer afford to rely on rhetoric to achieve understanding of contemporary socio-technological complexities, and we should get used to interpreting – everyone for himself – the information which in the past was exclusively the domain of experts, "learned" books and specialized journals.

What I am advocating here is not new: many paperbacks published in recent years have included much "hard" data, have been widely read by the general public as well as by the specialists, and have increased our awareness and understanding of complex phenomena* – a function I hope this paperback fulfills in the field of railway transportation in North America, and particularly in Canada.

J.L.
Ottawa, December, 1975.

* The controversial and internationally popular 1972 study *Limits to Growth* by M.I.T.'s Meadow's group (Meadows et al., 1972) is a foremost example of this type of publication.

ACKNOWLEDGEMENTS

This work grew out of my interest in various aspects of technological impact, an area of research which received support and encouragement from several directions. Carleton University has been sponsoring, since 1971, the development of interdisciplinary courses in Technology, Society and the Environment. Carleton's Norman Paterson School of International Affairs has been engaged, since 1974, in the investigation of international aspects of science and technology. Professor Davidson Dunton, Director of the Institute of Canadian Studies, and Professor Donald A. George, both of Carleton University, encouraged me to prepare a manuscript for publication. Results of research funded by the National Research Council of Canada, the Federal Departments of Energy, Mines and Resources and of the Industry, Trade and Commerce have contributed to this study. It is a pleasure to thank all of the individuals and organizations who have made the preparation and publication of this book possible. I am also grateful to the Canadian National, the Canadian Pacific, the Canadian Transport Commission, the U.S. Federal Railroad Administration and the National Railroad Passenger Corporation (AMTRAK) for their co-operation in obtaining information essential to this study, and to Messrs. F. Nouvion, Technical Director, Traction-Export, Paris (formerly Chief Traction Research Engineer, French Railways) and Mr. Y. Machefert-Tassin, Société MET, for information on railway developments in France and many valuable comments. Mr. Alfred Leeson provided me with valuable insights into practical aspects of railway operations. My sons Mark and Peter helped with correcting the manuscripts and proofs. I am greatly indebted to them and to many others who have assisted with this study.

INTRODUCTION

From the very beginning of railway development in Canada the government, realizing that without substantial subsidies the construction of railways could not attract private capital, proceeded to supply generous amounts of help from the public purse. At the same time, railway operation was left to profit-oriented private enterprise, and was expected to be governed by free-market competition. However, with the railroad virtually monopolizing overland transportation, tariff regulation became both a necessity and an effective political tool. The policies of subsidization, competition and regulation were often incompatible with profitable operation: subsidized and politically-motivated competition caused a proliferation of lines and a dilution of traffic below profitable levels, while tariff regulation restricted revenues. The inherently contradictory policies came to a head in 1923 when over one-half of the Canadian rail system was bankrupt and became nationalized – but the competition was maintained with one privately-owned (Canadian Pacific) and one publicly-owned (Canadian National) system. In the fourth decade of this century, as competitive modes of transportation developed, the railroad lost the attribute of a "natural monopoly." The truck, the passenger car, the bus, the airplane and the pipeline provided superior service and, although regulated, were furnished with very adequately developed, publicly-owned and maintained infrastructures, and benefited from generously funded research and development. Not so the railways: burdened with the costs of privately-owned 'ways' and extensively regulated, not allowed to amalgamate, deprived of government-funded research and development support, producing a small or negative return on investment, they had little possibility and incentive to modernize and combat competition. What has resulted over the years is *a highly unbalanced* transportation system with overemphasis on highways and airways, and a neglect of railroads, which often operate with old equipment on poor quality track and use obsolete facilities and operational procedures. Under the present "rules of

1

the game," which continue to emphasize intra-modal competition and profitability, railway modernization in Canada cannot take place. Government subsidies merely compensate for operational losses and – while sustaining unprofitable operations – inadvertently contribute to the preservation of obsolescence. They do not provide the capital necessary to modernize the railways – and neither does the private sector, which naturally invests in more profitable enterprises.

The situation of the majority of the U.S. railroads is quite similar. Just as in Canada, the profitability of the American railroading has been – on the average – decreasing, while the track and other facilities have been deteriorating. A crisis was reached in 1970 when the newly established (in 1968) Penn Central system announced bankruptcy (the largest in the history of the United States). The Penn Central was soon joined by seven other bankrupt railways in the northeast, and, in 1973, the Congress established the U.S. Railway Association, a government corporation created to reorganize the bankrupt lines. Two years earlier, the U.S. government has taken over the passenger rail operations through creation of AMTRAK. In spite of the professed adherence of both the American government and the public to the virtues and effectiveness of profit motivation, more and more railway operations in the U.S. are being managed and subsidized by the government.

The above is a very general view of the situation of railways in North America. Although it does not necessarily reflect the conventional wisdom, it is based on extensive evidence presented in Parts One and Two of this study.

Part One gives a brief account of the development of railways in Canada since 1850, establishes the fundamental characteristics of the Canadian railway system as it exists today and explains the origins of its basic deficiencies. In Part Two, Canadian railways are evaluated in terms of current developments abroad and the quality of service which they offer; their regulation and subsidization are also examined.

The evidence presented in Parts One and Two provides the basis for suggesting in Part Three desirable remedies and alternatives. They cover a wide spectrum of aspects, from organization and financing of railways to rationalization, technical modernization, management of energy resources and development of a long range policy.

As would be expected, comprehensive examination of railway transportation brings to light important issues which reach beyond the transportation scene. These issues – the questions of institutionalization of obsolescence and of inadequacies of traditional political process and journalism – are discussed in the Postscript.

The background materials are assembled in two appendices which follow the text. Appendix One contains schematic maps of railway lines in Canada. The maps indicate the chronology of railway construction and distribution of traffic (in 1970). In Appendix Two, typical reports on passenger rail services in Canada, the U.S. and France are collected.

Readers not familiar with railway and transportation terminology will find useful a short glossary of definitions and abbreviations. A list of references and a comprehensive index conclude the text.

The material presented in this study is complemented by a folio of photographs which illustrate various aspects of railway operations in North America, Europe and Japan.

PART ONE
THE ORIGINS OF THE MALAISE

A realistic evaluation of railway transportation in Canada today requires a clear understanding of the forces which, over a period of more than a century, were responsible for the evolution of the Canadian railway system. Indeed, the answer to the critical question of the economic viability of Canadian railways is to be found in the distant past.* The aspects which need to be considered include (i) the roles and the objectives that railways were originally assigned, (ii) the relations between railways and governments (the railway-government complex), (iii) the financing of railway construction and operation, and (iv) the evolution of networks of railway lines. The review of these four items is facilitated by first examining the basic components of the Canadian railway system. This is best done with the aid of schematic railway maps (Appendix One, Maps 1 to 5, pp. 255-260), which show the main railway lines and the dates of their completion.

*The following references served as the main sources of historical data included in Part One: Berton (1970, 1971a, 1974), Currie (1957), Fleming (1876), Fournier (1935), Glazebrook (1938), Innis (1971), Legget (1973), McDougal (1968), Skelton (1916), Stevens (1960, 1962, 1973), Thompson and Edgar (1933).

CHAPTER 1

THE BASIC NETWORK
OF RAILWAYS

Major Systems in the East: The Grand Trunk and the Intercolonial

The Great Western and the Grand Trunk (which absorbed the Great Western in 1882), Maps 1 and 2, were the first major railway systems in Canada. Developed in the 1850s and controlled by English capital, by 1860 they provided connections between Rivière-du-Loup (on the St. Lawrence) and Portland (Maine) in the east, through Montreal and Toronto to Sarnia, Windsor and Niagara in the west; in 1880 Chicago was reached from Port Huron. The Grand Trunk was acquired by the Dominion government in 1920.

The Intercolonial Railway (1858-76), Map 1, was built by provincial and Dominion governments as a strategic military railroad, as a link joining the Maritimes with each other and with Canada, and as an access to the Atlantic ports through Canadian territory. Completed in 1876, the Intercolonial connected Halifax, N.S. and St. John, N.B. with the Grand Trunk terminus at Rivière-du-Loup, and – over the Grand Trunk and Great Western tracks – with the Great Lakes. Since 1923, the Intercolonial has been part of the Canadian National system.

The triple transcontinental network

By 1915, three independent transcontinental railway systems had been developed in Canada: the Canadian Pacific, the Canadian Northern, and the Grand Trunk Pacific and National Transcontinental. The basic transcontinental lines can be traced in Map 1; for clarity, they are shown separately in Map 3.

The Canadian Pacific was the first transcontinental railway: by 1885 it extended from Quebec City to Vancouver, by 1890 it included a line from Montreal to St. John, N.B. With the exception of some 710 miles of track built by the liberal government of Alexander Mackenzie (1873-1878), the CPR was a heavily subsidized, private enterprise, constructed between the years

1882-1885, during John A. Macdonald's Conservative rule (1878-1891). The CPR provided the first fast transcontinental route located entirely on Canadian soil.

The two other transcontinental systems evolved more gradually under the auspices of Wilfrid Laurier's Liberal administration (1896-1911) through amalgamation, extension, and construction of a number of smaller railways; they were both built with the support of or directly by the Dominion government.

The Grand Trunk Pacific & National Transcontinental system was completed from Moncton, N.B. to Prince Rupert, B.C. between 1908 and 1915. The line from Winnipeg to Prince Rupert was built and operated by the Grand Trunk Pacific, a subsidiary of the Grand Trunk. The National Transcontinental, from Winnipeg through Quebec City to Moncton, N.B., was constructed by the Dominion government and, after completion in 1915, was to be operated by the Grand Trunk Pacific. However, in view of capital costs which largely exceeded the estimates, as well as poor prospects for profitable traffic, the Company refused to take over the line. The government had to assume its operations. The Grand Trunk Pacific was placed in receivership in 1919, and became part of the Canadian National system in 1920.

The Canadian Northern system had its origin in the partnership of William Mackenzie and Donald Mann, two talented enterpreneurs who, beginning in 1895 with lease, acquisition and later construction of a few local, short lines around Winnipeg, developed a railway that by 1902 reached east to Port Arthur and by 1905 west to Edmonton; by 1915 the line extended from Quebec City, Toronto and Montreal in the east, to Vancouver in the west. It was taken over by the Dominion government in 1917, and became part of the Canadian National system in 1923.

CHAPTER 2

RAILWAYS FULFILL
POLITICAL GOALS

The immediate and potential needs of the Canadian economy were not the only factors which governed the development of railways: there is abundant evidence that national and partisan political goals played an even more decisive role.* Perhaps more than in any other Western country, in Canada railways were the agents of national unification, the tools of partisan politics and the means to riches for enterprising businessmen. Railways were largely responsible for the settlement of the Canadian West (Mackintosh, 1934) and for exploitation of the country's resources. It has been said that the Canadian Pacific built the nation.

The Intercolonial

The concept of a railway as a unifying link between the provinces of British North America, as a boost to their development, and as a strategic defense measure, dates back to 1830s. In March, 1836, the legislatures of Lower Canada and Nova Scotia endorsed the resolution of the New Brunswick Legislative Assembly (of December 1835) which advocated the construction of a railway on the grounds that it would "promote the settlement of the country, greatly facilitate intercourse, extend the exchange of commodities between British possessions in America, increase the demand for British manufactures, afford facilities for the conveyance and settlement of emigrants and give additional employment to British shipping." Lord Durham's 1839 report on British American possessions, which recommended the unification of the Lower and Upper Canadas, ad-

---

* Transportation decisions continue to be made in Canada on political grounds. The support of the De Havilland of Canada Ltd. DHC-7 STOL (short-take-off-and-landing) aircraft development is a current example of this approach. (Marrens and Thomas; 1975; see also Chapter 23). Ontario's short-lived (1972-74) attempt to develop an exotic, German, magnetically-levitated GO-Urban rapid transit (see Chapter 21) is another example of political sense – as perceived by the party in office – making transportation nonsense.

8

vocated a trunk railway as an essential instrument in the growth of Canadian nationhood.

The first survey authorized to select a military route which would link the Maritime provinces with eastern Canada was completed by the Imperial government in 1844; a railroad linking Halifax with Quebec City was recommended. A second, definitive survey was finished in 1848; the route selected was essentially the one on which the railway was eventually built. Major Robinson, the chief of the survey, observed that the construction of the Halifax to Quebec Railway would constitute the first step towards unification of all the British North American provinces under one legislative government.

During the years 1849-62, several unsuccessful attempts were made to obtain Imperial aid for the construction of this railway. In 1863 the Province of Canada appointed Sandford Fleming (this appointment was endorsed by Nova Scotia, New Brunswick and Great Britain) to carry out new, detailed surveys (completed in 1865). Concurrently (1864), negotiations for the union of the Maritime provinces began, leading to the 1864 Quebec Conference. One resolution of the Conference stated that "the general Government shall secure, without delay, the completion of the Intercolonial Railway from River du Loup (sic), through New Brunswick, to Truro in Nova Scotia." In 1867 this became Section 145 of the British North America Act, which declared that "the construction of the Intercolonial railway is essential to the Consolidation of the Union of British North America," and that "it shall be the duty of the Government and Parliament of Canada to provide for the commencement within six months after the Union, of a railway connecting the River St. Lawrence with the City of Halifax in Nova Scotia and for the construction thereof, without intermission, and the completion thereof with all practicable speed."

The BNA Act received royal sanction on March 29, 1867; in April, the Imperial Parliament passed a second bill entitled "An Act for Authorizing a Guarantee of Interest on a Loan to be Raised by Canada, Towards the Construction of a Railway Connecting Quebec and Halifax." The act empowered the government to raise a loan of £4 million, the interest on three million of which was guaranteed.

For strategic military reasons, the Intercolonial was built well away from the U.S. boundary, thereby having to follow a much longer route than would have been chosen on the basis of commercial considerations (Map 1a, p. 255). In 1876, the Inter-colonial started operating between Halifax and Rivière-du-Loup; in 1879, through purchase of the Grand Trunk tracks, it was extended to Lévis opposite Quebec City. The railway be-came the mechanism linking the eastern provinces; it was soon to play an even more important role in the West.

The Canadian Pacific

In 1866, Vancouver Island joined British Columbia, and a year later the new colony voted for admission into the Dominion. B.C.'s delegation sent to Ottawa in 1870 asked that a railway survey be started at once, and a wagon road completed within three years following the Union. In 1871, British Columbia joined the new Confederation of Ontario, Quebec, New Bruns-wick, Nova Scotia and Manitoba (a member since 1870) on the generous terms of John A. Macdonald's Conservative govern-ment. The final agreement stated that:

> The Government of the Dominion undertakes to secure commencement simultaneously within two years from the date of Union, of the construction of a railway from the Pacific towards the Rocky Mountains, and from such point as may be selected east of the Rocky Mountains towards the Pacific, to connect the seaboard of British Columbia with the railway system of Canada; and fur-ther, to secure the completion of such railway within ten years from the date of Union.

The Act which was passed to implement the agreement with British Columbia stated that the railway should be built and operated by a private company, aided by land grants (up to 50 million acres) and subsidies (a maximum of $10 million). The railway was again to serve as an instrument of political union, but of a much larger scope than that of the Intercolonial: it was to be the backbone of "a transcontinental British nation in North America – a workable alternative to the United States" (Berton, 1974). This could not be possible without a transporta-tion link over which Canada had territorial control; moreover, the proposed railway was needed to check the power of the American Northern Pacific Railway, a real danger to the Cana-dian presence in the West.

Beyond political roles, the railway was to be the tool with

which exploration, settlement and exploitation of the empty country west of the Great Lakes was to be accomplished. It was also a necessary ingredient of partisan politics: it provided Macdonald with an objective and a diversion which he needed to stay in office. If the project succeeded, the Conservative party could wield power for many years.

The Intercolonial Railway was completed in the nine years following Confederation; 14 years passed since the admission of British Columbia to the Dominion until the Canadian Pacific Railway began operations in 1885. It accomplished the objectives which the Conservatives had set for the nation, and it exerted profound influence on the party fortunes, first toppling and then reinstating the Conservative government (see Chapter 3). It did this at a considerable expense to the public.

It can be argued that November 7, 1885 – the day on which the last spike was driven on the CPR line at Craigellachie (see Map 3, p. 258)—is a more appropriate day from which to date the existence of Canada than July 1, 1867:

> The idea of Canada as a nation made little sense without the great North West, and Canada's hold over the North West was extremely tenuous without a railway. That there would be a country, and what kind of a country it would be, was really only decided on November 7, 1885. 'Like a gavel,' in E. J. Pratt's words, the driving of the last spike 'closed off debate' (Chodos, 1973; Pratt, 1952).

The transcontinental railways of the Liberals

It is the Liberal party that wrote the next and the last major chapter in the history of Canadian railway development. Through successful construction and operation of the Canadian Pacific, the Conservative government "completely eclipsed anything that has been done by the Liberals. . . . It came to be accepted by both the government and the Canadian Pacific Railway Company that they were mutually dependent. It is not an unreasonable deduction that the Liberal Administration was ready to sponsor a fresh railway enterprise which would cancel their former mistaken, if honest, belief in the inability of the West to maintain a railway" (Glazebrook, 1938). The Liberals, who came into power in 1896, were keen to erase their anti-railway image. Wilfrid Laurier was unsuccessful in arranging

11

amalgamation or co-operation of the Canadian Northern in the West with the Grand Trunk in the East, a step toward the development of a transcontinental line. Such logical solution being denied to the Liberals, they embarked on a compromise policy which resulted in completion of two new transcontinental systems by 1915: the Grand Trunk Pacific & the National Transcontinental, and the Canadian Northern. Unlike the Intercolonial and the Canadian Pacific, it is doubtful whether these costly and uneconomic projects could have been justified in terms of broad national objectives; rather they appear as politically expedient, partisan ventures.

The PEI and the Newfoundland Railways

The Intercolonial, as well as the three transcontinental rail systems, are not the only ones which owe their origins to political objectives. The Prince Edward Island railway, started in 1871 as a provincial venture, was taken over, uncompleted, by the federal government in 1873; indeed, this was the condition necessary to induce PEI into the Union. The Newfoundland railway, built between 1881 and 1898, was also a heavily subsidized government venture; when Newfoundland joined Canada in 1949, the railway became part of the Canadian National system.

The Hudson Bay Railway

This railway, linking Winnipeg to Churchill, was developed between 1880 and 1931 (see Map 4, p. 259). The epic of this line is recorded here not because it has any particular significance within Canada's railway system, but because it is the ultimate example of a political, publicly-funded railway enterprise. The activities related to the Hudson Bay Railway spanned a period of 50 years and twelve Dominion governments, beginning with the incorporation in 1880 of two railway companies (before 1884, seven other companies were charted) and the involvement of Mann and Mackenzie, the promoters and owners of the Canadian Northern Railway, whose interest lay in obtaining the land grants rather than in forging a northern link to the Ocean. Between 1880 and 1929, when the line was completed on reaching Churchill (it was opened in 1931), the Hudson Bay Railway project was bandied in partisan bargaining between Liberals and Conservatives, the Dominion and the Prairie provinces;

several times, it served as a provincial and federal election issue. Lacking economic and national rationale, the construction of the line progressed slowly and spasmodically, subject to indecision, vacillations and sheer incompetence of succeeding governments and federal departments. Before 1910, when construction of the line from The Pas to Hudson Bay started (490 miles), the Laurier administration was advised that the freight saving on the maximum movement of grain via Hudson Bay would be $3.3 million a year, whereas the annual cost of operation and maintenance would be at least three times this sum; the line's operational period would be three months yearly. Nevertheless, the construction proceeded until it was halted in 1917 after completion of only 333 miles from The Pas. It was not resumed until 1927, when the Churchill terminal was finally chosen as more suitable than Port Nelson, Map 4 (p. 259), where some $6 million had already been spent. The total cost of the Hudson Bay Railway was $45.3 million (Canada, 1932).

In spite of a thousand miles saved in haulage and the benefit of Crowsnest Pass rates (see p. 108), the Hudson Bay route did not attract significant traffic; in 1956, only about 5% of all grain shipments from Canadian ports was loaded in Churchill. The traffic was essentially one-way: only 1.5% of the total was incoming cargo. The cost of the first grain shipment from Churchill to Liverpool was 14.95¢ per bushel; it was 10.95¢ on the Fort William-Liverpool route (Stevens, 1962). In the 1972-73 grain season, 25.3 million bushels of grain were shipped from Churchill, about the largest quantity ever. This represented 3.2% of all grain shipments from Canada, and 5.8% of all shipments excluding the Pacific ports.

CHAPTER 3

THE RAILWAY-GOVERNMENT COMPLEX: POLITICIANS IN THE SERVICE OF RAILWAYS

Although the generally-accepted point of view, often professed by politicians, legislators and railway promoters of the day, has been that the construction of railways was a national necessity, there is undoubtedly some merit in taking the opposite stand and viewing regional or national unity as a prerequisite necessary for the development of railways.

Before 1867, the Grand Trunk advocated political and economic union based on a transcontinental line. During a debate in the Provincial Parliament of Canada, A. A. Dorion observed that, the Intercolonial project "having failed (in 1862), some other scheme had to be concocted for bringing aid and relief to the unfortunate Grand Trunk – and the Confederation of all the British North American provinces naturally suggested itself to the Grand Trunk officials as the surest means of bringing with it the construction of the Intercolonial Railway. Such was the origin of this Confederation scheme." Later in the debate, when a reference was made to the Interoceanic Railway (whose charter was almost identical to the Canadian Pacific Railway charter), Dorion commented: "Yes, I suppose that is another necessity of Confederation. . . . Some western extension of the Grand Trunk scheme for the benefit of Messrs. Watkin and Company of the new Hudson's Bay Company" (Glazebrook, 1938). Similar views were expressed in the Canadian assembly by T. Scatcherd who stated that "this Confederation scheme is nothing more or less than a scheme to construct the Intercolonial Railway" (Glazebrook, 1938).

The Prince Edward Island railway provides another example of a railway whose fate depended on political union. The act authorizing an expenditure of £5,000 per mile of railway was passed by the PEI Legislature in April, 1870; construction began in October. As the number of miles to be built was not specified, the route was chosen by the contractors on the basis of maximum length and minimum construction costs to them; earthwork was avoided whenever possible. The line itself also reflected the parochial desires of the politicians, its meandering route designed to please their constituents (between George-town and Alberton, 84 miles apart, the railway was 147 miles long); patronage was rampant. By 1872, the costs of railway construction were coming close to the limit of PEI's resources, the government no longer being able to endure the drain of the railway debenture interest. A local bank was threatened with bankruptcy. The sturdy colonists, who in 1866 rejected the Quebec Conference resolutions and in 1870 declared that "the people [of PEI] are almost unanimously opposed to any change in the constitution of the colony", in true mercantile tradition in 1873 opted for Confederation on the condition that the federal government take over the railway and operate train ferry connections with the mainland (Stevens, 1960). The construction of the railway was completed in 1875 by the federal government. By 1919, when the PEI railway was merged with the CNR, the Canadian government's contribution stood at about $11 million.

Since many politicians and legislators were also active railway promoters, investing in railways and participating in their management, the suggestion that political aims were sometimes subservient to the goals of the railway companies appears entirely plausible.

This may not have been true of Joseph Howe, Nova Scotia's Provincial Secretary and a railroad promoter who advocated government ownership of railways. In 1854, after the British contractors withdrew from participation in the Nova Scotia railway venture, Howe introduced legislation which restored his original plan of government construction, operation and ownership of Nova Scotian railways and then resigned as Provincial Secretary to become the first Commissioner-in-Chief of the Nova Scotia Railway Board.

In Ontario, the main promoters of railways were also the government leaders. Francis Hincks, member of the first united Legislature of the Province of Canada and, after 1842, Inspector-General of Canada (a post equivalent to that of the Minister of Finance today), played a leading role in developing the aid-to-railways legislation (discussed in more detail in Chapter 4) which launched the railway boom in Canada in 1849. As Premier of the Province of Canada (1851-54) he was the main promoter of the Intercolonial, and, more importantly, of the Grand Trunk, originally planned to connect Montreal, Toronto and Hamilton. The legislation setting up the Grand Trunk was passed in 1852. In 1852-53, Hincks' government expanded the scope of the Grand Trunk to include a connection to Sarnia, a loop line from Belleville to Toronto, amalgamation with the Quebec-Richmond and Montreal-Portland lines, and other extensions which were beyond the original plan.

When the Grand Trunk Railway Company was first organized in 1853, the government felt that inasmuch as the province was guaranteeing some of the bonds of the Company, it should have the right to appoint six of the twelve directors resident in Canada and to have its two bankers on the London Board of six members. John Ross, Solicitor of Canada, became President and Director; Hincks and four cabinet ministers became Directors. Because of the interlocking membership, in a broad sense it was true that a group of men acting as directors of the Grand Trunk asked the government for aid and then the same men in their capacities as cabinet ministers voted such aid.

In 1854, Hincks was forced to resign his premiership, and a special committee to investigate charges against Hincks and some members of his cabinet was appointed by the Legislature. Hincks was accused of receiving shares in the Grand Trunk, of speculating in the stock of the St. Lawrence and Atlantic Railway, of making illegal profits on City of Toronto bonds, and of locating a line so as to increase the value of some land which he had bought. Characteristically, after considering evidence the committee of the Legislature concluded that Hincks had been interested in the purchase of securities and of land in the same manner as members of previous administrations, and absolved him from wrongdoing.

Hincks was succeeded as Premier by Sir Allan MacNab, Director, President, and from 1853, Chairman of the Board of the Great Western Railway Company, a railway promoter who was among the original 1834 incorporators of Great Western's predecessor. Except for Hincks and one or two others, MacNab's ministry had the same members and was supported by Hincks, who retained his parliamentary seat. In 1854, the Great Western investors applied to Parliament for legislation to permit doubling the amount of common stock, and the bill was approved in 1855. MacNab was awarded £4,000 by the Canadian Board of the Great Western Railway for "special services;" in 1856, he received a further £5,000.

Before becoming Premier, MacNab was a member of Canada's Legislature. In 1848, A. T. Galt, a fellow railway promoter, and MacNab, then Speaker of the House, presented to Parliament a joint petition for assistance. A group of parliamentarians was empowered to hear such appeals and thus a situation developed in which "Allan MacNab, as Chairman of the Committee of the House, listened sympathetically to Allan MacNab, Chairman of the Great Western Railway" (Stevens, 1960).

George Etienne Cartier, Conservative leader of French Canada and member of several cabinets, was another politician whose career was closely linked to railway development. Cartier was one of the original incorporators of the Grand Trunk (in 1852), was salaried solicitor of this Company and was counsel for Peto, Brassey, Jackson and Betts, the English contractors for the Grand Trunk.

The political climate in Canada during the railway development of the 1850's was succinctly described by Skelton (1916):

The eight or ten years which followed 1849 are notable not only for a sudden outburst of railway construction and speculative activity throughout the provinces, but for the beginning of that close connection between politics and railways which is distinctively Canadian. In this era Parliament became the field of railway debate. Political motives came to the front: 'statesmen' began to talk of links of Empire and 'politicians' began to press the claims of their constituencies for needed railway communications. Cabinets realized the value of the charters they could grant or the country's credit they could pledge, and contractors swarmed to the feast. 'Railways are my politics,' was the frank avowal of the Conservative leader, Sir Allan MacNab.

Such government-railway coziness continued to influence railway construction and operation for many years. In the case of the first transcontinental railway – the largest rail venture ever undertaken in Canada – it reached catastrophic proportions and culminated in the Pacific Scandal.

When the contract admitting British Columbia to the Dominion was signed in the summer of 1871, Macdonald's Conservative government was looking for a group of Canadian capitalists to undertake the task of constructing the Pacific railway. The

17

job was given to Sir Hugh Allan, reputedly the richest and most powerful financier in Canada (It was Hincks, at that time Macdonald's Finance Minister, who first approached Allan). Allan was the front man for an American syndicate composed of Northern Pacific Railway directors. A secret agreement signed with Allan in December, 1871, stipulated a line running between Sault St. Marie and the Manitoba border in U.S. territory. Allan's task was to secure the charter, and he was generously supplied with funds to insure success. Allan did not succeed in buying off Senator MacPherson, who was organizing a rival (Interoceanic) railway company, but Allan did donate some $350,000 to election funds of Conservative ministers (this did not prevent Liberals from gaining seats in the August, 1872, election).

Cartier, a close associate of John A. Macdonald and an influential member of his cabinet (as Minister of Militia and Defense), drew heavily on Allan's funds and promised that "any amount that you or your Company shall advance for that [election funds] purpose shall be re-couped to you."

In June, 1872 both Allan's and MacPherson's companies were officially organized. The government was in an awkward position: while Allan's American connections were objectionable, a charter could not be given to MacPherson's Ontario-based group. When an attempted amalgamation of the two "rings" did not succeed yet another charter was drawn up by the government in February, 1873, naming the Canadian Pacific Railway Company and mentioning as subscribers Allan and other Canadians who were members of the two old companies. With American connections severed, the new group attempted to raise funds in England; before it could succeed, the "Pacific Scandal" exploded. Shortly after opening of the new session of Parliament, the Liberals made charges of corrupt relations between the government and the Allan ring. Correspondence revealing the use of Allan's funds was published in the press. In August, 1873, a Royal Commission to inquire into the Pacific Railway negotiations was appointed. The government, attacked for alleged corruption, resigned in November, 1873.

In the United States, the early railroad owners – Vanderbilt, Hill, Morgan, Harriman, Huntington and others – were known as "railway kings" and wielded enormous influence. As the British historian James Bryce observed in 1888:

They have power, more power – that is, more opportunity of making their will prevail – than perhaps anyone in political life except the President and the Speaker who, after all, hold theirs only for four years and two years, while the railroad monarch may keep his for life.

Those men commanded great empires. Montana, North Dakota, and Nebraska were referred to as James J. Hill's feudal states. When railroad monarch Leland Stanford rode in his private car, railroad workers all along the tracks lined up and stood at attention as he passed by. State legislatures were often subservient to the railroad kings.

An uneasy balance of power existed among railroads, and, as with governments, the balance often shifted, sometimes causing wars. Occasionally a railroad king dealt directly with the President of the United States. For example, when President Theodore Roosevelt, reacting to a public outcry, brought antitrust proceedings against J.P. Morgan's holding company, the Northern Securities Company, an upset Morgan with remarkable candor reportedly told Roosevelt face to face, "If we have done anything wrong, send your man [Attorney General Philander Knox] to see my man, and they can fix it up." In this case, Morgan was rebuffed, but only after a split Supreme Court decision. (Southerland and McCleery. 1973, pp. 56.).

CHAPTER 4

THE RAILWAY-GOVERNMENT COMPLEX:
FINANCING RAILWAYS

> It has been suggested that if a British economist in 1830 had been able to calculate a cost-benefit analysis on the subsequent history of railways, they would never have been built. The private cost would have exceeded the private benefit to the owners. Yet clearly the railway system provided an enormous social benefit to the nation.
>
> Jenkins (1972)

From the very beginning, significant railway projects in Canada relied heavily or totally on the support of governments and municipalities. In 1871,

> John and Edward Trout, the earliest historians of Canadian railways, listed fourteen ways in which public monies could be expended on them: (1) government debenture issues transferred to railways as loans, (2) government-guaranteed loans, (3) government guarantee of interest on railway bond issues, (4) government guarantee of railway bonds, (5) direct issue of bonds to railways against mortgages, (6) government guarantee of share capital, (7) subsidy of crown lands, (8) revenue of crown lands transferred to railways, (9) release of government claims against railway, either outright or by resigning priority of claim, (10) composition of government claims to nominal figure, (11) municipal loans, (12) municipal bonuses, (13) municipal purchases of common stock, (14) assumption by government of municipal liabilities of railways and cancellation thereof (Stevens, 1960).

The first initiatives towards construction of a main line between St. Andrews (west of St. John, N.B.) and Quebec City, were made in 1836, but unable to secure the help of the Imperial government in London, they failed. It was not until the Railway Guarantee Act became law in 1849 that the railway boom was launched in Canada. The act "to Provide for Affording the Guarantee of the Province to the Bonds of Railway

Companies on Certain Conditions, and for Rendering Assistance in the Construction of the Halifax and Quebec Railway" enabled the government of the Province of Canada (formed in 1841 through the union of Upper and Lower Canada) to: (i) guarantee a rate of interest up to 6% on the bonds of any railway venture which owned at least 75 miles of line, (ii) guarantee, either to private investors or to the Imperial government, a sum of up to £20,000 per annum to meet interest charges upon the capital expended upon any railway which linked the Maritime provinces with Canada, (iii) offer to the Imperial government, in exchange for its backing, the title to all crown lands for ten miles on either side of the projected railway and to other lands required for right-of-way and terminals.

The 1849 Municipal Act allowed municipalities to take stock in railway companies and to make loans to them. In 1851, the Main Trunk Line of Railway Act cleared the way for an inter-provincial railway: the Province of Canada would build the Sarnia/Windsor-Toronto-Montreal-Quebec section (which included St. Lawrence and Atlantic Railway line from Montreal to Richmond), whereas the Halifax-Quebec City Line would be a joint enterprise of New Brunswick, Nova Scotia and Canada.

If it were not for the 1849 Act, the St. Lawrence and Atlantic portion of the Main Line – a private venture of A. T. Galt – could not have been completed to Richmond in 1851 for the lack of funds. The line was finished in 1853 (to Stanhope, on the Vermont border); the capital raised for it (a total of £740,000) included 54% in provincial and 14% in Montreal City bonds, or 68% under the 1849 Act. The first two Canadian main lines, MacNab's Great Western (Toronto-Windsor, 1855) and Hinck's Grand Trunk (Toronto-Quebec, 1856) had incurred a provincial debt of $29.5 million by 1867. The eastern section of the main line, the Intercolonial Railway from Halifax, N.S. to Rivière-du-Loup on the St. Lawrence, completed in 1876 at a cost of $22 million, was paid for entirely from public funds, as was the Prince Edward Island Railway: between completion in 1875 and merger in 1919 with the Intercolonial, the PEI Railway's total cost came to $10.8 million.

Not only the establishment, but also the operation and expansion of Canada's railways required a generous and continuing access to the public purse. The Grand Trunk was often desperately short of working capital. By 1855, in its third year of construction, the Grand Trunk had spent all its money and had great difficulties in paying its contractors. An 1855 loan of £0.9 million supported construction for less than a year. In 1857, Parliament relegated the claims of the Province of Canada (£3.1 million) to the status of a secondary liability and thus gave the holders of the 1856 Grand Trunk debentures priority in interest payments. The Relief Act of 1856 provided £0.8 million in cash towards the completion of the Victoria Bridge in Montreal and authorized the issue of £2 million in guaranteed preference bonds.

During the first few years after its nominal completion, the Grand Trunk was continually on the verge of bankruptcy. In 1861, the Company again petitioned the government for help. In 1862, the Grand Trunk Arrangements Act was passed which provided new resources, including a ten-year breathing spell during which the Company was allowed to capitalize the interest on its bonds. By 1867, Grand Trunk's debt amounted to $25.6 million. In 1873, another Grand Trunk Arrangements Act was passed providing further resources, which enabled purchase of new, coal burning locomotives and also enabled the gauge to be narrowed.

Grand Trunk's competitor, the Western Railroad (since 1853, the Great Western Railway), also relied on public funds. In 1849 it, too, took advantage of the Guarantee Act (£0.77 million), and in 1853 the Hamilton and Toronto Railway (amalgamated with the GWR in 1856), although only 40 miles long, was able – as an exception – to qualify for assistance. In 1859, the Company defaulted on its interest payments to the government, and in 1869 was allowed low interest rate payments until the debt was paid. In 1882, after years of financial struggles, the GWR succumbed to its competitor and was amalgamated with the Grand Trunk Railway.

Construction of the Canadian Pacific, the first transcontinental railway, required new and extensive support from public funds. The Company was launched on February 17, 1881; the terms of contract with the government called for completion of the road on May 1, 1891 and included subsidies of $25 million cash and 25 million acres of land, and some 700 miles of completed line, built at a cost of $38 million. Land was also granted for the road bed, stations, etc.; the material required for construction and operation, and the capital stock, were exempted from taxation forever, and the land was exempted for twenty years. Further protection was given Canadian Pacific by a "monopoly clause" (repealed in 1888 under Manitoba's pressure), which guaranteed that for twenty years no other line could be constructed south of the CPR to run within 15 miles of the U.S. border.

In 1882, under William Cornelius Van Horne, the new General Manager, a record 500 miles of CPR track were completed. But the costs of construction were much higher than expected. By September, 1882, the CPR syndicate was in trouble.* CPR's President George Stephen reported to the Prime Minister that "the road . . . is costing us a great deal more than the subsidy.... We are just about even with the world at the moment, but to reach this position, we have had to find 5 million dollars from our resources. To enable me to make up my quota I had to sell my Montreal Bank stock."

Towards the end of 1882, when only about one-quarter of the projected 2000 miles of line construction were completed, the financial crisis reached panic proportions as is apparent from the CPR President's letters to the Prime Minister. Stephen wrote, at the end of November, 1882, that:

> I . . . cannot move until I have patents for the lands earned, up to this time . . . we shall need every acre of the grant to enable us to find the money . . . delay will be fatal to us – we cannot wait. . . . The demand on us for money is something appalling. $400,000 went to Winnipeg last week and one million more to be there on the 10th. Our pinch is now.

The crisis of 1882 marked only the beginnings of CPR's financial difficulties; they continued to be compounded until construction was completed in 1885. Towards the end of 1883, the railway was again in serious trouble; it was desperately short of money, and had no cash to pay its employees. At Brandon, the staff of the freight office had not been paid for three months. An estimated $30 million was needed to pay off the debts and complete the line. International credit was no longer available to the CPR.

Stephen told the Prime Minister that unless something was done at once, he would be forced to give up and let the government take over the railway. The Company's total debt was $15

---

*The continuing financial struggles during construction of the CPR are here summarized following Berton's (1970, 1971a, 1974) detailed account.

million; payments totalling $10.5 million had to be made during January, 1884. The Company requested a $22.5 million loan and a number of other financial concessions; the proposal was approved by the government on January 31, 1884, and the way was again open for construction to proceed during the 1884 season.

Predictably, the next crisis occurred before the year was out. Construction costs were again running ahead of the estimates; CPR's credit at home and abroad was gone. In 1884, Stephen crossed the Atlantic three times in search of help from England. By October, 1884, when it had become apparent that the Company might not have enough funds to complete the line, it was feared that government subsidy payments might stop altogether. The Company began paying the construction crews by cheques, hoping that they would not be cashed until conditions improved. By January, 1885, the crisis deepened; Stephen notified the Prime Minister of "Imminent danger of sudden crisis unless we can find means to meet pressing demands." In order to raise the $650,000 needed to pay the dividend and $1 million for a short-term note to provide funds for the coming weeks, Stephen and Smith (Lord Strathcona, financier and CPR director) pledged the remainder of their personal assets. On March 18, 1885, Stephen applied for a loan of $5 million to the privy Council; the application was rejected. Resigned, he wrote the Prime Minister: "I need not repeat how sorry I am that this should be the result of all our efforts to give Canada a railway to the Pacific Ocean. But I am supported by the conviction that I have done all that could be done to obtain it."

The next two months represent probably the most dramatic period in the construction of the CPR. Stephen was persuaded to continue negotiations with the Privy Council on the basis of a new proposal, submitted on March 27, 1885. On the same day, the news of the March 26 Duck Lake tragedy, in which ten members of police and volunteer force were killed and 13 more were wounded, reached Ontario. The first indication of an impending rebellion in Saskatchewan (the Second Riel Rebellion) appeared in the Ottawa press on March 23, but the possibility of an Indian revolt in the Prairies was not entirely unexpected. Earlier in the year, Van Horne suggested to John Henry Pope, Minister of the Railways, that he could get troops from Quebec and Kingston in ten days to Qu'Apelle (east of Regina). He now volunteered the services of the CPR to the Privy Coun-

24

cil, and his offer was accepted. In spite of four gaps in the line (totalling 86 miles), some 3,300 men, their equipment and supplies were transported a distance of 1600 miles west from Ottawa. As pledged by Van Horne, the first troops to leave Ottawa arrived in 9 days at Qu'Apelle. The railway, while in dire financial straights, had now demonstrated that it was indispensable to the security of the country, and expected the government's help to continue.

The situation was paradoxical: while the country in general was enthusiastic about the railway and the talk of useless expenditure of money had ceased, CPR could not immediately collect the close to a million dollars it had spent on shipping the troops west, and its negotiations with the Privy Council showed little progress. In the construction camps, complaints over lack of pay led to work stoppages and riots.

. On April 15, 1885, Stephen gave up negotiations with the government and left Ottawa for Montreal. CPR's situation was summed up by Van Horne in a wire which reached Stephen the next day: "Have no means paying wages, pay car can't be sent out, and unless we get immediate relief we must stop. Please inform Premier and Finance Minister. Do not be surprised, or blame me if an immediate and most serious catastrophe happens." Minister of Railways Pope, when notified of this situation, informed the Prime Minister. Macdonald's private request to the Bank of Montreal to loan $5 million to the CPR was ignored, but on May 5th, $750,000 was advanced on the government's request. It was not a solution to the financial difficulties, but it provided funds for the overdue March and April wages. On June 1, interest on the Ontario and Quebec Railway bonds was due; less than a week before the deadline, the government guaranteed the required loan. "The advance we are now making is quite illegal and we are incurring the gravest responsibility in doing so," Macdonald wrote to Stephen. The melodrama continued until July 10th, 1885, when the Commons voted in favour of railway relief. The entire issue of the new CPR bonds was bought by the London financial house of Baring Brothers. Adequate funds were now available to carry CPR's construction to completion on November 7, 1885.

Following completion of the Canadian Pacific in 1885, railway expansion in Canada continued – this time under the auspices of Laurier's Liberal administration (1896-1911) – on the basis of extensive government subsidies, and resulted in development of the second and third transcontinental systems (see Map 3, p. 258).

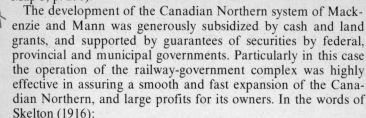

The development of the Canadian Northern system of Mackenzie and Mann was generously subsidized by cash and land grants, and supported by guarantees of securities by federal, provincial and municipal governments. Particularly in this case the operation of the railway-government complex was highly effective in assuring a smooth and fast expansion of the Canadian Northern, and large profits for its owners. In the words of Skelton (1916):

> The financial and political aspects of this great enterprise were as striking as was the construction. Governments have many a time given lavish aid, promoters have often built roads entirely out of the proceeds of bond issues, financiers have dominated great railway systems by a majority or controlling interest in the stock. But never before did a group of men plan to unite, on such a scale, all three arrangements – to build ten thousand miles of railway without themselves investing a dollar and still retain control. The men behind the Canadian Northern not only planned such a project, but carried it through, displaying in the process, and at every stage of the undertaking, a mastery of political diplomacy, an untiring persistence, and great financial resourcefulness. They are, therefore, entitled to a special place among the world's railway builders.
>
> Their plan was simple in principle, if wondrously complicated in working out. It was to build the road by government subsidies and the proceeds of the bonds guaranteed by government, and to control the road by issuing to themselves, for their services of promotion and management, practically all the common stock. To carry out this audacious plan, political influence, public enthusiasm, and the confidence of outside investors in Canada's future were all required and were all forthcoming.
>
> Dominion and province vied in aid. This aid took many forms. The Dominion had abandoned in 1894 its policy of giving land – grants, but the original companies which combined to form the Canadian Northern had previously been promised and later received over four million acres: up to 1914 about eighteen million dollars had been real-

ized from the sale of parts of this land, and the grants unsold were worth at least ten millions more. In addition, Ontario gave two million acres and Quebec one-third as much. Cash subsidies were not wanting. The Liberal government of Sir Wilfrid Laurier voted something less than two millions in cash to aid in building the link between Winnipeg and Lake Superior. It declined to recognize or aid the extension to the Pacific coast; but in 1912 the Conservative government of Sir Robert Borden gave over six millions for this work, and in the following year fifteen millions more for the Ontario and western Alberta sections of the main line. The provinces were less lavish, Quebec, Ontario, and Manitoba offering all told six millions.

But it was neither to land-grants nor to cash subsidies that the Canadian Northern looked for its chief aid, but to government guarantees. This device, the main form of state aid given in our first railway era, had long been discredited by the unlucky fate of the Grand Trunk and the Northern guarantees, and had been sparingly used since. To the Canadian Northern its revival was chiefly due. It was a seductive form of aid: provided that the railway thus helped had good traffic prospects, the government stood little chance of loss and the railway greatly gained by the certainty of the sale of its bonds and the higher price secured. But, like other forms of the extension of public credit, such as the issue of paper money, state guarantees are difficult to keep within bounds, and compel ever-fresh extensions to save the old liability. So Dominion and province alike found. From 1903 to 1911, under Sir Wilfrid Laurier, the Dominion guaranteed bonds of the Canadian Northern system to the extent of fifty-six millions; from 1912 to 1914, under Sir Robert Borden, it endorsed the Canadian Northern's notes for forty-nine millions more. Nor were the provinces behindhand. Mainly in the seven years from 1908, the five westernmost provinces pledged their credit on behalf of the same system to the astounding amount of over one hundred and thirty millions, British Columbia leading; Nova Scotia made a loan of another five millions. Thus endorsed, usually as to both principal and interest, the bonds of the Canadian Northern were floated with little difficulty, so long as money was to be had at all by any seeker.

In the meantime, while the road was being built by state gifts and bondholders' lendings, the great bulk of the stock of the parent road and of the chief subsidiaries was conveyed to Messrs Mackenzie and Mann for their services in promoting and managing the system. This method of financing had its dangers. It meant that there was no large commitment of shareholders' capital, to secure support in difficulty and compel responsibility in management. It meant that the control of the vast enterprise was in the hands of a few men, unchecked by public inquiry or the criticism of independent shareholders – whatever that might be worth. It meant that with all the cash capital taking the form of bonds, any failure to make ends meet, any lengthened depression, would bring risk of the mortgage-holders' foreclosure and receivership – not merely the shareholders' waiting for a turn of the tide – except in so far as the burden could be shifted to the governments that had endorsed the notes.

The development of the third transcontinental system (see Map 3, p. 258) was based on a 1903 agreement between the federal government and the Grand Trunk Railway. The agreement provided for (i) construction of the Grand Trunk Pacific Railway (owned by the Grand Trunk) from Winnipeg to Prince Rupert on the Pacific, at the expense of the parent company assisted by important government guarantees; (ii) construction of the National Transcontinental from Winnipeg across unopened country via Quebec City to Moncton, N.B. (where connection with the Intercolonial Railway provided access to Halifax), entirely at public expense; (iii) lease of the National Transcontinental to the Grand Trunk Pacific, for a period of 50 years at an annual rate of 3% of construction costs. In addition, the Grand Trunk was to build a connection from Superior Junction to Fort William. The cost of both the eastern and western sections greatly exceeded estimates. The cost of the eastern division finished in 1913 (Winnipeg to Quebec), exceeded the estimate of $61.4 million by $100 million (without interest on capital during construction), or over 160%. The cost of the road was so enormous – $88,300 a mile – that a Royal Commission was appointed to investigate. The construction of the Quebec-Lévis bridge (a separate contract from the railway line), started in 1900, was taken over by the government after the bridge collapsed in 1907; rebuilt, the bridge again fell in 1916. It was finally completed in 1917, at a cost of $22.6 million to the taxpayer.

By 1914, the uncompleted transcontinental lines were in serious financial difficulties. The Canadian Northern, in spite of a government guarantee for nearly half the amount, was unable to secure the $100 million estimated as necessary to complete the line. The Grand Trunk Pacific, which by 1916 received $115 million from public funds (cash, credit and proceeds of land sales, Table 4.1, p. 30) declared that the only alternative to further assistance was receivership.

In 1916 a "Royal Commission to Inquire into Railways and Transportation in Canada" was appointed; in 1917, the majority of commissioners recommended assumption of control by the government of both the Canadian Northern and the Grand Trunk group (Canada, 1917). In November, 1917, the government acquired complete control of the Canadian Northern. The Canadian National Railway Company, designed to absorb all railways owned or controlled by the government, was incorporated in 1919. In the same year, the government took over the bankrupt Grand Trunk Pacific; in 1920, it assumed financial responsibility for the Grand Trunk. Unified operation* of the Canadian National Railways system began on January 1, 1923; it comprised the following lines: The Canadian Northern Railway; The Grand Trunk System (including the Grand Trunk Western Railroad and the Central Vermont Railroad); The Grand Trunk Pacific, and the lines comprising the Canadian government railways: The Intercolonial Railway; The National Transcontinental Railway and its Lake Superior Branch (leased from the GTP Railway); The Prince Edward Island Railway, and the Hudson Bay Railway.

The above review, while incomplete, indicates that development of all railways in Canada depended critically on extensive public subsidies. Their magnitude (including cash, credit and proceeds of land sales) is shown in Table 4.1. As of June 30, 1916, $1.9 billion was invested in Canadian railways; of this, almost exactly one-half, ($955 million) came from the public

---

*As distinct from corporate and legal structure, which preserved the identity of constituent railways.

purse. Except for the Grand Trunk, public investment ranged from 40 to 100%.

Since the government takeovers of bankrupt lines (between 1917 and 1923), public outlays for railways had substantially increased, as shown in Table 4.2. By December 31, 1931, Dominion government contributions had reached an aggregate sum (cash expenditures and credit guarantees) of $2.653 billion;

TABLE 4.1 INVESTMENT (CASH, CREDIT AND PROCEEDS OF LAND SALES) IN CANADIAN RAILWAYS AS OF JUNE 30, 1916 (CANADA, 1917; STEVENS, 1962)

Total* investment: $1,927,645,650   100%
Total* public investment: $954,982,733   49.5%

	Route mileage	Total investment per mile $1000	% Total investment	Public investment as % of total investment in each line	Public investment as % of total public investment
Canadian Pacific	7,779	68.2	27.5	43.0	23.9
Canadian Northern	9,002	55.0	25.5	60.3	31.2
Grand Trunk	3,351	126.6	22.0	6.6	3.0
Grand Trunk Pacific*	1,962	98.0	10.0	59.5	12.0
National Transcontinental	1,810	88.3	8.5	100.0	16.7
Intercolonial and P.E.I.	1,789	70.3	6.5	100.0	13.2
Total or average	25,693	75.0	100	49.5	100

*G.T.P. branch lines, with a public investment of $13.47 million, not included.

provincial and municipal subsidies amounted to $48.9 million, for a total of $2.7 billion. The Canadian National system, including subsidies received by constituent railways before nationalization, accounted for $2.488 billion ($1.201 billion cash and $1.287 billion credit) or 92% of the total. With a route mileage of 42,075 miles, the average subsidy (cash and credit) per mile amounted to $64,500; the subsidy on the Canadian

TABLE 4.2 PUBLIC OUTLAYS FOR RAILWAYS IN CANADA AS OF 31 DECEMBER, 1931 (CANADA, 1932, p. 89)

	Total Subsidies, $ million			Land grants, million acres		
	Cash	Credit	Total	Dominion	Prov.	Total
Canadian National (including constituent railways before 1923)	1,201.5	1,286.5	2,488.0	5.727	1.806	7.533
Canadian Pacific	104.5	–	104.5	24.953	10.612	35.565
Hudson Bay	48.7	–	48.7			
Other	11.4	–	11.4	1.102	3.090	4.192
Total Dominion	1,366.1	1,286.5	2,652.6	31.782		
Provincial and Municipal	46.2	2.7	48.9	–	–	–
Total Canada	1,412.3	1,289.2	2,701.5	31.782	15.508	47.290

National lines (21,785 route miles) was $114,000 per mile, compared to Canadian Pacific's $6,400 per mile. In addition, land grants of 47.3 million acres were made by Dominion and provincial governments to the railways (Table 4.2). Canadian Pacific received 75% of the land grants.

Given the economic nonviability of the railways which have formed the Canadian National system since 1923, and the fact that, as discussed below, the system has remained virtually intact over the years, it is not surprising that the problem of the capital structure of the publicly-owned railways in Canada has defied solution. In 1937, the situation was revised when the government wrote off $1,167 million of CN's old debts and deficits accrued since 1923. Another recapitalization took place in 1952, when one-half of the long-term debt was changed into a 4% stock to be held by the government, the payments by CN being contingent on earnings after interest and income tax. In addition, $100 million was interest-free until 1962. By 1961, the funded debt of the CN was $1,675 million, or 2.75 times what it was after the recapitalization of 1952. The net cash deficit from 1952 to 1961 was $251 million, and in 1963 another recapitalization was proposed. The net deficits over the years 1962-66 exceeded $186 million. In 1959, a Royal Commission, chaired by M. A. MacPherson, was appointed to investigate the railway problem, and published its findings (Canada, 1961), which led to the 1967 National Transportation Act (Canada, 1967, 1970a). The new legislation, which came into force on March 23, 1967, provided for continued subsidization of railways through payment of most of the losses sustained in operations (on recommendation of the Canadian Transport Commission), maintenance of uneconomic branch lines, etc. Over the 1967-73 period, total payments to railways under the NTA amounted to $771 million, and have continued to increase every year since 1970 (see Chapter 12 and Table 12.2). As discussed in Chapter 12, the 1967 Act provides for continuing subsidy of obsolescent rail technology in Canada.

The financing of railway development from public funds has continued beyond the formation of the CN system. The British Columbia Railway (BCR) represents an on-going case of a province's involvement in railway construction and operations, with the objective of promoting economic and political goals. It was chartered in 1912 as the Pacific Great Eastern Railway (PGE; the name was changed to BCR in 1972), a line (based on the British capital) intended to connect Vancouver with Prince George (on the new Grand Trunk Pacific link to Prince Rupert, see Map 4, p. 259). Although British Columbia guaranteed bonds to the amount of about $20 million, the contractors were unable to finish the work; the province took control of the property and completed construction between Squamish (40 miles north of Vancouver) and Quesnel in 1921, stopping some 130 miles short of Prince George. As described by Leggett (1973), " . . . for the next twenty eight years the isolated little line just existed, . . . the butt of sorry jokes, names such as . . . "Past God's Endurance" being popular explanations of 'PGE'." It was not until 1953 that the line was upgraded and extended to Prince George; the link to Vancouver was completed in 1956, 44 years after the charter was granted. The railway building continued, Fort Nelson being reached in 1971. In 1972, an extension to Dease Lake (see Map 4) was planned by B.C.'s New Democratic Party government, based on promise of a $100 million federal subsidy. As of 1975, in view of soaring cost estimates and unfavourable economic climate, the future of the Dease Lake link appeared uncertain; 1977 has been mentioned as the year of completion.

Between 1957 and 1972, the BCR's accumulated deficit amounted to nearly $100 million. In 1975, B.C.'s Premier David Barrett stated that the Fort Nelson line was not properly planned and constructed; it had 57 derailments in 1974 alone. Referring to the Social Credit ministry which preceded his own, Premier Barrett noted "incompetence and political chicanery" in management of the BCR "which have cost and will continue to cost the people of B.C. hundreds of millions of dollars."

The Alberta Resources Railway (see Map 4, p. 259) is another provincial line which did not live up to expectations. It has failed to break even every year since it was opened in 1968 because interest charges on its debt far exceed freight revenues. By 1974, it has accumulated a deficit of $46.4 million.

In the United States, railway development was also based on public subsidies. The enormous land grants given to the railroads by the federal government – rather than the transportation business – lured aggressive speculators and enterpreneurs:

Such grants were made during the pre- and post-Civil War era, 1850 to 1871, a time when the nation was impatient to open new economic, technological, and territorial

33

frontiers, and the railroads could expect to receive anywhere from 10 to 40 sections of land *per mile* of track constructed, depending on terrain and location. (A section is one square mile, or 640 acres; 40 sections adds up to 25,600 acres.) The land thus granted was in a checkerboard pattern, the government hoping that the non-railroad-held portions would be homesteaded.

In this fashion the federal government gave to some 80 railroads more than 187 million acres, some of it the richest in resource value of any in the world – and grants from states added another 50 million acres. Northern Pacific received the most land of any railroad: 49 million acres. Texas gave away an amount larger than the state of New York. Also, growing communities and established cities offered railroads land, and sometimes cash, as inducements to get rails through their towns – not for the convenience of passengers, but so that livestock and lumber and grain and coal and other products could be hauled to market. Additional land was sometimes offered for depot sites. Not all the federal grants were of western land; chunks of Alabama, Florida, Illinois, Michigan, Mississippi, and Wisconsin were included. (Southerland and McCleery, 1973, pp. 56-57).

CHAPTER 5

FRAGMENTATION
VERSUS INTEGRATION

Private ownership and independent operation of a multiplicity of systems is a distinctive feature of rail transportation in North America. In light of the experiences of other industrialized countries, it is also an anachronistic trait. The fragmented structure of railways on the North American continent is maintained as a mechanism which – according to conventional wisdom – insures competition and efficient operation, and prevents the abuses of a monopoly. Despite extensive evidence which indicates that the supposed benefits of competition have failed to materialize, today there is little thought given in Canada to rationalization of railways through effective, complete integration. In fact, this issue was much more alive at the time of nationalization of the bankrupt railways (Canada, 1917) and during subsequent investigation of railway transportation in Canada by the Duff Commission (Canada, 1932) than it is today.

The first, and the only major integration of railway operations in Canada followed from recommendations of the Drayton-Acworth Report (Canada, 1917) and resulted in nationalization of virtually all lines (except the Canadian Pacific) and their unification within the Canadian National system in 1923. The policy of competition supported by public subsidies, which in the first place led to overcapacity and bankruptcy of the railways taken over by the Canadian National, was not eliminated, although only two competitors remained. An alternative plan of integration, the minority report (Canada, 1917) by A. H. Smith, President of the New York Central Railroad, proposed consolidation of the bankrupt lines into three groups, for operation by the Grand Trunk in the East, and by the Canadian Northern in the West, with the government running the connecting lines. The principle of competition was also preserved under this design.

A different plan – also rejected by the government – was outlined in 1921 by Lord Shaughnessy, Chairman of the Board and President of the Canadian Pacific. He proposed that the government acquire the rail properties of the Canadian Pacific, guarantee a certain fixed return to the shareholders, and enter into a contract with the Canadian Pacific to administer all railways, so that operations would be unified under a single, private management.

A second proposal for the unification of Canadian railways, similar to the above, was made in 1925 by a special committee of the Senate charged with investigation of the railway situation. The plan provided for unified management of the two (CP and CN) systems, recapitalization of the CN and a guarantee of dividends for the CP. As business conditions and railway revenues improved, nothing became of this project.

As described in the next chapter, CN-CP rivalry and competition in the 1920's resulted in further unwarranted expansion of the two systems and continued growth of deficits. At the suggestion of E. W. Beatty, Chairman of the Board and President of Canadian Pacific, a Royal Commission was appointed in 1931 (Canada, 1932) to again investigate railways and transportation in Canada. On the issue of consolidation of railways, the Commission recommended that while the identity of the two railway systems and a degree of competition should be maintained, machinery should be provided for cooperation and elimination of duplicate services and facilities. Detailed counterproposals were made by Canadian Pacific, urging completely unified management of the two railways by Canadian Pacific and a division of net earnings on a basis to be agreed upon with the Dominion government. These plans echoed the first CP unification proposal made in 1921 by Lord Shaughnessy, which was fully endorsed by Beatty. Speaking in Toronto in 1933, Beatty said that if the 1921 plan had been accepted, "hundreds of millions of dollars would have been saved to Canada, and we would, even under present conditions, not have had a serious railway problem on our hands" (Fournier, 1935).

The Canadian Pacific's case was well summarized by Fournier (1935):

> It is argued . . . that there would be no likelihood of a decline in efficiency because the railway administration would be responsible to the shareholders and to the Government for the production of adequate returns from the unified properties. Moreover, the unified properties would not be in a position of complete monopoly because com-

petition from water transport, the motor vehicle, the aeroplane and the railways of the United States (in respect to certain traffic and for standards and practices), would provide ample checks on inefficiency. The point is also made that competition between two immense railway systems, one privately and one publicly owned, does not promote operating efficiency in any way. It only results in an unfair struggle for traffic with resulting practices which are not economical. Under such conditions "healthy competition" is impracticable. Any limitation of competition short of complete unification is difficult to accomplish without the danger of placing more of the burden on, or giving less of the advantage to, one company than the other. For years the privately-owned railway has been subjected to a most unhealthy type of competition, resulting in uneconomical expenditures by both companies which could be avoided if the properties were unified.

If a general scheme of co-operation between the two competing systems were to be worked out on a large scale, carrying with it an assurance of permanency, it would have to be on the principle of equality of sacrifice and equality of advantage. Conditions vary to such an extent in different sections of the country, and are so subject to modification from time to time, that the difficulties in negotiating a mutually satisfactory arrangement on broad lines would be almost insurmountable. In short, competition and co-operation are in practice irreconcilable.

Beatty saw the following advantages in unification:

The more favorably situated lines, the better facilities and equipment of the two companies would be available to carry out the combined operation in the most efficient manner and at the least expense. There would be none of the conflicting interests which are ever present in endeavoring to secure economies by co-operative effort. In every case where the two companies are performing similar services, if either company is more advantageously placed, that advantage would be secured for the operation of the unified property. Gradually duplication in facilities would disappear with resultant decrease in maintenance expense. Duplicate expansion, involving unnecessary competitive expenditure, would be avoided in the future. Supervisory and general expenses would be materially lessened. An important feature . . . is that these advantages can be achieved, I believe, without material detriment in service to the public and with a minimum disturbance to labor (from testimony before the Royal Commission, quoted by Fournier, 1935).

CP studies estimated annual savings of $75 million as a result of unified operations (which envisaged abandonment of about 5,000 miles of railway); the CN estimate run at $56 million.

Proposals for unification were dismissed by the Royal Commission without an impartial study of relative merits. The Commission stated rather curtly that "the time is not opportune for giving serious consideration to this particular remedy; neither complete public nor complete private ownership is possible." The consolidation was opposed by the CN; S. J. Hungerford, the Acting President, stated that "the consolidation of practically all railways into one system would inevitably result in a serious decline in the energy, initiative and enthusiasm of the officers and employees . . . the resultant loss would largely, if not wholly, offset any savings that might be effected." The answer was to "economize in every possible way, and simply hope for return to normal times." As would be expected, organized labor also opposed unification and endorsed the Royal Commission's recommendations.

In Parliament, legislation based on the Royal Commission's report was introduced. During debate it became clear that all parties were solidly opposed to the principle of railway amalgamation. The argument was essentially grounded in the conviction that the people of Canada would not stand for unification, which was therefore considered politically inexpedient. And so the Royal Commission's recommendations were implemented under the Canadian National-Canadian Pacific Act of 1933, which directed the railways to agree on co-operative measures, and set up a mechanism for compulsory arbitration over disputes involving joint use of terminals, running rights and joint use of tracks and other facilities, construction of new lines, and pooling of freight and passenger trains. In effect, competition between the two principal systems was safeguarded again, but moderated by arbitration.

In practice, the extent of cooperation which resulted from the 1933 Act was quite limited, and essentially consisted of pooling CN and CP passenger services between Montreal and Toronto,

Montreal and Ottawa (initiated in 1933), and Montreal and Quebec (in 1934); the pool operation was abolished in 1967. The powers of the arbitration tribunal were never invoked. Although the Royal Commission believed that cooperation would lead to annual savings of $35 million, during the first five years the actual joint economies amounted to only $1.8 million per annum. In 1967, the 1933 Act was repealed.

Since the passage of the CN-CP Act in 1933, the issue of unification of railways in Canada has been dormant. A 1938-39 Senate study emphasized voluntary cooperation. During World War II, Beatty's successor announced that CP had dropped its campaign for unification. The 1951 Royal Commission (Canada, 1951) made some suggestions for improving the functioning of the 1933 Act, but favoured the existence of two distinct railway systems. This arrangement has been continued under the 1967 National Transportation Act (Canada 1967, 1970a).

In his analysis of railway nationalization in Canada, L. T. Fournier, an economics professor at Princeton University, observed in 1935 that:

> . . . the solution of Canada's railway problem calls for more drastic measures . . . under the traffic conditions that exist in Canada, railway competition has more disadvantages than advantages. An examination of the problem, and the factors surrounding it, leads to the conclusion that unified management of the two railways, by such means as will retain the profit motive, is the only practicable way of reducing costs of operation sufficiently to provide the financial relief that is so urgently needed.
>
> Under the CN-CP Act of 1933, the policy of cooperation is being given a trial. . . . Yet indications are that it will yield little financial relief. . . . Possibly when this has been fully demonstrated . . . Canada will be ready to accept unified management, both as a means of rectifying some of the mistaken policies of the past and of putting its railways on a paying basis.

In spite of mounting evidence over the past forty years, Canada has not been yet able to adopt—as discussed in Chapter 23 —the required "more drastic measures." Regulation and fragmentation of the railway industry, and competition have been also emphasized in the United States, or noted by Mertins (1972, p. 19).

During the period from 1880 to about 1920, the transportation resources of the nation grew enormously. But the role of the federal government took a somewhat different course. The primary emphasis of national transportation policy shifted to almost singular concern with regulation of the railroads. This largely represented a reaction to abuse and to what were considered "violations of the public trust." The imperative for action was a widespread fear of high cost transportation, dominated by an uncontrolled group of railroad managements. As a consequence, a long series of stumbling, trial-and-error steps was initiated to bring the industry under control.

The railroad problem also became confused with, and aggravated by, national reactions to monopolies and trusts. This gave further rise to the idea, increasingly supported by the federal government, that there ought to be ready substitutes for the individual modes. The strategy adopted was to promote competition, even where basic economic conditions might have justified a "natural monopoly."

CHAPTER 6

THE 1915 HERITAGE:
DUPLICATION AND OVERCAPACITY

The government could, no doubt, construct a network of State railways parallel with the existing railways. . . . The State could then undersell the separate private companies and take all their traffic from them. That would be the competitive method. There would then be two railways . . . one of them carrying nearly all the traffic, and the other carrying only its leavings and holiday overflows until it fell into hopeless and dangerous decay and ruin.

But can you imagine anything more idiotically wasteful? The cost of making the competing State railway would be enormous, and quite unnecessary. The ruin of the private railway would be sheer destruction of a useful and sufficient means of communication which had itself cost a huge sum. The land occupied by one of the railways would be wasted. What government in its senses would propose such a thing when it could take over the existing railways. . . . ?

– George Bernard Shaw (1928), p. 272

There is yet another course a government could follow, one that even Shaw, with his fine sense of the absurd, did not think of. With one private railway company operating profitably, the government could charter two new private railways to compete with it. When these two go bankrupt, as they inevitably must, since there is not enough traffic to sustain three roads, it could take them over and try to mould them into a workable national railway, leaving the first one alone to make its profits. Would any government in its senses propose such a thing? But we leap ahead of ourselves.

– Robert Chodos (1973), p. 29

From the early days of railway development in Canada, private competition supported by generous public subsidies resulted in the construction of excessive rail mileage. This led to two types of duplication: (i) functional, through lines which although physically more or less remote, catered to the same traffic, and (ii) physical and functional, through closely paralleled lines operated by competing carriers.

In Ontario, the Grand Trunk and the Great Western (see Map 2, p. 257) duplicated many services, struggled with inadequate revenues, and finally amalgamated in 1882 only to face shortly thereafter Canadian Pacific's competition; bankrupt, they were taken over by the government in 1920.

The duplication of railroads on a continental scale resulted from construction of the second and third trans-Canada systems, under the auspices of a Liberal government; the major parallel lines are evident in Maps 1, 2 and 3 (see p. 255 *et seq.*) In the Maritimes, the National Transcontinental between Moncton, N.B. and Quebec City, completed in 1915, duplicated the Intercolonial (in operation since 1876), and added a third line to the Eastern ports. Between Quebec, Montreal, Ottawa and Toronto, Toronto and Sudbury, Montreal/Ottawa and Sudbury, Niagara Falls/Fort Erie and Windsor, a multiplicity of lines was built. At one time, four connections were available between Quebec and Montreal, Ottawa and Montreal, and also between Toronto and Montreal. (After the First World War, 144 miles of the Canadian Northern track were lifted east of Toronto, on the Montreal line). Further west, three "bridge" lines were built over the rocky terrain north of Lake Superior, all leading to Winnipeg. The original (1885) CP line from Sudbury to Winnipeg was duplicated in 1914 by Canadian Northern while National Transcontinental, running farther north from Quebec City, was completed in 1913. Between Winnipeg and Edmonton, functionally parallel lines were built by the Canadian Northern, the Grand Trunk Pacific and the Canadian Pacific; Canadian Northern paralleled Canadian Pacific from Winnipeg to Regina. Duplication, both in space and time, attained the peak of absurdity on the Edmonton-Tête-Jaune (Yellowhead) section. Over a distance of 305 miles, the Canadian Northern and the Grand Trunk Pacific were laying tracks side-by-side, while concealing their intention to use the Tête-Jaune pass. In places, the two lines were so close that they could be taken for a double-track line; they crossed at Chip Lake. The National Transcontinental line opened in 1914; the Grand Trunk Pacific in 1915. But less than two years later, in May, 1917, 90 miles of the Canadian Northern track were abandoned (rails were removed to help with the war effort); by the end of 1918, less than 20% of the Canadian Northern trackage remained; today, only a single track line is operated by Canadian National between Edmonton and Red Pass Junction (25 miles east of Tête-Jaune). While separated by a span of 28 years, a similar case of duplication occurred between Kamloops and Vancouver, the Canadian Northern (1913) paralleling the Canadian Pacific (1885) tracks on the opposite banks of the North Thompson and Fraser rivers.

Extensive duplication of railroads is reflected in the rate of track mileage expansion. During the two decades from 1898 to 1917, 23,900 miles of track were added, at an average rate of almost 1200 miles per year, or over 3 miles per day. Between 1898 and 1915, Canadian Pacific alone built new branches at a rate of 380 miles per year, or more than a mile a day for 18 years.

The overexpansion of transcontinental railways in Canada was well recognized by the Duff Royal Commission (Canada, 1932). Describing the establishment of the second and third systems, the Commission observed that "there developed by the authority of the Parliament of Canada, the tragedy of three transcontinental railways (providing, with branches, over four thousand miles of unnecessary lines), when two were all the business of Canada required or could support."*

The last and the final period of vigorous expansion of railways in Canada occurred between 1920 and 1930, when Canadian National and Canadian Pacific embarked on competitive expansion of their branch lines in the Prairie provinces. During that decade, almost 4000 route miles were added in Manitoba, Saskatchewan and Alberta, an increase of 27.4%, as compared with only an 8% increase in the total mileage in Canada. As described in the Duff Report (Canada, 1932) this was the time

> . . . of intense rivalry between the two systems in new territory. . . . The construction program of one company was responded to by an equal or greater program of construction of the other. The development of this territory did not meet expectations, and the railways now [1931]

---

*The U.S. railway system has also suffered from proliferation of lines. For example, between Chicago and St. Louis, a distance of 284 miles, no less than six railroads were constructed, comprising 1,828 miles of main tracks (Williams, 1971).

find themselves with additional traffic mileage and an increased burden of capital charge. It would be fruitless at this stage to apportion the blame for the competition, and it is imperative that conditions be imposed that will make impossible a repetition of the rivalry in the extension of railway mileage that marked the period from 1923 to 1931.

Although rivalry – in terms of network expansion – was arrested during the Depression years, the damage had already been done, and its consequences persist to this day, the railways still maintaining a large mileage of uneconomic, low-density traffic lines.

The Duff Report (Canada, 1932) stated that in 1931 42% of the route miles operated at a density smaller than 250,000 net tons per year and carried only 5% of the traffic. "Were it possible to abandon this economically unsound mileage (17,658 miles), the mileage remaining and now carrying 95% of the net ton miles, would be about 58% of that now in existence."

During 1926-35, 40% of the Canadian National mileage carried only 5.7% of the system's gross ton-miles, at an average density of 289,000 gross tons per year. In 1956-59, the same

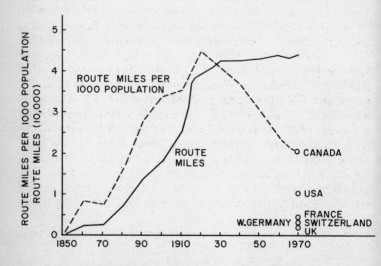

Fig. 6.1   Growth of railway lines in Canada.

mileage carried only 4.4% of the traffic, at an average density of 405,000 gross tons per year (Canada, 1961). Thus, while the contribution of branch lines has diminished, the traffic density has remained at a low level. In 1961, the MacPherson Commission (Canada, 1961) found that a traffic level of at least 200,000 gross tons per year was required to assure economic operation, and that about 8600 routes miles (or 20% in 1961) were being operated in Canada below that density. Nevertheless the redundancy of Canadian railways has been continued under an Order-in-Council (May 4th, 1967), which prohibited abandonment of 18,103 miles of track in Manitoba, Alberta and Saskatchewan (or 90.5% of total route miles in the Prairies, and 42.5% of mileage in Canada) until the end of 1974. In December, 1974, the government announced extension of the prohibition of abandonment of 18,696 miles of tracks in the Prairie provinces: 12,413 miles will be protected until the year 2000, while the remaining 6,283 miles will remain "frozen" for at least one year pending evaluation of their future. Only the lines which were no longer in use (525 miles) were left unprotected and could be abandoned, subject to the Canadian Transport Commission's approval.*

As described above, as a result of subsidized competition, Canada's railway network consists almost totally of single track lines, often parallel to the exclusion of more efficient, double trackage. In fact, there exist today only three major double track lines (see Map 6, p. 261): (i) Sarnia-London-Hamilton-Toronto-Kingston -Montreal (CN, 509 miles), (ii) Thunder Bay-Winnipeg-Portage-la-Prairie (CP, 475 miles), (iii) Glen Tay-Smith Falls-Montreal (CP, 135 miles), for a total of 1119 miles, or 2.7% of the total route mileage (43,644 miles) in 1970.** At present, because of the independent operations by two major carriers, single track lines are used for two-way traffic by utilizing numerous passing loops. In view of the extensive duplication of lines, if the operations were integrated one could envisage single track lines carrying only one-way traffic between major centers, thus providing effec-

*In July, 1975, CN was granted permission to close 55 railway stations in Saskatchewan. The freeze was extended to the end of 1976.

**In 1970, there was a total of 2,018 miles of second and other main track in Canada, or 4.6% (Statistics Canada, 1970, pt. I).

tively the benefits of double track. This intriguing possibility is discussed further in Chapter 20.

The growth of railway mileage in Canada over the years is shown in Table 6.1 and Fig. 6.1: it was extremely fast until about 1915, when the network attained some 35,000 route miles (about 40,000 miles of main track). During this period, the length of railway lines was growing much faster than the population: by 1915, a record 4.5 route miles per 1000 persons was reached. Although by 1970 this figure had dropped to 2 route miles per 1000 population, Canada still operates more track per capita than other industrialized countries (see also p. 55 and Table 8.1, p. 57).

TABLE 6.1 CONSTRUCTION AND ABANDONMENT OF RAILWAY TRACKS IN CANADA (CANADA 1973)

MILES OF RUNNING TRACK

Year	Opened*	Closed*	Net
1840	30	—	30
50	80	—	80
60	2506	11	2495
70	3132	11	3121
80	6938	14	6924
90	14177	87	14090
1900	19184	167	19017
05	22627	242	22385
10	27833	292	27541
15	39591	348	39243
20	41184	490	40694
1925	43101	695	42406
30	45730	985	44745
35	46916	1524	45392
40	47033	2320	44713
45	47075	2522	44553
50	47142	2595	44547
55	47858	2847	45011
60	48822	3224	45598
65	49047	4149	44898
1970	50022	4367	45655

*Cumulative to year shown; net mileage is opened minus closed mileage

Plate 1. LEFT: *The Colonist*, Canadian Pacific's first class parlour car, 1888-1895 (*CP Rail*). At the turn of the century, Canadian railways offered luxurious travel in sumptuous and elaborate surroundings. BELOW: Canadian National engine 6218, here shown at Victoriaville, Quebec station in July 1971, was operated in Ontario and Quebec on day excursions in the years 1964-1971 (*W. R. Linley, Ottawa*). Today, modern passenger rail transportation is not available in Canada, but old steam trains—relics of an earlier romantic era of railway technology—are popular with the Canadian public.

Plate 2. Trains in Western Europe and Japan offer fast (up to 130 mph in Japan), smooth travel and modern comfort. ABOVE: Trans Europ Express *Le Mistral* passengers en route from Paris to Nice (*SNCF*). BELOW: *Le Mistral* bar-boutique car resembles a modern shopping plaza or hotel (*SNCF*).

Plate 3. Electric traction is superior to diesel. ABOVE: TEE *Le Mistral* is pulled from Paris to Nice by one electric locomotive (*SNCF*). In 1975, French intercity trains run at average speeds up to 102 mph. BELOW: Electric, 74 mph *Metroliners* are the only high speed trains operating (since 1969) in the U.S. (*AMTRAK*). They are tomorrow's trains running today on yesterday's track: their speed potential of 160 mph cannot be realized under present conditions.

Plate 4. The operation of expensive, slow and unreliable transcontinental trains in Canada reflects an earlier era of transportation technology. ABOVE: The CN *Super Continental* is pulled by three diesels along the Fraser river, B.C. (*Canadian National*). In 1972 only one-third of the trains made the 40 mph schedule. From Montreal to Vancouver the engine crews change 21 times, the train crews – 9 times. BELOW: Transcontinental trains are likely to follow the fate of transatlantic liners. *France*, the flagship of the French line, was withdrawn from service in 1974 (*Guy Reuland, Luxembourg*).

Plate 5. In North America, long and heavy trains move efficiently bulk shipments over large distances. But many uneconomic operations continue ... ABOVE: A CP Rail unit grain train – a seemingly endless string of government-owned, covered hopper cars is pulled by four diesels over the Lethbridge viaduct, Alberta, in 1974 *(CP Rail)*. BELOW: At the eastern periphery of Canada, apparently two narrow gauge engines are required to propel a four-car mixed train as it returns to Clarenville from Bonavista, Newfoundland in 1973 (*W. R. Linley, Ottawa*). The last car is a passenger-caboose combination featuring hardback seats and wood stoves.

Plate 6. ABOVE: A CP Rail coal unit train alongside Columbia Lake in British Columbia in 1972. The mid-train diesels are controlled by the robot unit, directly ahead, which responds to radio commands of the train engineer (*CP Rail*). BELOW: An aerial view of CN classification yard in north Toronto in 1974 (*Canadian National*). Although Canadian and American railways operate extensive, highly automated facilities for sorting cars and assembling trains, the freight cars sit idle for much of the time in marshalling yards.

Plate 7. Two systems of efficient, intermodal rail-road transportation have been developed: containerization and "piggy-back". ABOVE: Piggy-back trailers being loaded onto CN flatcars (1953, *Canadian National*). BELOW: A CP Rail container being loaded from a flatcar onto a truck (1975, *CP Rail*).

Plate 8. Intermodality may also be the key to viable long distance passenger train operations. *Auto-Train*, started in 1971, provides comfortable and inexpensive transportation from Virginia and Kentucky to Florida for automobiles with their passengers. It is the only passenger train in North America which makes money. ABOVE: A movable ramp is used by *Auto Train* to load automobiles onto the upper deck of ex-CN carrier cars (*Auto-Train Co.*). RIGHT: Coach passengers travel in domed cars equipped with comfortable, reclining, first class airline type seats with leg rests. A pillow and a blanket awaits each passenger. Compartments sleeping two are available at extra cost. Buffet and night-club cars are included in the train (*Auto Train Co.*).

Plate 9. The past decade has seen vigorous development of new railway technology in Western Europe and Japan. ABOVE: The world's fastest (130 mph max.) passenger trains operate on Japan's *Shinkansen* system of dedicated lines. (*Japanese National Railways*). BELOW: *TGV (Train Grande Vitesse)* is under development by the French National Railways for service at speeds up to 163 mph. The prototype *TGV-001*, here shown, attained 198 mph in 1972 (*SNCF*)

Plate 10. ABOVE: French 125 mph *RTG* gas turbine trains entered AM-TRAK service in 1973. In 1974, AMTRAK decided to acquire a total of 13 *RTG* trains in preference to the American *Turbotrains*, originally produced by the United Aircraft Corporation, and no longer manufactured (*AMTRAK*). BELOW: Prototype locomotive and coach of the *LRC* (*Light, Rapid and Comfortable*) 120 mph train under developement by a Canadian consortium. The design conforms to standard North American practice but allows higher speeds on existing tracks. Tilting of the passenger compartment ensures comfort on curves at high speeds. As of 1975, no *LRC* trains have been ordered in Canada, or elsewhere (*Montreal Locomotive Works—Worthington, Ltd.*).

Plate 11. In Britain, modern passenger trains provide fast (80 mph average) passenger service on main intercity runs. Faster equipment is being developed for use on electrified and non-electrified lines. ABOVE: British Rail's 125 mph *High Speed Train* is decreasing travel times on non-electrified lines. In 1973 the train broke the world record for diesel traction by running at 141 mph (*British Rail*). BELOW: British Rail's *Advanced Passenger Train (APT)* will enter service on electrified routes in 1978. The *APT-Experimental*, here shown, attained 152 mph in 1975. The articulated suspension of the train is clearly visible (*British Rail*).

Plate 12. Modernization of railwa[y]
Western Europe and Japan ha[s re-]
quired a considerable research an[d de-]
velopment effort, and has led to t[he in-]
troduction of many novel techni[ques.]
BELOW: British Rail's Tech[nical]
Centre in Derby, with a staff of 2[500,]
probably the largest railway R&[D es-]
tablishment anywhere. (*British* [Rail.]
LEFT: An innovation adopted i[n the]
APT, the *LRC* and other designs [is the]
body tilt, which allows fast trav[el on]
curves with no discomfort due to c[entri-]
fugal force. Here *APT-E* is seen [tilting]
while negotiating a curve at high s[peed.]
Note also the modern track con[struc-]
tion featuring concrete ties an[d im-]
proved rail fasteners (*British Rail*).

Plate 13. In the 1960s and early 1970s considerable effort went into the development of fast surface transportation systems. ABOVE: Artist's concept of an electromagnetically supported urban transportation system of West German design, which was being developed from 1972 by the Ontario government. The *GO-Urban* project was cancelled in 1974 when work was discontinued in West Germany (*Wide World Photos*). BELOW: The French *Aérotrain* intercity vehicle attained a record speed of 257 mph. It was supported on air cushions and propelled by a jet engine. *Bertin & Cie*).

Plate 14. ABOVE: As of 1975, Canada has the dubious distinction of being the world's only industrialized country *without* a single piece of new passenger intercity rolling stock on order. The only modern passenger trains operating in Canada are the *Turbotrains*, leased by CN from Pratt & Whitney of Canada, Ltd. Because of inadequate track and signalling, the 125 mph trains achieve an average speed of only 80 mph (*W. R. Linley, Ottawa*). RIGHT: The C.N. Tower, the world's highest (1815 ft) free-standing man-made (at cost of $50 million) structure and a symbol of CN's diversification, nears completion in Toronto in 1975. Low earnings have encouraged North American railways to seek more profitable, off-the-track ventures (*Canadian National*).

Plate 15. From their inception in 1968, CN *Turbotrain* operations have been continually plagued with problems. LEFT: This CN advertisement appeared on December 9, 1968 to announce the beginning of "a whole new travel experience" on the *Turbo*. "*Turbo* is unlike anything you've known before"—it said. It enticed the public to "Experience the *Turbo* Excitement" (*Canadian National*). BELOW: The next day, on December 10, 1968, the premiere press run of the Montreal-bound *Turbo*, intended to show the most luxurious rail travel in North America, ended in an accident which demonstrated that level crossings are not compatible with passenger operations. This prize-winning picture was taken from the rear observation dome: it shows debris flying over the train's roof moments after the *Turbo* sliced through a tractor-trailer at a level crossing in Kingston. Due to technical difficulties, *Turbo* service was discontinued in January, 1969 (*Ernie Lee, London Free Press*).

Plate 16. ABOVE: Technical difficulties continued during CN's attempt at operating *Turbotrains*. In July, 1970, 188 Montreal passengers boarded a *Rapido* train after a CN *Turbo* stalled at Pickering (*Davis, The Globe and Mail, Toronto*). BELOW: In July, 1973 a *Turbo*, on test run before delivery to AMTRAK, collided with a CN freight near Montreal and was destroyed by fire (*Canada Wide Feature Service Ltd.*).

Between 1915 and 1970 (inclusive), a total of some 13,000 miles of new track was laid in Canada; about 50% of this growth occurred in Saskatchewan and Alberta before 1937, and during the same period (1915-1937), about 1750 miles of track were abandoned. Subsequent growth, mostly after 1952, was due to construction of railways for the exploration of the Canadian North. About 3,100 miles (including 2,900 miles since 1952) were built, mostly in Quebec, Alberta and British Columbia; these major new lines are shown in Maps 4 and 5, pp. 259-260. Up to 1970, a total of 4,367 miles were abandoned in Canada (Canada, 1973). Therefore, assuming the mileage taken out of service to have been built before 1915, we find that 71% of the 45,655 miles of running track operated in 1970 in Canada were in use before 1915. If the mileage of the northern railways is excluded from this comparison, this figure increases to 77%. A similar calculation shows that 89% of the track operated in Canada in 1970 was built before 1930; the proportion increases to 96% if the northern lines are excluded. Clearly, the rail network in Canada today essentially dates back to the First World War, and has undergone only small changes during the past 45 years. Up to 1970, only 8.7% of the track has been abandoned in Canada. This includes a small mileage of low traffic branch lines, and a few tracks on the main lines (between Edmonton and Jasper, Winnipeg and Portage-la-Prairie, Toronto and Ottawa, Ottawa and Montreal). It is apparent that only a minimal rationalization of the railway network has taken place over the years. The extravagance of three transcontinental systems and the redundancy of a multiplicity of branch lines have been well preserved.

Because of duplication and large overcapacity, and in spite of huge subsidies, the financial performance of railways in Canada has usually fallen short of expectations.

The first two main-line systems, The Grand Trunk and the Great Western Railways (whose initial development was completed between 1853 and 1856), suffered chronic financial setbacks.

The capital cost of all railways in Canada exceeded the estimates by a large factor. The Great Western, one of the few early railways that ever showed a profit (but nevertheless amalgamated in 1882 with the Grand Trunk as a result of financial difficulties), cost £1.8 million above the estimate for the main line alone. The cost of the Intercolonial exceeded the estimate by $14 million.

The anticipated rail traffic never materialized, due in part to competition from waterways. In 1862, only 6.6% of the western grain at Montreal went over the Grand Trunk. The operating ratio (operating expenditures/revenues) of Canadian railways stayed at a high level. Based on British experience, Grand Trunk's operating ratio was placed at 40%, but actually never dropped below 58% and in the years 1856-59 remained between 89% and 92%. By 1860, the Grand Trunk was virtually bankrupt; its deficit amounted to $13 million in 1861. The Company was referred to as "the world's worst business."

Competition between railways was often responsible for the dilution of traffic, as for instance between the Great Western and The Grand Trunk on the Toronto-Sarnia/Windsor lines. Moreover, both railways failed to attract a significant volume of the east-west United States traffic: the long-sought prize of American trade escaped them.

While the Grand Trunk and the Great Western relied heavily on English capital, subsequent Canadian railway ventures were all based on public (provincial, municipal and federal) financing or outright government ownership, and cannot be therefore considered as ordinary business enterprises. The Intercolonial Railway, running between Halifax and Quebec, since 1876 was the next major Canadian system and the first experiment by the Dominion in public ownership of railways. By 1916, the Intercolonial had 1450 miles of track constructed at a cost of $108 million. Built expensively to carry fast through traffic, it was never able to achieve a sufficient volume to carry the capital investment. Neither could it attract adequate local traffic in the sparsely populated areas of eastern Quebec and northern New Brunswick. From 1890 on, with the opening of the Canadian Pacific "short line" through Maine to Saint John, N.B., the Intercolonial had to compete not only with shipping but also with a much shorter rail connection. Predictably, the Intercolonial was never a profitable enterprise.

Subsequent major railway systems, whether privately-owned (the Canadian Pacific, 1881-1885*, the Canadian Northern, 1897-1915 and the Grand Trunk Pacific, 1908-1914) or publicly-owned (the Prince Edward Island Railway, 1870-1875, the

* Period of the initial major construction is indicated.

Newfoundland Railway, 1881-1884, and the National Trans-continental, 1908-1914), were built – as already discussed – with very substantial assistance from governments. Had the private investors believed that the railroads would be profitable, they would have built them without subsidy. The Canadian Pacific has been the only major railway system which consistently rewarded the private investor.* In view of the large subsidy it received, the significance of its apparent profitability has been questioned. The results of studies conducted by George (and noted in his *Foreword* to Innis, 1971) suggest that in terms of private rates of return on CPR investment during the first decade of operation (1886-1895), the CPR was unprofitable. Conversely, it was found that the Company received "excessive" subsidies, to the extent of $40 to $61 million in 1885, when the market rate of return on investment was assumed to be 10% to 6% respectively. Traditionally, it has been assumed (e.g. by Innis, 1971), that the "economic benefits" of the railroad were "substantial", and that the railway was "likely to yield large social returns** on investment but only low levels of private income to the Company" but, as noted by George (in Innis, 1971), there has been as yet "no attempt to calculate the social rate of return on CPR investment, or 'social savings' attributable to the railroad."

The information here reviewed indicates that without subsidies only a small fraction of the railway network as we know it today would have been constructed. It is also likely that, had an unsubsidized competition been allowed to freely operate, a railway system commercially more viable would have been developed. But this is not to say that such a system would have served adequately the needs and aspirations of a developing Canada.

---

* 1932 was the first year in which CPR did not pay dividends on common stock; in 1933 the preferred stock dividend was withheld.

** The numerator in the "social rate of return" calculation is equal to "the net earnings of the railraod plus the unpaid benefits", or "the increase in the national income brought about by the road but which failed to be reflected in the company's net earnings" (George in Innis, 1971, p. viii).

CHAPTER 7

THE PERTINENT PAST:
A SUMMARY

Summarizing the development of railways in Canada we should first note that railway development has not been primarily governed by the forces of competitive, free market economy. Rather, the motivation has often been political, on both a national and partisan level. The Intercolonial, linking Halifax with Quebec, was planned (starting in 1836) and completed (in 1876) as a link between the Maritime Provinces and eastern Canada, and as a strategic, military line. Its construction was stipulated in the 1867 British North America Act. The Canadian Pacific (completed between Montreal/Toronto and Vancouver in 1885), the first transcontinental railway, was built in fulfillment of the 1871 agreement which admitted British Columbia to the Canadian Confederation. While Canadian Pacific played a major role in opening up the Canadian west, it was also the major project and achievement of the Conservatives. Starting in 1896, the second and third transcontinental lines were developed under the auspices of the Liberals, who needed to match the Conservatives' success. Thus Grand Trunk Pacific & the National Transcontinental (from Moncton, N.B. to Prince Rupert, B.C.) and the Canadian Northern (from Quebec to Vancouver, B.C.) were completed by 1915. The completion of the PEI railway, started in 1871, was a condition necessary to induce PEI into the Union in 1873.

Throughout the era of major railway development in Canada (before 1915), the relationship of railway companies and governments (federal and provincial) was very close; today it would carry the "railway-government complex" label. Prime ministers, ministers, high government officials, and members of legislatures often served as officers of railway companies or as their salaried counsels, and frequently held significant blocks of shares. Railways were generous contributors to party funds. No doubt, political aims were sometimes subservient to the goals of the railway companies.

The railway-government complex provided railways with very generous subsidies for construction and operation. The railway boom was launched in Canada when the Railway Guarantee Act became law in 1849. Cash and land grants, loans and guarantees of credit by federal, provincial and municipal governments were the major forms of assistance. In many cases, railways were built entirely with government funds, and operated by governments (Intercolonial, National Transcontinental, PEI). By 1916, the total investment in Canadian railways amounted to $1.9 billion; of this, $955 million, or 49.5%, came from the public purse.

Heavy subsidization of several independent and competing, politically-motivated railways resulted in the construction, by 1915, of an inefficient system of a much larger traffic capacity than economically justified. Much of the network and many services, were duplicated. There were three transcontinental systems and as many as four different connections between major centers in eastern Canada (e.g. Montreal-Toronto, Montreal-Ottawa). Instead of the efficient double track, practically the entire network consisted of single track lines.

In spite of large subsidies with the exception of the Canadian Pacific all railways operated at a loss; in 1923 these railways were absorbed into the government-owned Canadian National system. However, the subsidized competition, although reduced to two systems (CP and CN), was not arrested. In the 1920s both systems greatly expanded their networks in the Prairies. Proposals for unified management of the two railways were rejected in 1920s and 1930s. By 1931, CN (including constituent railways before 1923) received $2.5 billion in subsidies. The density of the traffic was below the minimum economic level on a large portion of the network: 42% (17,600 miles) of it carried only 5% of the traffic. The redundancy of the rail lines was continued under a 1967 order which prohibited abandonment of 18,100 miles (41% of the total network) of uneconomic tracks in the Prairie provinces; the order was extended in 1974 to cover 12,413 miles until the year 2000, and 6,283 miles for at least another year. It is estimated that about 70% of the railway mileage operated in 1970 was in use before 1915. Today's network of railways in Canada essentially dates back to World War I.

Realizing that the development of railways in Canada was not grounded in sound economics, but rather in national and partisan politics, and that the Canadian railway network, as it exists today, has undergone little change since World War I, we should not be tempted to view the Canadian railways as an efficient system capable of competition with other and newer transportation modes.

PART TWO
THE STATE OF THE ART

In the early days of the last war when armaments of all kinds were in short supply, the British, I am told, made use of a venerable field piece that had come down to them from previous generations. The honorable past of this light artillery stretched back, in fact, to the Boer War. In the days of uncertainty after the fall of France, these guns, hitched to trucks, served as useful mobile units in the coast defense. But it was felt that the rapidity of fire could be increased. A time-motion expert was, therefore, called in to suggest ways to simplify the firing procedures. He watched one of the gun crews of five men at practice in the field for some time. Puzzled by certain aspects of the procedures, he took some slow-motion pictures of the soldiers performing the loading, aiming, and firing routines.

When he ran these pictures over once or twice, he noticed something that appeared odd to him. A moment before the firing, two members of the gun crew ceased all activity and came to attention for a three-second interval extending throughout the discharge of the gun. He summoned an old colonel of artillery, showed him the pictures, and pointed out this strange behavior. What, he asked the colonel, did it mean. The colonel, too, was puzzled. He asked to see the pictures again. "Ah," he said when the performance was over, "I have it. They are holding the horses."

– E. E. Morison (1966)

The condition of railway transportation in Canada today reflects the historical development as reviewed in Part One more than it does the progress in railway operations and technology achieved over the past decade or two, mostly in Western Europe and Japan. Indeed, before modernization of Canadian (and North American) railways can be considered (in Part Three), their operations should be evaluated relative to the progress made elsewhere, particularly in comparison to technical performance and quality of service. Other aspects, related to engineering research, manning of trains, regulation by government and efficiency in the allocation of transportation services, also need to be considered.

TABLE II.1   CN AND CP SHARE OF RAILWAY TRANSPORTATION IN CANADA IN 1970 (CANADA YEARBOOK, 1972)

	CN	CP	CN AND CP
Length of lines operated, %	52	38	90
Gross ton-mile hauled, %	51	38	89
Operating revenues, %	51	37	88

In reviewing the "state of the art" of railway transportation in Canada, frequent reference is made to the Canadian National and the Canadian Pacific, the two organizations responsible for operating practically all railways in Canada (they account for about 90% of the traffic, operating revenues and track length, see Table II.1) and to the Canadian Transport Commission (CTC), the regulatory agency created to implement the 1967 National Transportation Act (see p. 32) and having, as its principal objective, the "co-ordinating and harmonizing the operations of all carriers engaged in transport by railway, water, aircraft, extra-provincial motor vehicle transport* and commodity** pipelines" (Canada, 1967, 1970a).

---

*Part 3 of the NTA, designed to bring extra-provincial trucking under federal regulation, has never been implemented. The trucking industry continues to be under the ruling of the provinces and is subject to a variety of provincial laws.

**Commodity pipelines do not include pipelines for the transmission solely of oil and/or gas. Oil and natural gas pipelines are under the authority of the National Energy Board.

CHAPTER 8

RAILWAY OPERATIONS IN INTERNATIONAL PERSPECTIVE

Railway operations in North America have been seldom – if at all – compared to the operations of other systems. It has been often said that little wisdom could be gained from such comparisons because conditions in North America have been quite different from those in Western Europe and Japan. Indeed, in North America the distances between population centers are greater, and the population density is much smaller than in Western Europe and Japan. It is also true that, at least since the Second World War, the development of Canadian and American railways followed a substantially different path from that taken by the Western European systems. The divergence came about largely as a result of expansion of car, truck and air traffic (all helped by the availability of cheap oil) in North America, and substantial modernization of Western European railways in the wake of destruction inflicted during the war.* Nevertheless, it is useful to enquire whether – differences in the geo-demographic and economic environments notwithstanding similarities exist in some of the fundamental characteristics of railway transportation in North America and Europe. If this were the case, it would not be possible to ascribe the present, often unsatisfactory state of north American railway technology to objective deterrents to modernization. On the contrary, it would be necessary to look for such deterrents within the transportation policies that have been followed in North America over the past three decades.

A selection of statistical data relevant to comparisons of Canadian, U.S. and other railway systems is given in Tables 8.1 to 8.8. In terms of the Gross National Product (GNP), the railway activity (revenues) in Canada (Table 8.1) amounts to 2.3% and is larger than in any other country (no data is available for the USSR); it matches closely the next highest figure of 2.2% for Switzerland. The significance of railway transportation is also reflected in the level of traffic. Except for the USSR, Canadian

---

*In France, for example, some 82% of the motive power, 80% of coaches and 64% of freight cars had been damaged or destroyed; about 2500 bridges and viaducts had to be rebuilt.

railways move more gross ton-miles per year per capita than other systems, about 3 times the amount typical of Western Europe. The same is true of rail freight traffic alone: the USSR excepted, Canada shows the highest ton-miles of freight per capita, about 6 times the amount for Switzerland and West Germany. Thus, in terms of the overall economic activity and population, even though their share of intercity passenger traffic is very small (3%, Table 8.2), railways in Canada play a more significant role than in other industrialized countries, with the possible exception of the USSR. This is also apparent in the capital investment in railways per capita, which is highest in Canada (20% more than in Switzerland and West Germany, twice the U.S. value, 5 times the U.K. value), and in the length of track* per capita: 2 miles of running track per 1000 population (see also Fig. 6.1, p. 46), about four times more than in Western Europe, twice as much as in the U.S., and five times the amount in the USSR. With 1.9 miles per 1000 population, Australia is a close second to Canada.

Although railway investment in Canada appears to be very large on a per capita basis, when related to the traffic volume and track length, it is among the lowest. For example, investment per gross ton-mile/year in Canada is one-third of the investment in West Germany, while the investment per mile of running track is about one-quarter of the West German figure (the corresponding U.S. figures are even smaller). On the other hand, the level of track utilization (or traffic density, measured in gross ton-miles per year, per mile of running track), although on the low side, is comparable to the levels achieved in Western Europe (identical to France and only slightly lower than in West Germany).

Such relatively low investment levels in Canadian and U.S. railways may reflect not only the obsolescence of the railway plant in North America but also its efficiency. As discussed in more detail below, North American railways are obsolete in some respects, but highly efficient in others. For example, freight operations in Canada are highly productive (Table 8.3): trains carry 5 to 8 times the loads common in Western Europe

---

*In Canada (CN and CP), there are only about 2,000 route miles with more than one track (see Map 6 and Chapter 6), so that "route miles" amount to 95% of the "running track" length (Statistics Canada, 1970, I). The latter represents about 75% of all track; a somewhat lower proportion (63%-68%) is typical of Western Europe (IUR, 1971).

(1650 tons compared to 200-350 tons)*, 80% of train capacity is used (compared to 65% in West Germany), larger net loads are moved (52% compared to 37-40% in Western Europe), and trains run over much longer distances (533 miles versus 75 to 175 miles). However, while annual revenues (Table 8.4) represent in Canada – as in Switzerland, West Germany and Japan – 23% of the investment, revenues per unit track length and freight revenues per ton-mile are low in Canada, and amount to only 20 to 50% of the revenues of Western Europe.

Unlike in Europe and Japan, in Canada and U.S. passenger rail traffic is negligible when compared to rail freight, or other modes of passenger travel. In North America, passenger rail revenues (Table 8.5) represent only about 5% (versus 76% for Japan, 39% for France and Switzerland) of freight revenues. Passenger traffic per unit track length is lowest in Canada, some 30 times smaller than in West Germany and France. In terms of gross ton-miles, passenger traffic in Canada represents only 10% of the total, compared to about one-third in France and West Germany, and one-half in Switzerland and Italy.

The absence of passenger traffic, and the previously mentioned use of much larger freight trains, is the cause of another major difference in railway operations: in North America, the average frequency of trains (Table 8.6) is some ten times less than in Western Europe and Japan.

The manning of Canadian railways (Table 8.7) reflects the steam locomotive era (see Chapter 11) and is extravagant when compared with modern practice elsewhere. Canadian railways employ the largest number of persons per train-mile (about twice as many as West Germany) and pay them the most money (more than twice the European amounts). However, in terms of the "units of traffic" (the sum of freight ton-miles and passenger-miles), the manning of North American railways is at the lowest level (0.5 (U.S.) and 0.8 (Canada) persons per million units of traffic, compared to 2.7 in France, 3.6 in West Germany and 5 in the U.K.). This reflects a negligible volume of passenger traffic and the previously mentioned high efficiency of freight operations.

The modernization of railways through electrification (Table

---

*The use of very long trains (6,000 tons are common) in North America reflects crew rules which result in over-manning of trains (see below and Chapter 11); high capacity, automatic car couplers (125 ton capacity) make such operations possible. (I Mech. E., 1975, p. 74).

8.8) has yet to start in Canada and the U.S. In West Germany, France and the USSR, from 25 to 40% of running track is electrified, and carries up to 75% of the traffic (gross ton-miles).

The information here reviewed indicates that, compared to other industrialized countries, the utilization of railways in Canada is at a high level, and railway transportation is particularly important in the overall economy. Indeed, Canada's largest investment per capita in railways and low freight revenue per ton-mile should provide a strong incentive to conduct rail operations with the highest possible efficiency.

TABLE 8.1   COMPARISON OF RAILWAY UTILIZATION AND INVESTMENT IN 1968-1970 (IUR, 1968; SBB, 1971b)

	Can.	Switzl.	W. Ger.	Fr.	UK	USSR	Japan	USA
Rail revenues as % GNP	2.3	2.2	2.0	1.8	1.2	–	1.6	1.2
Gross ton-miles per year per capita (1000)	9.1	3.4	2.7	3.1	–	18.2*	1.8	8.2
Freight ton-miles per year per capita (1000)	4.6	0.7	0.8	1.0	0.3	7.1	0.4	3.7
Running track (mile per 1000 population)	2	0.43	0.47	0.68	–	0.39	0.16	1.16
Running track traffic density (million gross ton per year)	4.5	7.9	5.7	4.5	–	4.8*	0.3	7
Investment per capita (1000 Sw. Fr.)	1.46	1.22	1.19	0.42	0.28	–	0.52	0.74
Investment per mile running track (million Sw. Fr.)	0.7	2.8	2.6	0.6	–	–	3.2	0.6
Investment per gross ton mile per year (Sw. Fr.)	0.15	0.37	0.45	0.14	–	–	0.3	0.09

*Estimated

The main differences between railway operations in Canada and the U.S. on the one hand, and Western Europe and Japan on the other, concern the much larger frequency and smaller weight of trains in the latter countries, as well as a much larger volume of passenger traffic, and extensive use of electric traction. Thus it could be anticipated that modernization of railways in North America would involve electrification of high density lines and significant augmentation of passenger services.

TABLE 8.2   DISTRIBUTION OF INTERCITY TRAFFIC IN CANADA IN 1970 (LUKASIEWICZ 1975)

Mode	Passenger-mile (10^9)	%	Freight (10^9)	Ton-mile %
Rail	2.3	3	110	35
Water	–	–	96.5	31
Pipeline*	–	–	86.3	27.6
Truck**	–	–	19.8	6.3
Bus	3.5	4.5	–	–
Auto	66	85	–	–
Air +	5.7	7.5	0.3	0.1
Total	77.5	100	312.9	100

* Gas and oil
** Urban trucking excluded
+ Common carriers only

BLE 8.3 COMPARISON OF RAIIL FREIGHT OPERATIONS IN 1970 (SBB, 1971b)

	Can.	Switzl.	W. Ger.	Fr.	UK	USSR	Japan	USA
n net load train (ton)	1650	237	346	342	222	–	346	1780
n train (mile)	533	90	123	175	75	538	204	516
n wagon acity (ton)	60	29	32	36	20	–	22	67
load ss Weight (%)	52	37	38	40	–	–	48	46
n load n capacity (%)	80	42	65	71	–	–	90	82

ABLE 8.4 COMPARISON OF RAILWAY REVENUES in 1970 (SBB, 1971b)

	Total Revenues			Freight Revenues per Ton Mile Sw. Fr.
	As % of Capital Investment	Per Mile of Running Track 1000 Sw. Fr.	Per Employee 1000 Sw. Fr.	
Canada	23	64	51	0.06
Switzerland	24	348	40	0.22
W. Germany	23	266	30	0.16
France	53	168	28	0.11
U.K.	43	197	19	0.14
Japan	26	390	28	0.07
U.S.A.	35	110	89	0.06

TABLE 8.5   PASSENGER TRAFFIC

	Revenues* Passenger	Passenger miles per mile of route*	Gross ton-miles† Passenger
	Total %	(million)	Total %
Canada	6	0.05	10
Switzerland	39	2.8	47
W. Germany	33	1.5	33
France	39	1.6	31
U.K.	54	2	–
Japan	76	9	55
U.S.A.	5	0.2	4

*In 1970 (SBB, 1971b) † In 1968 (IUR, 1968)

TABLE 8.6   DAILY FREQUENCY OF TRAINS IN 1970 (SBB, 1971b)

	All Trains +	All Trains*	Passenger*	Freight*
Canada	5.2	5.5	1.5	4
Switzerland	58	85	55	30
W. Germany	38	57	37	20
France	24	36	18	18
U.K.	33	66	48	18
Japan	67	90	64	26
U.S.A.	–	6.8	1.2	5.6

+ Computed as the ratio of train-miles per day to the total running track length

* Computed as the ratio of train-miles per day to the total network route miles

TABLE 8.7   MANNING OF RAILWAYS IN 1970 (SBB, 1971b)

	Employees per 10^5 train-miles	Mean annual salary (1000 Sw. Fr.)	Employees per 10^6 units of traffic*
Canada	141	53.4	0.8
Switzerland	72	22.6	2.8
W. Germany	103	23.6	3.6
France	103	18.1	2.7
U.K.	93	14	5
Japan	108	39.7	1.8
U.S.A.	108	54.3	0.5

*Units of traffic equal the sum of passenger-miles and freight ton-miles

TABLE 8.8   ELECTRIFICATION OF RAILWAYS: STATUS IN 1972 (IUR, 1972)

	Electrified Track, %	Electric Traction Traffic, %
Canada	Negligible	Negligible
Switzerland	100	100
W. Germany	43	75
France	35	77
U.K.	21	—
U.S.S.R.	25*	—
Japan	60	78
U.S.A.	Negligible	Negligible

Data Based on Running Track Length and Traffic
Volume in Gross ton-miles

*Based on route length (SBB, 1971b)

CHAPTER 9

ADVANCES IN TECHNOLOGY

Modern technology is highly pervasive: it spreads easily across national boundaries and competes internationally. This is true in fields such as aviation, computers, plastics and communications, to mention only a few – but not of North American railroading. Curiously, Canadian and American railways have remained isolated from some of the significant developments abroad and have yet to take advantage of innovations adopted by many contemporary foreign systems. The more important among those innovations are mentioned in this chapter.

The "technology gap," however, does not apply in all areas of railway engineering, and these comments are not intended to deny the excellence of certain aspects of North American railroading. For example, it is generally recognized that significant progress has been made in containerization, "piggy-back" and unit-train operations, computerization and automation of car location identification and yard operations, among other things. While these advances contribute to the efficiency of rail freight, they nevertheless do not preclude obsolescence in other important areas, such as traction, suspension, structural efficiency or weight of rolling stock, track construction, signalling and traffic control.*

Traction: Electric versus diesel

The development of traction technology is one of the fundamental issues of rail modernization. Suprisingly, in North America it followed a different course than in the rest of the world (see I. Mech. E., 1975, pp. 73-84).

In North America, the steam locomotive has been replaced by diesel-electric (or diesel, for short) engines.** Compared to

---

* For a comprehensive review of all aspects of modern railway technology see I. Mech. E. (1975).

** When equipped with direct drive, the diesel engine is very limited because it cannot adapt to variable load requirements. Also, it cannot start from rest under load. These difficulties have been overcome by the use of electric transmission, the diesel engine being connected to an electric generator which in turn drives electric traction motors. This is known as the diesel-electric design.

steam, this has been a significant advance: it has meant an increase in energy efficiency from about 6% to 35% (Summers, 1971), less frequent servicing, smaller locomotive crews, cleaner and less polluting trains. However, with the conversion from steam to diesel completed in 1960 (see Fig. 9.1), the modernization of traction on Canadian and American railways has come to a halt.**

NO. OF LOCOMOTIVES

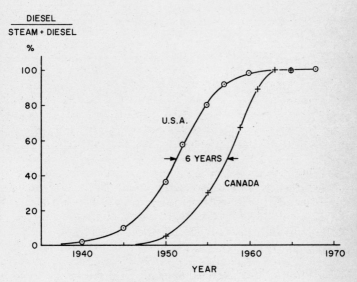

Fig. 9.1   Progress of railway dieselization in the United States and Canada.

In Europe, Japan, South Africa and elsewhere, the diesel-phase of modernization has been largely bypassed in favour of direct change to electric traction, as illustrated below for France.

** Incidentally, it is interesting to note that in Canada rail dieselization (modernization) lagged the U.S. by about 6 years (Fig. 9.1).

% gross-tons hauled

Year	1953	1962	1972
Steam	31	28	0.2
Electric	62	64	77.0
Diesel	3	8	22.8

SNCF Annual Reports; IUR 1972

Although electric traction is historically older than the diesel,* it is nevertheless a basically superior technique which, moreover, has been further improved in recent years through application of solid-state devices. The advantages of electric traction have been recognized in Europe, Japan and elsewhere but have yet to be generally appreciated in North America. I can only record them briefly here; the interested and more technically inclined reader should consult recent, extensive literature, e.g. Emerson (1968), Friedlander (all references), Fisher (1971, 1972), I. Mech. E. (1975), Little (1974), Middleton (1975), Nouvion (1971, 1972, 1974), RSMA (1974). The papers by F. F. Nouvion, who played a major role in the electrification of French railways, are particularly informative.

Power, weight and adhesion
Electric traction is basically superior to diesel because its function is merely to convert electrical energy into mechanical pull (by means of an electric motor). Diesel-electrics, on the other hand, must also produce the electrical energy from fuel and therefore, in addition to electric motors, have to carry the fuel, the prime mover (diesel engine) and the generator. In the case of electric traction, heavy equipment is located in an electrical utility plant miles away, and the energy is drawn from a catenary** supplied from the electrical grid. In effect diesel locomo-

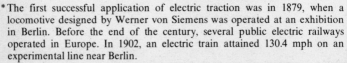

---

* The first successful application of electric traction was in 1879, when a locomotive designed by Werner von Siemens was operated at an exhibition in Berlin. Before the end of the century, several public electric railways operated in Europe. In 1902, an electric train attained 130.4 mph on an experimental line near Berlin.

The pioneer diesel-engine locomotive of any size was a 1000 HP unit built by the Diesel-Klose-Sulzer company in 1912. The first commercially successful diesel-electric locomotive was produced in 1925 by the American Locomotive Company.

** An overhead wire; a third rail has also been used, on rapid transit and suburban railways.

tives are the equivalent of small mobile power stations and are therefore more complex, more expensive and much heavier.

Electric locomotives cost approximately 80% as much per horsepower as diesels: a 3000 HP diesel locomotive costs approximately $400,000; an electric unit of 6600 equivalent horsepower costs about $700,000 (Little, 1974). Nouvion (1971) estimated that, for a given duty on a high traffic volume line, the cost of diesel locomotives would exceed the cost of electric ones by 75%.

For the same weight, electrics exert a larger pull than the diesels and develop more power: 70 HP/ton (French railways) compared to only 13.5 HP/ton for the standard CN (GM) diesels (Fig. 9.2). Putting it in terms of obsolescence, the present American diesel locomotives develop as much power per unit weight as did electric locomotives in Europe in the 1920s.

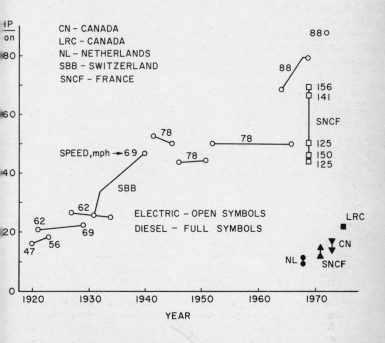

Fig. 9.2   Power/weight ratio and speed of electric and diesel locomotives (1920 to 1973).

65

The larger weight of diesels in relation to their power has several serious disadvantages: it means a smaller pull upgrade and a poorer acceleration and braking performance than is available with the electrics. The weight of fuel which diesels must haul further reduces their performance.

Yet another deficiency of diesel traction is related to the so-called adhesion, or the ability of a locomotive to exert pull or tractive effort. The maximum pull which a locomotive of a given weight (on the driven wheels) can develop at any speed – provided it can generate sufficient power – is determined by the frictional resistance between the wheels and the rails; if a larger force is applied to the wheel rim, wheel slip results and traction is lost. The ratio of the frictional resistance to the weight is known as the *adhesion coefficient*: the larger the adhesion coefficient, the greater the pull that locomotive of a given weight (on the driven wheels) can exert. However, its ability to do so is limited by the maximum power it can develop. This is because power equals the product of pull times speed, so that, with the maximum pull determined by the locomotive weight and adhesion, little power means low speed. Thus diesel locomotives, which are underpowered for their weight, can take advantage of their weight only at low speeds.

The above effects of power/weight ratio on the performance of diesel and electric locomotives are shown in Figs. 9.3 and 9.4, in each case for locomotives of similar weight. "If one sums up [this evidence] by saying that the work which can be performed by an electric locomotive is three times greater than for a diesel, this is probably a fair assessment", (Nouvion, 1971).

Electric locomotives are more efficient than diesels not only because of their higher power/weight ratio, but also because they achieve higher values of the adhesion coefficient, i.e. they are capable of using their weight for traction more effectively than the diesels. This is due to a more sophisticated design of traction motor controls, which allows the motors to operate at all times on the threshold of wheel slip, and to a better design of the bogies or trucks, which reduces dynamic loads and assures equal weight distribution on all axles (see also p. 70). The superiority of traction available with the electric locomotives, well-known in Europe and Japan, was recently verified by G. T. Fisher (1971) of Canadian Pacific, who conducted exten-

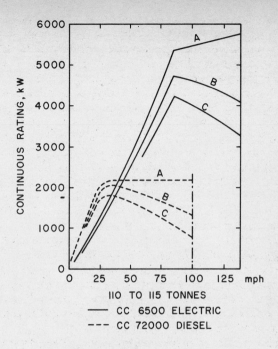

Fig. 9.3   A comparison between the continuous rated output of SNCF diesel and electric locomotives of similar weight. Curves B and C show that the locomotive's own weight reduces the power at the draw-bar on a rising gradient more drastically in the case of the diesel. Also, the diesel locomotive reaches its maximum power at a much lower speed than the electric (Nouvion, 1971).

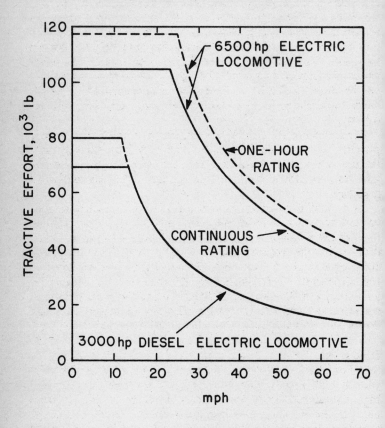

Fig. 9.4   Comparison of tractive efforts of six-axle, 195-ton diesel-electric and electric locomotives, geared for the same speed range. Diesel-electric: 3,000 HP (2,460 HP at wheels); electric 6,500 HP (7,400 HP one-hour). Note that at a typical running speed of 45 mph, the one-hour tractive effort of the electric locomotive is approximately three times that of the diesel (Fisher, 1971).

sive tests of Swiss and Swedish electrics in Switzerland and Norway. His results have shown that "on railways using modern electric locomotives, trains can be dispatched for average weather conditions similar to those in Canada at train tonnages requiring adhesion in excess of 27%, which is 50% more than that achieved by conventional diesel-electrics [18%]. On certain European railways even higher figures are routine." In other words, the diesel locomotive – in order to develop the same pull on the level – must be at least 50% heavier, and its performance, particularly in mountainous terrain, is accordingly reduced.

But this is not all: electric locomotives, inherently much more powerful than the diesels, can be overloaded for short periods (in the range of 10% overload for one hour to 60% for five minutes), for acceleration and negotiation of steep and short gradients.

As a specific example of gains which would result from conversion to electric traction, the following estimate was made for the Canadian Pacific operations in the Rocky Mountains: "One of the [CP] unit coal trains destined for Roberts Bank may have 105 wagons, each loaded with 105 short tons of coal, giving a trailing load of 13,600 short tons. At present, 12 diesel-electric locomotives of 3000 HP are needed to move the train at 15 mph up and down the steepest grades. Six electric locomotives can do the same job at speeds up to 25 mph" (Fisher, 1971).

High speeds
Superior characteristics of electric traction are especially relevant at high speeds. In view of large power/weight ratio and high adhesion, electric locomotives have small axle loadings and use low unsprung weight bogie design* – conditions necessary to insure a comfortable ride and an acceptable rate of track deterioration. Modern electric and gas turbine locomotives and train sets, (see below) such as the United Aircraft Corporation *Turbotrain* (operated by CN and AMTRAK), the French TGV 001, the British Rail APT (Advanced Passenger Train), the Jap-

---

*Unsprung weight is the weight of those components which are not isolated from the track through suspension; for example, wheels, axles, axle bearings, wheel brakes, etc. fall in this category. Unsprung weight is substantially increased if electric motors are mounted directly on the axles, as is the North American practice.

anese New Tokaido Line train, all carry only 16 to 17 tons on the driven axles.

In America, axle loadings twice as large are common. For example, GM diesels (1750 HP, 130 ton), such as those used by CN, carry 32.5 ton/axle (the standard American maximum axle load is 33 tons); the LRC diesel-electric locomotive (now under development in Canada, see Chapter 14) is designed for 27 ton/axle. Such high axle loadings aggravate the speed and comfort limitations and are in no small measure responsible for the poor condition of track on many lines in North America.

Electric traction is also particularly well suited for very high speeds (in excess of, say, 150 mph):* it can accommodate the opposing requirements of small axle load and large power. The small axle load, and the experimentally-observed deterioration of the adhesion coefficient as the speed increases, both limit the power that can be transmitted by an axle. At the same time, because of air drag, train resistance to motion rises more steeply as the speed augments; in fact, it tends to increase as the square of the speed; therefore, the power (equal to resistance x speed) required to drive the train rises even more sharply, as the third power of the speed. Fortunately, electric traction helps to resolve these conflicts: it allows distribution of drive to a maximum number of wheels (through individual electric motors, as in modern train sets), and thus permits utilization of all available weight for traction.

Another advantage of electric traction, particularly significant at high speeds, relates to braking. As speed increases, the task of slowing down or stopping a train within prescribed distance (for example, as imposed by existing signalling systems) becomes increasingly difficult because the amount of kinetic energy to be dissipated augments as the square of the speed. Also, the higher the speed, the more critical is the braking performance from the point of view of safety and operational reliability.

With electric traction, regenerative (electrodynamic) braking can be used in addition to conventional friction brakes (acting through shoes on wheel tread or on axle- or wheel-mounted discs). In a regenerative system, the electric traction motors, used as generators, absorb the train's kinetic energy and convert it into electric current, which is then fed back into the grid or

---

*As evident from Table 21.4, p. 216. World's speed record for wheel-to-rail traction (206 mph) was established in 1955 by French electric locomotives.

dissipated in resistors as heat. In the former case, not only better braking performance is obtained, but also energy is saved.

Braking systems which act on the wheels are ultimately limited by adhesion between the wheels and the rails: excessive braking may result in wheels becoming locked and sliding on the rail, which damages the wheels through formation of 'flats' and limits the braking force. With electric traction, non-adhesion braking is possible through linear induction motor (LIM) brakes, a technique which makes use of currents induced in the rails by brake electromagnets; the latter are always separated from the rails by an air gap. The main advantages of the LIM brakes are the provision of a substantially constant braking effort at high speeds (at low speeds LIM brakes are ineffective since the current induced in the rails vanishes at zero speed) and non-reliance on adhesion. The energy to power LIM brakes is supplied by traction motors operated as generators when braking. Thus the two electric braking techniques: the regenerative braking and the LIM brakes complement each other well and provide the performance required at high speeds (Machefert-Tassin, 1975)*.

Advances in electrical engineering
Recent developments in solid state technology have had a two-fold impact on electric traction: they improved the performance of electric locomotives and reduced the costs of railway electrification. Silicon rectifiers and thyristor controls are more reliable (no moving parts) than conventional equipment which was used before. With thyristors, the traction current can be controlled smoothly and instantaneously, and electrical failures quickly isolated, before permanent damage occurs to the locomotive.

Before solid state rectifiers became available, electric railways were operated from direct current or from low-frequency alternating current, either of which had to be produced by special generating plants or converted from commercial power at considerable capital and conversion expense. Today, electric traction can be supplied with high voltage (up to 50 kV), a-c

---

*Advanced mechanical brakes are being also developed for use at high speeds. For example, brakes in which energy is dissipated through fluid motion (hydrokinetic or fluiddynamic brakes) are used on the 150 mph British Advanced Passenger Train (see p. 212).

power at commercial frequency, at a much reduced price.* The electrification of railways at high voltage (25kV) and commercial frequency was pioneered in France after World War II, and was subsequently adopted in U.K., Japan and elsewhere (viz. CP proposals for the Calgary-Vancouver route at 50 kV, Fisher, 1971). Solid state technology has also reduced the costs of the fixed plant, including catenary sub-stations and signalling equipment. Regarding the collection of current from the catenary, recent experience in France (Morris, 1972) and Japan suggests that satisfactory performance is obtained at speeds at least up to 200 mph.

Operational aspects
In the railway balance sheet, such factors as life, maintenance and availability of locomotives play an important role.

The life of an electric locomotive, which contains only rotating, as opposed to reciprocating, machinery, and is therefore mechanically much simpler (a diesel locomotive has some 3000 parts) is known to be much longer than the life of a diesel. The useful life of electrics exceeds that of diesels by a factor of 2 to 3.

Similar gains are recorded as regards maintenance costs. Diesel maintenance costs exceed electrics costs (including power distribution maintenance) by 100 to 250%. The French (SNCF) experience in this area has been summarized as follows:

> The reason for this big difference [between diesel and electric locomotives] is not only the diesel engine itself, which accounts for about a third of the maintenance charges. It results also from the cramped internal layout of the diesel which makes access for maintenance difficult, as well as vibration, heat, and the presence of oil and grease. These all contribute to the ageing of components and thus to their unreliability.
>
> On a system like the SNCF where 80% of the traffic is handled by around 2000 electric locomotives and 20% by a not dissimilar number of diesels, one finds that – for modern units – maintenance costs per kilometre run are 1.8 times higher for the diesel. If the load hauled is taken as a basis for comparison rather than distance run, the

---

*The world's first 50 kV, commercial frequency (60 Hz) railway, the Black Mesa and Lake Powell in Arizona, was formally opened in March, 1974 (RGI, 1973a).

ratio rises to 2.8. When performance is also taken into account the diesels turn out to be three times as expensive to maintain as the electrics (Nouvion, 1971).

Even higher relative maintenance costs of the diesel have been estimated in Canada:

In round terms, the average maintenance cost of the diesel locomotive is about four times that of the longer-life electric. If expressed in terms of useful performance (the electric unit having more than double the capability of the diesel) one could reach the conclusion that the relative maintenance cost is as high as 8 to 1 for the diesel over the electric unit.

This is, perhaps, an over-simplification because all of the excess performance of the electric unit over the diesel cannot be utilised continuously. A more conservative ratio of maintenance costs on a locomotive fleet basis is that electric units of equivalent size and weight to high-horsepower diesels will cost roughly one-sixth in total maintenance expenses" (Fisher, 1971).

The high level of maintenance required by diesel locomotives reduces significantly their availability as compared to the electrics. "Availability of diesel locomotives for use on trains is commonly taken as 85%, leaving 15% of the time for running inspections, running shop repairs, and workshop repairs. The comparable figure for electric motive power is often around 95%, thus the availability factor becomes an important element in estimating the total investment required in locomotive units" (Fisher, 1971).

Maintenance costs of electric traction are further reduced – as compared to diesel traction – through application of energy-saving, regenerative braking (see p. 218). According to French experience (Nouvion, 1974), the introduction of regenerative braking has reduced by one-third the rate at which wheel-sets have to be replaced, and by three-quarters the rate of brake shoe replacement. Similar gains would be expected with the linear motor brakes (see p. 71).

Automation

As pointed out elsewhere (see p. 79 and Chapter 21), railway is the mode of transport which lends itself best to complete automation, and modern electric traction is particularly well-suited to automatic, remotely-controlled driving. Solid state, thyristor controls are flexible, respond instantaneously to varying power requirements, and efficiently protect electrical equipment. As Nouvion (1974) observed, "One walks with a diesel; one flies with thyristors."

Environmental quality

Last but not least, electric traction is more desirable than diesel for preservation or enhancement of environmental quality. Electric locomotives do not pollute the atmosphere, and it is more practical to apply and maintain stringent pollution controls at large electric generating plants than on each diesel locomotive. Acoustic pollution is also lessened with the electrics.

Superiority of electrics

The many operational advantages of electric traction have been re-stated recently as follows: " . . . improved [traction] control systems, made possible through use of thyristors, prevent wheel-slip, and permit electric locomotives to accelerate more rapidly, climb steeper grades, and travel faster than diesels, thus achieving faster schedules without exceeding existing speed limits. Finally, because refueling is eliminated, turn-around time is also greatly reduced. Tighter schedules permit more trips, and improved use of locomotives as well as of cars" (Little, 1974).

A similarily favorable assessment of electric traction was given in Canada by Fisher (1971), who wrote: "The silicon-controlled rectifier or thyristor had . . . been perfected to the point where locomotives were being produced with full electronic stepless control of motor current and tractive effort, yielding performance and reliability unknown in North American diesel technology."

Summarizing, electric traction is seen to offer performance and economy far superior to diesels, a situation which was described by Nouvion (1971): " . . . the electric railway almost invariably operates on a plane which is just not accessible to the diesels. It is far from certain that a diesel will ever be produced that equals today's electric locomotive, and from this point of view the modern diesel can be regarded as obsolete before it is built."

Its obsolescence is also assured – at least insofar as high density traffic applications – through increasing scarcity of oil. The energy crisis, as discussed in Chapter 22, is a powerful factor which favours both rail transportation and electrification.

Finally, it should be noted that – because electrification involves a large initial investment but reduced running costs – even the rising inflation tips the balance in favour of electric traction (Nouvion, 1974; Little, 1974).

Gas turbine traction

The gas turbine traction fits between the electric and the diesel: less economical than electric, it offers performance superior to the diesel. Application of gas turbines appears advantageous in passenger operations where traffic volume does not warrant electrification, or as an interim measure before electrification is accomplished. Although gas turbine locomotives have not yet reached the degree of perfection achieved by the electrics, they are currently undergoing intensive development and have already been proven reliable in France, and the U.S. Gas turbine, fast passenger trains are being increasingly used in Western Europe on non-electrified lines, by AMTRAK in the United States and by CN in Canada.

Rolling stock

The benefits of reduced locomotive weight with electric traction have already been indicated. An efficient structural design of rail cars is also essential for achieving high performance. In general, light weight structure results in several advantages, such as better braking and acceleration performance, smaller wear, less damage to track, smaller maintenance costs and higher safety. New passenger car designs use aircraft-type construction and materials to achieve light weight. Traditionally, the North American passenger equipment has always been much heavier than the European. (see also Chapter 22 and Table 22.2 re standard Pullman train). Typical U.S. and Canadian passenger cars have a unit weight of about 1 ton/seat, compared to European coaches at 0.35-0.6 ton/seat.

The overall power/weight ratio is a significant measure of train performance. For standard, "fast" Canadian passenger trains it is in the 3 to 4.5 HP/ton range. Standard fast European trains, such as the TEE, achieve 9-11 HP/ton, or more than twice the Canadian value. The future "interim trains," such as Canada's LRC, will have power loading similar to the current European practice (10 HP/ton). The gas turbine trains, and modern electric designs, achieve very high power loadings, in the 15 to 25 HP/ton range.

The desire to operate at higher speeds has led Europe and Japan to introduce improved methods of suspension of railway vehicles, necessary to assure passenger comfort and prevent excessive dynamic loading of tracks and rolling stock. New designs are the result of extensive theoretical and experimental efforts which have been underway in recent years in France, Japan and the U.K. At present, much higher competence in this area exists in Western Europe and Japan than in the U.S. and Canada.*

Improved suspension is particularly significant when using existing, standard or low quality lines for fast passenger trains. Ideally the suspension should feature full articulation, body tilt, and a low unsprung weight. These objectives have been met in various degrees by different designs recently developed for fast passenger trains.

The future British Advanced Passenger Train (APT, Gunston, 1972), and the new French and Japanese fast trains use articulation.** Body tilt is an innovation which, by compensating for lateral acceleration, allows higher speeds on curves without passenger discomfort. It is employed on the JNR's new narrow gauge equipment, the British APT, the German fast diesel train (VT 614), and the new Italian equipment, among others. In North America, only the *Turbotrain* uses both articulation and body tilt. The Canadian LRC design incorporates body tilt only.

Track

The development of lighter, higher-powered and faster rolling stock has been paralleled in Europe and Japan by the applica-

---

* Disturbing evidence of this situation was provided by the derailment in February, 1975 of the first E6OCP electric locomotive built by General Electric for AMTRAK. The accident, which occured at 100 mph on a straight portion of track, was due to violent oscillation of the leading bogie (RGI, p. 286, August 1975).

** A design which allows the wheels to be steered by the car ahead in the direction of the curve. The APT train bogies allow the two-wheel sets to yaw relative to each other while steering always along the local direction of the rails, with no flange contact. Articulation is not required for high speed trains intended for operation on specially constructed, dedicated tracks, which feature particularly high standards of alignment and small curvature. Thus the New Tokaido Line equipment in Japan does not use articulated design.

tion of new methods of track construction and maintenance. Concrete ties, concrete slab beds and improved rail fasteners are being introduced, as well as more efficient and sophisticated techniques of track maintenance, cleaning and reinforcing conventional ballast. In West Germany, less than half of the ties are wooden. In Canada, CN's first permanent installation of concrete ties (a 45-mile track doubling project between Winnipeg and Portage-la-Prairie) is to be completed in 1976. The use of continuously welded rail (cwr), which improves the quality of the ride, is a practice long-established in Europe. In Canada, the conversion to cwr was initiated by CN in 1954, and by 1973 about 5200 miles of cwr have been installed. This amounts to about 12.5% of all track, compared to West Germany's 64% and Switzerland's 52%.

These advances have yet to be widely established in North America, where many railway tracks are not only of obsolete construction, but – through lack of adequate maintenance (so-called "deferred maintenance") – are often unsafe even for slow traffic. In October, 1973, when the new federal track standards came into force, the bankrupt Penn Central Railroad announced that 6,900 miles, or almost 20% of its 38,000 miles of track, was substandard. Service was suspended on 2,000 miles of the system, and was resumed under a 6 mph restriction after a reprieve was granted by the federal government. In 1974, "slow orders" (i.e. speed restrictions) prevailed on 8,000 miles of Penn Central track, making on-time train operation impossible and pushing up costs. In 1973, only 29% of AMTRAK Chicago-Florida trains arrived on time. In 1974, accidents were occuring at a rate of 500 per month.

In Canada, the CTC noted in December, 1973, inadequate maintenance of CN and CP tracks as a cause of frequent derailments, and suggested limiting the car loads and train speeds until conditions were improved. Paradoxically, in spite of inferior track quality, North American railways operate cars about twice as heavy as those in Europe, at much higher axle loads (as noted in Chapter 8, Table 8.3, and p. 70 above).

The emphasis on freight operations, using very heavy cars and long, relatively slow trains, has affected the track geometry and track suitability for fast passenger train operations. It has been pointed out (Fletcher Prouty, 1974) that in the U.S. the railways have been engaged in "flattening" the track on curves that were superelevated* or banked to allow a train to take curves faster while maintaining passenger comfort. This was desirable since the track on superelevated curves had to be replaced – on the lower side only – five times more often than the upper track and two to three times more often than on the "flattened" curves. Extensive "flattening" of the tracks resulted in a track geometry which is incompatible with fast passenger train operations, and which now restricts speeds on many lines. For example, between Concord, N. H. and Boston, Mass. passenger trains which once operated at 90 mph had to be slowed down to 40 mph, and eventually abolished.

Traffic Control

Another important area of railway technical progress is that of traffic control. The early form of train control (still widely used today) consisted of informing the train crew, by means of way-side signals, of track conditions ahead and actions to be taken, the crew providing the link between the controller and the train. This was an "open-loop" system, in which information flowed only in one direction, from the controller via the wayside signals and crew to the train; the controller could not ascertain whether the train behaved in accordance with his orders. Major improvements have included interlocking signals and switches and block signalling (manual and automatic), prohibiting the train from entering the next section of the track until the train ahead has left it. It was common to program train operation on the basis of a strict timetable and, in unusual circumstances, to issue orders by telegraph to keep trains moving (the so-called "time-table-train order" system) – a system still used in the U.S. and Canada on lighter traffic lines.

While the original function of train control was to indicate to the engineman when it was unsafe to proceed, the aim today is to maximize the capacity of a railway system to handle traffic. This led to development of the centralized traffic control (CTC), a system under which a controller, through the completely remote operation of switches and signals, directs the

---

* Superelevation is defined as the vertical distance between the heights (measured from a horizontal reference) of the outside edges of the outer and inner rails of a curving track. Superelevation may amount to several inches. Its function is to help the train turn by reducing lateral loading of the rails due to centrifugal force.

movement of all trains while observing at all times their location and progress on a miniature track layout on the control panel. The territory of a CTC operator may extend over several hundred miles. The CTC eliminates any need for written train orders or manual operation of block signals and permits the elimination of telegraph or signal stations – all significant economies.

Unlike earlier control systems, the CTC is a closed-loop system, in which the controller can monitor at all times the compliance of trains with his orders. The human element – the train crew – forms a vital, albeit often fragile, link in the CTC system.

The performance of the CTC can be further improved through substitution of automation for one or both of the two remaining human links: the train engineer and the traffic controller. With the automatic train control (ATC), the human element in the controller-train loop is eliminated to a certain extent. The ATC provides the locomotive engineer with audible and visual information on track conditions, and should a restrictive indication be ignored, it applies the brakes automatically to slow or stop the train. Continuous automatic control of train speed is a further extension of the ATC. Under the ATC system, the control of the train does not rely on observation of wayside signals by the train crew – a very difficult task at high speeds or under adverse weather conditions.

A further extension of the ATC leads to fully automatic train operations (ATO), the motion and routing of all trains being totally controlled from remote centers. Ultimately, the ATO renders the driving crew as well as the traffic controller superfluous, the functions of the latter being automated through application of suitably programmed computers.

In Europe and Japan, continuing increase of train speeds and frequency has been accompanied by extensive modernization of traffic controls, with widespread application of CTC, and gradual introduction of ATC and ATO systems. French, W. German, Dutch, Swiss, Swedish, British and Japanese railways are all engaged in upgrading traffic controls, and important segments of main lines operate under CTC and ATC modes (see e.g. Friedlander 1974b, d, f, 1975b).

Japan's Shinkansen trains, which, since 1964, have been providing the fastest rail passenger service in the world, operate without wayside signals and use ATC-type controls. On the

New Tokaido Line (Tokyo-Osaka), these trains run at speeds up to 130 mph, and at an average frequency of one train every 13 minutes on each track. A computer-augmented CTC system is used in Paris' Gare du Nord, to control commuter as well as mainline traffic. Holland is moving towards complete centralization and, eventually, automation of rail traffic.

In North America, the progress towards automation of main line traffic control has been slower, despite the existence of a most advanced communications and information processing industry. The movement of most trains still depends almost exclusively on the observation of wayside signals by the train crews, a highly unreliable technique which leads to frequent accidents (see Chapter 10). In Canada, about 6100 route miles operate under CTC; this represents some 14% of the network, and about 60% of the high density traffic line mileage. Even on such busy routes as Montreal-Toronto the CTC installation has yet to be completed (over about 60 miles east of Kingston).

Completely automated ATO operations have been introduced on urban transit systems, suburban commuter lines and industrial railways. The San Francisco Bay Area Rapid Transit system (BART) is an example of the former. The longest fully-automated freight line is the 78-mile Black Mesa & Lake Powell railway in Arizona, opened in March, 1974 (RGI, 1973a). Full automation is being developed around several major railway terminals in Europe. Amsterdam will be the first complex junction in the world where the computer will run the railway.

CHAPTER 10

SERVICE QUALITY:
THE WIDENING GAP

The technological obsolescence of North American rail, evident from the above-discussed data, can perhaps be best appreciated by examining the quality of services offered. Strangely enough, this is an aspect seldom addressed in American and Canadian transportation studies, which are more often concerned with advanced technologies, such as air cushion vehicles or magnetic suspension systems. Neither is it normally considered by regulatory railway legislation.

Freight

As noted, rail freight operations are highly efficient in North America. Indeed, the cost of shipping a ton of freight one mile (revenue per ton-mile, see Table 8.4) is the lowest, by a large factor, on American and Canadian railways.* Nevertheless, some of the techniques (see p. 62) which make freight operations more efficient have undesirable side effects. For example, long, infrequent and heavy trains are a major factor contributing to low car utilization, slow and unreliable delivery schedules, and a high incidence of accidents and damage to cargo and equipment (heavily loaded special cars may be damaging the roadbeds at an excessive rate). In 1971, the average freight car in the U.S. moved only 15 loads of traffic, was in motion (whether loaded or empty) less than 3 hours per day, and hauled from origin to destination at only 3.1 mph (Meyer and Morton, 1974).

A U.S. Federal Railroad Administration survey in 1969 indicated that only one-third of rail carloads moved "on time"; 47% were one day or more late. By comparison, trucks offered a 95%

---

* In a recent study (Mendelsohn, 1972) it was estimated that for all Canadian railways in the period 1957-1968, the output per manhour increased at an average annual rate of 7.7%; the total factor productivity (including labor, capital, and purchased materials and supplies) increased at 3.7%. These results were achieved with a work force that declined by 35% between 1957 and 1963, and remained stable through 1968. The decline in employment reflected the replacement of steam traction with diesels (see Fig. 9.1).

punctual service (TRF, 1972, p. 475). The average speed of CN freight trains increased from 22.6 mph in 1963 to 23.5 mph in 1972, or less than 1 mph in 10 years. On the other hand, the average speed of trucks (in the U.S.) was augmented by 38% between 1945 and 1969 (largely as a result of improved highways and equipment, TRF, 1972, p. 490).

The slowness of rail freight is partly due to the frequent interchange of shipments between carriers: in fact, 70% of freight ton-miles is interline, i.e. is carried over two or more rail lines (Ford, 1973).

The marshalling yards of St. Louis – the second largest American rail centre – typify this situation. They are served by 19 companies operating 63 marshalling yards and a network of connecting lines. The rail facilities occupy prime city center land, but perform poorly: an average wagon transit time is 36 hours. If the operation were consolidated in a master yard, which could be built for $150 million, the transit time could be reduced to 11 hours and a benefit/cost surplus of 50% would be realized (RGI, 1974b).

Between 1960 and 1971, the railway share of intercity freight traffic in the U.S. dropped from 44% to 39%, while the freight revenue share decreased from 19% to 13%. These losses reflect the poor quality of railway service as compared to that offered by trucks.

In Canada, the railway share of intercity freight has also been declining, from a peak of 74% in 1944, to 35% in 1970. Although trucks' share has increased from 3% in 1944 to 6.3%, pipelines (oil and gas), which now carry some 28% of freight, have been the major cause of freight redistribution (Canada, 1970; see also Table 8.2 and Fig. 16.2).

The evidence suggests that freight trains, at least in the U.S., may already be too long for either reducing costs or developing a competitive marketing strategy, and that the key to further progress is faster, more frequent and more dependable, damage-free service.

Passenger Rail

It is generally appreciated that the quality of passenger rail in North America falls far short of the standards achieved in Western Europe and Japan. This view is supported by the accounts of typical passenger experiences on Canadian, American and French railways; several recent impressions and comments are reproduced in Appendix Two.

Service quality – as perceived by the passenger – involves such mundane aspects as reservation procedures, ticketing, access to the trains and platforms, payment for services, information on arrivals and departures, food, and cleanliness of trains and stations, among other things. For example, CN uses airline-type tickets, instead of preprinted ones, forcing passengers to spend more time than necessary when purchasing transportation. Unlike more modern enterprises, CN does not accept internationally recognized credit cards.

Many of the above shortcomings are evident from the material included in Appendix Two. Here, we shall consider the much more serious deficiencies of the passenger rail services in Canada, which concern (i) the nominal, scheduled speeds; (ii) the actual speeds, or on-time performance; and (iii) the frequency of service.

Scheduled speeds
The scheduled speeds of some of Canada's fastest passenger trains (see Fig. 10.1) are low and have been increasing only slowly, if at all. From 1930 to 1960, the speed on the Montreal-Toronto run was virtually constant at 55 mph. In 1972, the average scheduled speed of Canada's fastest trains on runs not exceeding 350 miles was 56 mph. At present, except for the *Turbotrains*, 67 mph is the maximum *scheduled* speed of any train (*Rapido*, between Montreal and Toronto). The average speed increase over the 1950-1970 period has been 6 mph per decade on the Montreal-Toronto line, and zero on the Ottawa-Montreal run.

CN *Turbotrains* began their fifth (since 1968) attempt to operate between Montreal and Toronto in December, 1973 (see p. 152) at an average scheduled speed of 80 mph. Their speed would have been much higher if it were not for drastic slowdowns at both extremities of the trip. The time gained in running over 311 miles at an average of 90 mph is lost between Montreal and Dorval (11 miles at 25 mph) and Guildwood and Toronto (13 miles at 46 mph). Clearly, no effort has been made to preserve a significant speed advantage, which translates into a saving of 27 minutes (between 80 and 90 mph average) on the Montreal-Toronto run.

In the U.S., the fastest rail service (74 mph) has been offered

83

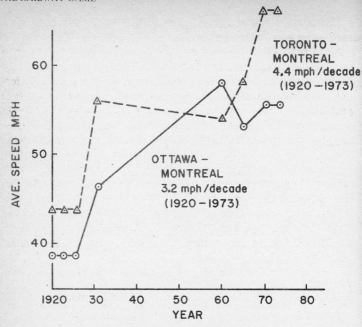

Fig. 10.1   Average scheduled speed of CN fast passenger
trains, 1920 to 1973.

since 1969 on the electric *Metroliners* between New York and
Washington. *The Adirondack*, introduced in August, 1974 between Montreal and New York (via Albany), operates at an
average speed of 38 mph, and takes 75 minutes longer than its
predecessor which made the same run until 1971. Greyhound
buses take 2 hours less to make the trip.

The Canadian transcontinental trains (Fig. 10.2) have been
much slower: over the past 87 years, their speed has been increasing at a snail's pace of 2.2 mph per decade, to reach an
average of 40(!) mph in recent years.*

* Similarly low speeds are achieved on other transcontinental lines. In Australia, the *Indian-Pacific* covers a distance of 2,461 miles between Sydney
and Perth at a scheduled average speed of 38 mph. The Trans-Siberian
Railway clocks a scheduled average 26 mph on the 5,787 mile line between
Moscow and Valdivostok. In New Zealand, the luxurious Japanese-made
Silver Star travels between Auckland and Wellington (427 miles) at an
average scheduled speed of only 36 mph. AMTRAK's *Southwest Limited*,
operating between Chicago and Los Angeles, is scheduled at a relatively
high speed of 55 mph, but it takes 50 minutes longer to make the run than it
did in 1936.

The above performance of Canadian trains comes nowhere close to modern railway practice. In 1970, fast French passenger trains (Fig. 10.3) operated (on lines analogous to the Toronto-Montreal run) in the 80-86 mph range, and in the last 20 years their speed has been increasing at 11.5 mph per decade. The Paris-Dijon freight express runs at an average of 64.5 mph, or 11% faster than Canada's fastest passenger trains. In terms of scheduled speeds, Canadian rail lags French performance by two (*Rapido*) to three (average short-distance train) decades!

The fastest trains in Canada operate, on the average, at a scheduled speed which is smaller by 26 mph than that of the corresponding French trains; the latter run at a speed 46% greater than achieved in Canada. By any standard this is a very large difference; it equals the relative difference in speed which was realized when commercial jets replaced propeller aircraft beginning in 1958.*

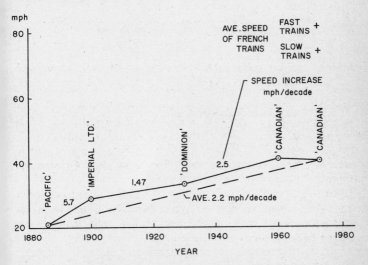

Fig. 10.2   Average scheduled speed of CPR transcontinental trains, 1886-1972 (Hammond, 1964; CPR, 29 October 1972 Time Table).

*The reciprocating engine, propeller aircraft (such as the DC-7) attained speeds of about 310 mph; the turbo-props operated at about 370 mph; both types were superseded by pure jets (Boeing 707 and Comet were the first in service), flying at 550 mph.

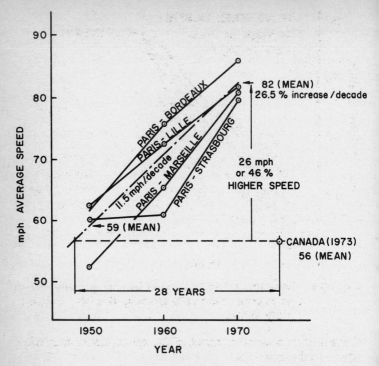

Fig. 10.3   Average scheduled speed of fast passenger trains in France, 1950-1970 (*Railway Gazette*, August 21, 1970, p. 625).

Even more impressive progress was made in France (Fig. 10.4) with the slower trains, which in 1970 operated at an average speed of 77 mph, or at a speed 37.5% higher than the *fastest* Canadian trains and almost equal to that of the CN *Turbo*. The speed of the slower trains has been increasing in France at 14.5 mph per decade since 1950. The steady augmentation of high speed passenger travel on French trains in the 1961-1971 decade is summarized in Fig. 10.5, which gives the miles travelled at speeds above 60 mph. In 1975, France operated fastest trains in Europe, at average intercity speeds up to 102 mph (RGI, 1975a).

Speed is *the* major factor in the competition for passengers and it is clear that the Canadian railways rate poorly when compared with their counterparts elsewhere. The situation in

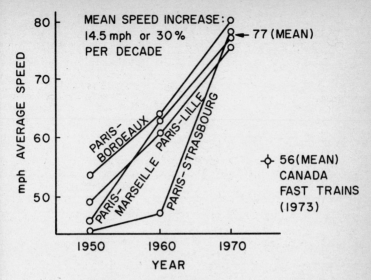

Fig. 10.4   Average scheduled speed of slow passenger trains in France, 1950-1970 (*Railway Gazette*, August 21, 1970, p. 625).

Canada is even worse in terms of the *actual*, rather than scheduled, speed of railways.

On-time performance
"On-time performance"* information is not publicized by CN and CP (although it is regularly published by the U.S. AMTRAK), but thanks to the cooperation of CN, data were obtained for some of the important trains.

In 1972, only 72% of CN's trains between Toronto and Montreal arrived "on time" (Fig. 10.6); during the four winter months, only 50% made the schedule with less than 6 minutes delay; in February, only 29%, or less than one-third of the trains were "on time." In this, the worst month, one train (No. 55) arrived "on time" only once (3% performance!).**

While no information on causes of delays was obtained, a

---

*"On-time performance" is defined by CN as arrival no later than 6 minutes after the scheduled time (5 min. is used by AMTRAK).

**Surprisingly, the reliability of trains on the Montreal-Toronto run was judged good by the CTC (1970).

87

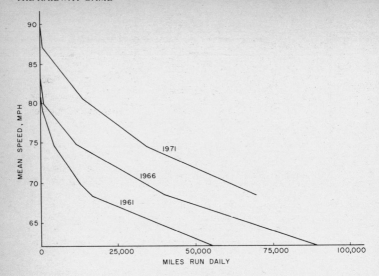

Fig. 10.5   Decade of progress on SNCF (France): Mean speed and distance travelled by passenger trains (Nouvion, 1972).

good correlation (Fig. 10.7) was found between the percent of "on-time" performance, the mean monthly minimum temperature, and the mean monthly snowfall. For the *Rapido* trains in 1972 (Fig. 10.8) the percent "on-time" performance has decreased by 20 percentage points for every 10 inches of snowfall, or alternatively for every 10°F temperature drop below freezing.

The "on-time" performance of long-distance trains is much worse, as indicated by the record of CN's *Super Continental* (Montreal/Toronto-Vancouver, Fig. 10.9). In 1972, no monthly "on-time" performance exceeded 80%, and for seven months it stayed below 32%. The westbound train achieved a year's average of 24%, and both trains, an average of 34%. Under these circumstances, one must wonder why schedules for the *Super Continental* are not revised to correspond more closely to reality?

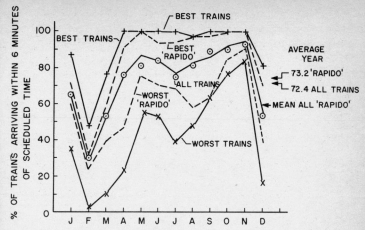

Fig. 10.6   On-time performance of CN trains between Toronto
and Montreal in 1972.

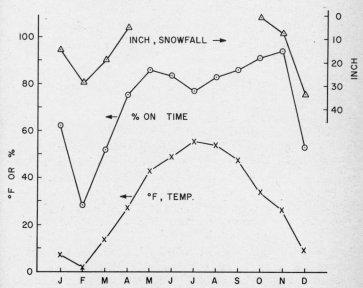

Fig. 10.7   Weather conditions and on-time performance of CN
Rapido trains in 1972.
Snowfall: Mean of monthly snowfall in Montreal,
Kingston and Toronto.
Temperature: The lowest (among Montreal, Kingston
and Toronto) mean monthly minimum temperature.

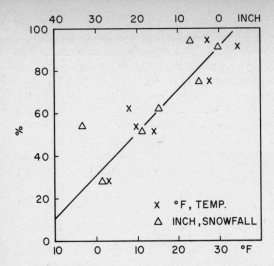

Fig. 10.8   Correlation of on-time performance (%) of CN *Rapido Trains* in 1972 with snowfall and temperature.
.Snowfall: Mean of monthly snowfall in Montreal, Kingston and Toronto.
Temperature: The lowest (among Montreal, Kingston and Toronto) mean monthly minimum temperature

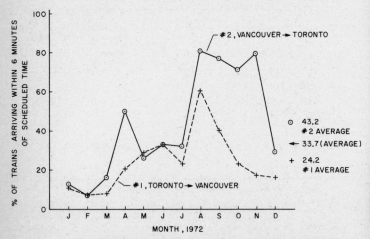

Fig. 10.5   On-time performance of CN *Super Continental* in 1972.

The data discussed thus far tell little about the performance of trains delayed for more than 6 minutes, an aspect of obvious interest to the passengers. In the worst period in 1972 (February 22 to March 7), two of the transcontinental trains never reached their destination,* others were delayed by 50 hours, or 65% of the scheduled trip time. The average delay amounted to 12 hours!** The *Rapido* performance was somewhat better, but delays as long as 3½ hours occurred, 73% of the trains were late, and the average delay was one hour. During the "best" periods (August-September), transcontinental mean delay amounted to 39 minutes whereas on the Montreal-Toronto run it was reduced to 11 minutes.

There can be little doubt that a detailed study of weather conditions and "on-time" performance would uncover many specific problems which require attention. One can only conclude that neither were adequate studies performed, nor were the deficiencies corrected. It is surprising that the Canadian (and U.S.) railways have not succeeded in mastering winter operations in spite of over 130 years of experience.† In fact, railway personnel in North America have become completely conditioned to delays resulting from weather, real or imagined, as one irate passenger discovered:

> The 8:18 out of a suburban town was 25 minutes late when it limped into New York's Grand Central Station one winter morning. A long-suffering commuter asked the conductor what was wrong this time. The answer: "This train is almost always late when it snows."
>
> "But there is no snow today," the puzzled commuter pointed out.
>
> "Yeah," admitted the conductor. "But snow was *predicted*." (Sylvester, 1974).

* The passengers were flown from Edmonton to Vancouver by Air Canada.

** Could this be the performance advertized by CN as "Dependable – CN's all-weather reliability gets you there safely"? (CN *Timetable*, October 29, 1972, p. 1).

† This would have also surprised Keefer, who as early as 1849 praised the railways' "extra-ordinary regularity" and their ability to work "the whole year round, without delay of . . . winds . . . , fog, frost or rain. . . . " (Keefer, 1972, p. 13).

The on-time performance of American trains has been similar to the CN's: the fast *Metroliners* achieved a 76% "on-time" performance (compared to 73% for the *Rapido*), and the long distance trains 54% (compared to 34% for the *Super Continental*).

The CN shuns any responsibility for the punctuality of its trains. Under "Train Service," we read the following in a *CN Timetable* (29 October 1972, p. 19): "CN endeavors to operate its trains punctually according to schedules shown in this timetable. In the event of delay or detention, your indulgence will be appreciated. CN cannot accept responsibility for such occurrences or any inconvenience caused by them." The rail ticket is apparently nothing more than a contract for getting a passenger from A to B, in a time unspecified.

By any reasonable standard, the punctuality of CN trains must be considered dismally unsatisfactory. It certainly falls a long way behind the standards achieved elsewhere, as in France, where in 1968, 86.4% of the fast trains arrived on time, and only 3.6% were delayed more than 14 minutes.*

The intrinsic ability of the railway to provide a higher degree of punctuality and reliability than air and road transportation has been completely neglected in Canada but well exploited elsewhere. The following is a typical example of railway performance in Europe under difficult conditions, as reported by the *New York Times* of January 5, 1971. It concerns the effects of a storm which blanketed a large area of south-east France with heavy snow at the end of December, 1970:

---

*The significance of punctuality in railway operations is not necessarily appreciated even on railway systems which have undergone considerable modernization, as evident from the following 1975 comment on British Rail operations:

Living on an island, the Southern's [Region] management has probably never wondered why it is that every Continental station from Brest to Istanbul is plastered with clocks, every one of which features a large red secondhand. Pulsed centrally by the post office, these secondhands turn as one. As any production engineer knows, to achieve a given tolerance a man must be given measuring devices more accurate by one order of magnitude. In Paris or Tokyo it is taken for granted that train crews trying to observe a timetable in 30 sec units require clocks accurate to $+ - 3$ sec. Most British Rail clocks don't even have secondhands, and in consequence it is not uncommon to find trains leaving up to 2 min early, never mind late. Inevitably, this leads management to believe that key lines and junctions are congested, and it is symptomatic of our age that costly solutions involving computers are sought before simple expedients shown to be effective elsewhere get a look in. (RGI, 1975b).

RAIL SYSTEM IS HERO IN FRENCH STORM CRISIS

Paris, Jan. 4 – Countless thousands of holiday motorists stranded by the snow that had cut the country's main north-south route for eight days returned to work today, thanks to the railroad. In a special effort some hundreds of their cars were hauled home by rail as well.

Trains Get Through

The national authorities are widely accused of negligence. They did not assign military and civilian forces from the Alps and Marseille until well into Wednesday.

But everyone hailed the work of the nationalized railroad system which got all its rolling stock moving and kept it moving through the crisis. Yesterday alone, it brought 434 trains to Paris.

A railway union suggested today that the authorities consider this performance when they are making up their investment budgets. It pointed out that the closing of branch lines – a trend in France as elsewhere – was deeply felt by the many communities still isolated by snow and ice on roads.

As if to make a point, the *New York Times* printed below the above dispatch the following item:

Weather Stops Muskie

London, Jan. 4 – Senator Edmund S. Muskie paid an unexpected visit to London today as he started a planned tour of Europe and the Middle East. The fog caught him. The Maine Democrat, now his party's leading prospect for the 1972 Presidential nomination, was on a flight from Washington to Frankfurt. It made a scheduled stop at London Airport this morning – and then could not take off because of the weather.

As would be expected, the quality of service, in terms of high scheduled speed and punctuality, or high effective speed, has an appreciable effect on traffic volume.

Between 1962 and 1970, rail traffic in France grew by 28%, while the mean speed of trains increased by 10 mph. In England, the London-Midlands line was electrified in 1966. The journey time was reduced by a third with average speeds of 80 mph and a maximum of 100 mph. Almost overnight, passenger traffic increased by 20%, and air traffic dropped by two-thirds. Six years of electrification has seen a 90% growth in traffic, of which 60% was newly-generated by the reliable, fast rail service, 25% came from airlines, and 15% from highways.

In Japan, the New Tokaido Line "had a tremendous impact on air travel between Tokyo and Osaka, the percentage of travellers using the air route dropping from 15% to 8%. Although recovering slowly, air travel has not experienced the growth that would have been its due before the NTL was constructed. Even a new auto route between Tokyo and Osaka has not syphoned off a significant number of NTL passengers" (McLaren and Myers, 1971). When in March, 1975, the Okayama to Hakata Sanyo Shinkansen was opened, a sharp drop in bookings was recorded by the two principal airlines. Osaka-Kyushu flights were reduced from seven to three daily, Osaka-Hiroshima from nine to three, and the Hiroshima-Fukuoka route was closed down.

In the U.S. North-Eastern Corridor between August 1971 and August 1972, Washington-New York rail traffic increased by 60%, and New York-Boston traffic by 78%. On both runs modern equipment has been used: electric *Metroliners* to Washington and UAC *Turbotrains* to Boston. Started in 1969, the 74 mph (average) *Metroliner* New York-Washington service has been expanded to a train every hour in each direction. In the first quarter of 1974, New York-Washington patronage was up 24% over the same period in 1973. Railway modernization policies (see Chapters 15 and 20), which are now being developed for an integrated high speed network in Western Europe, stress speed as the decisive factor in the competition with the other modes.

Trip frequency and schedule

The frequency of trains and convenience of schedules are the other crucial indicators of service quality. Here again, Canadian railways are totally uncompetitive. In 1973, on the Montreal-Ottawa run, there was a daily total of 7 (each way) direct trains, compared to express bus service every hour between 7 a.m. and midnight (18 runs), and 17 flights. No trains were scheduled to leave later than 6 p.m. from either city. On the Montreal-Toronto run, there were only two (each way) non-stop trains daily, compared to 38 flights and 7 bus runs. Moreover, one of the two *Rapido* trips was scheduled between noon and 5 p.m., as if designed to waste the passenger's entire day.

The scheduling and exploitation of the CN's ill-fated *Turbotrains* is perhaps the prime example of rail's indifference to passenger needs. When operated for short periods in 1968-69 and 1970-71, the *Turbotrain* was making up to two daily round trips between Toronto and Montreal; with the five trainsets available, this amounted to a utilization of 13.3%. The three *Turbotrains* CN put into service in 1973 make only one daily round trip, replacing one of the existing *Rapido* runs, and achieving a utilization of 11.1%. Since August, 1974, one *Turbotrain* has been used on the Ottawa-Montreal run, making one daily trip. The utilization of the three *Turbotrains* has been thus increased to 16.7%.*

Safety

The quality of railway services and their social costs are related to the level of safety realized in railway operations. When compared to other systems, North American rail's safety performance appears to be inferior.

In the U.S., Senator R. A. Taft, Jr. (Ohio) observed that "Tragically, the efficiency of America's railroads has been jeopardized by deteriorated track and roadbeds. Such deterioration presents a serious safety problem for the American people. Between 1963 and 1970 train derailments caused by defects in track and improper maintenance of track increased by almost 250 percent. Freight loss and damage claims paid out in 1970 are almost double the amount ten years earlier" (Southerland and McCleery, 1973).

As already noted in Chapter 9, some of the U.S. systems' tracks have been declared unsafe and speed restrictions have been applied – a course of action well-justified by the growing frequency of accidents. In 1973, on the Penn Central Railraod, derailments attributable to defective track were up 83% over 1972. In August, 1974, after 1,329 track defects were found on the 419 mile Chicago-Louisville, Ky. line, 67 miles of the route were closed to all traffic. During the first four months of 1974 there were 2149 derailments on Penn Central, double the figure for the same period in 1973.

---

* *Turbotrain* service has been augumented with the introduction of a second daily run between Montreal and Toronto (in October, 1974), and Ottawa and Montreal (in April, 1975). All *Turbo* service between Ottawa and Montreal was discontinued following damage by fire to a *Turbotrain* in September, 1975.

In Canada, an inquiry into the safety of railway operations was launched in 1970 (CTC, 1972a), in the face of an alarming rise in accidents caused by poor track conditions. In 1972, the number of derailments was three times that in 1959, and nearly double that in 1969 (CTC, 1973).

TABLE 10.1   RAIL ACCIDENTS IN CANADA AND FRANCE (IUR, 1971, 1972, 1973)

Accident category*	Year	Canada	France	Canada / France
Number of derailments	1971	2.54	0.21	12.1
per million train-km	1972	3.53	0.29	12.2
Number of collisions †	1971	1.7	0.81	2.1
per million train-km	1972	2.16	0.67	3.2
Number of collisions † and	1971	4.25	1.03	4.1
derailments per million	1972	5.7	0.97	5.9
train-km	1973	6.18	1.02	6.1
Passengers killed and	1971	0.062	0.045	1.4
injured per 10 millions	1972	0.145	0.084	1.7
passenger-km	1973	0.05**	0.025	2**
Rail employees killed and	1971	2.73	0.26	10.5
injured per million motive	1972	2.45	0.16	15.3
vehicle – km ††	1973	1.62**	0.17	9.5**

* Data relates to operating accidents only (on main lines and sidings as a result of the running of rail vehicles).
† Includes all collisions with railway rolling shock (between trains, during shunting operations, at level crossings, etc.)
†† Trains and shunting operations
** CP only

In comparison to modern railway systems, Canadian railways show an unusually high rate of accidents and casualties, as indicated in Table 10.1 which gives data for Canada (CN and CP) and France (SNCF).* In 1972, Canadian railways experi-

* U.S. railways accident data is not reported in International Railway Statistics. In 1974, AMTRAK experienced 0.76 derailments per million train-km, or about one-quarter of the Canadian figure (Table 10.1). The general level of derailments on U.S. railways ranges from 3 to 15; the lines which show the best record (Denver and Rio Grande Western, Union Pacific, Florida East Coast, etc.) are in the 1.3 to 3 bracket, i.e. at a level comparable to the Canadian practice, which – in the North American terms – must be judged as good (RGI, p. 1, January 1975).

enced 12 times the number of derailments, 3 times the number of collisions, and 6 times the number of collisions and derailments that occurred on French railways (per train-kilometer). The losses in life and injuries were also heavy: 15 times higher than in France among railway personnel, and 70% higher among passengers.** The same trend prevailed in 1971 and 1973. Accidents cause frequent and extensive disruption of rail services in Canada, as evident from the following recent Canadian Press wire:

600 airlifted around
break in CNR line

JASPER, Alta. (CP) – About 600 passengers were airlifted between Edmonton and Vancouver yesterday after a derailment on Sunday closed the Canadian National Railways main line near Mount Robson, B.C., 54 miles west of Jasper.

Alex Rennie, a CN spokesman, said 14 cars containing potash on a westbound train left the tracks about 3 p.m. The potash was stored in self-contained units and did not spill.

However, passengers on four trains, including a transcontinental and two cancelled trains from Vancouver, were affected.

Another derailment on Sunday involving 34 empty cars 13 miles east of Biggar, Sask., closed the CN line for a 24-hour period and caused the rerouting of trains between Saskatoon and Edmonton through North Battleford and Lloydminster.

Meanwhile, about 50 men were repairing the CP Rail line near Provost, Alta., 155 miles southeast of Edmonton, after heavy rains washed out a section of the track Friday.

Twenty-four cars on a 50-car train left the track as a result of the storm, which uprooted trees and smashed aircraft in the area. (*The Globe and Mail*, July 8, 1975).

** A most impressive safety record has been established by Japan's Shinkansen New Tokaido Line, on which world's fastest passenger trains are operated since 1964. No Shinkansen passenger has yet (1974) been killed through the fault of the railway; in terms of passenger-miles, this is equivalent to running the French passenger rail for over six years without a single fatality (RGI, p. 455, December, 1974).

In both Canada and the U.S., serious accidents often occur at poorly protected grade crossings. A comparison of the situation in Canada (Statistics Canada, 1970) and Switzerland (SBB, 1971a) yields interesting results. Although Canada has only a small number of crossings per mile of line (23% of the Swiss figure), over 75% of them are unprotected (without barriers or automatic signals)*, compared to 20% in Switzerland. Canada has only 7.5% of separated grade (bridge or subway) crossings versus Switzerland's 58%; of the protected crossings, only 2.2% have barriers in Canada, compared to 19% in Switzerland. Significantly, 57% of rail crossings in urban areas in Canada are unprotected; only 16% of urban rail crossings in Canada are grade-separated.

In the light of these statistics it is not surprising to find that in 1970 the relative frequency of collisions at grade crossings** in Canada was twice as high as it was in Switzerland. In fact, grade crossing accidents account for about one-fifth of all train-related mishaps and non-fatal injuries in Canada, and about two-thirds of the fatal injuries. The same proportion of fatalities is registered in the United States (USA, 1974).

Clearly, Canadian and American railways (and governments) have been deficient in meeting their share of social costs in relation to other modes of travel. When compared to Switzerland, where there were only 220 cars per 1000 persons in 1970 versus 320 in Canada, this is an even larger deficiency than indicated by the above figures. Railways and governments in Canada continue to interpret literally and unrealistically rail's "right of way", as if rail still monopolized surface transportation. Characteristically, a different attitude prevails when super highways are built: limited access and separated crossings (rail and road) are standard practice.†

Comparing the progress made from 1966 to 1970 in eliminating and protecting crossings in Canada and Switzerland, we find that with the total number of crossings substantially constant during this period, level-separated crossings increased by

* Euphemistically referred to as "otherwise protected" by Statistics Canada (1970, 1973, Pt. I).

** Calculated as the ratio of the average number of accidents per grade crossing per year to the average frequency of trains based on total network route miles (see footnote, Table 8.6).

† But there are exceptions. In Canada, a level crossing, protected only by warning lights, is occasionally found even on a freeway.

4% in Switzerland, but only by 0.7% in Canada; the number of unprotected level crossings in Switzerland decreased by 7%, but only by 5.7% in Canada. Although the number of protected crossings in Canada increased by 31%, the proportion of unprotected crossings changed only from 80 to 75.5%. This decrease was hardly significant when compared to the small fraction of unprotected crossings in Switzerland (21.5% in 1966, and 20% in 1970).

Although the above data indicate that a major thrust would be required to improve railroad crossings protection in Canada, there is no evidence which suggests that Canadian railways or governments intend to embark on any such policy.* Under the 1967 National Transportation Act, rail crossings (which are at least 3 years old) can be improved through financing by the Railway Grade Crossing Fund (CTC 1967R-74R). Since 1969, the average payment was at $17 million p.a. and the tendency has been to diminish the amount ($25.6 million in 1969 compared to $10.1 million in 1974).

Summarizing, the above data show that Canadian standards of railway safety and service, as judged on the basis of the protection of road crossings, the frequency of derailments and collisions, and the toll in human life, fall short of standards typical of Western Europe. Significantly, unsafe conditions often limit train performance, as in the case of the 125 mph CN *Turbotrains*, which are restricted to 95 mph between Montreal and Toronto, and to 70 mph between Montreal and Ottawa.

The safety of Canadian rail operations not only hasn't been improving over the past several years, but has been deteriorating. **

It was only in 1970 that the CTC recognized this situation

---

* Instead, cheap solutions of limited effectiveness have been sought. "Working on the theory that accidents might be reduced if motorists had a better chance of noticing oncoming trains", CTC, CP and CN had NRC develop a superior locomotive warning beacon (NRC, 1971-72, p. 50). Recently a CTC investigator suggested "changing the color of diesel engines to make them more noticeable" (Canadian Press wire service, 6 February, 1974). It was only after nine persons died and twenty were injured in a train-bus collision on December 12, 1975, that the Federal government allocated its share of funds ($5.2 million) for the construction of underpasses at two level crossings in Scarborough (including the one at which the accident occured).

** Also in the early days of railroading in Canada, the safety left much to be desired, as evident from the following account of Great Western's operations (Stevens, 1960):

99

and launched an inquiry into the safety of railway operations. Their investigation (which is more fully examined on p. 132 *et seq.*) was prompted by three serious train wrecks which occurred within a period of eight days and "seemed to the [Railway Transport] Committee [RTC] to be the culmination of a long series of derailments, collisions and other mishaps on Canada's railways that had been multiplying at an alarming rate" (CTC, 1972a). The inquiry showed that in general no adequate safety standards existed, and that many railway operating practices were basically dangerous. For example, it had been CN's practice to disconnect slide detector fences. On February 15, 1971, a CN eastbound freight train consisting of two diesel units and 100 cars encountered a rockslide in the Fraser Canyon at Boothroyd, B.C. Three members of the head-end crew were killed, and the locomotives and six cars fell 200 ft into the river gorge. "It was established that the slide detector fence had been out of service for several weeks prior to the accident as the result of having been activated by snow accumulations from

A Shocking Toll of Accidents. During 1854 no less than nineteen serious accidents had occurred, culminating on the night of October 27th in a collision in which fifty-two were killed and forty-eight injured. This latter disaster led to an official committee of inquiry, whose report threw a strong light on the impact of a railway on primitive communities. The pioneer mentality, in which none is deemed master and in which every man tends to be a law unto himself, was at the root of most of the accidents. In seven instances the victims were plainly culpable because of drunkenness, lunatic behaviour, or stupidity. In nine cases the servants of the company were at fault; they had been arbitrary, careless or criminally negligent.

Perhaps the most characteristic behaviour was in regard to livestock upon the line. In a number of derailments the evidence was plain; the driver had seen the beasts in time to slow down; instead, he had speeded up in order to knock the animals off the tracks . . . Trains were run in many instances according to the whims of the crews. Engines arrived at watering points to find empty tanks, at fueling points to find no cordwood; signals were ignored, maintenance of way was neglected. (One accident occurred because a ganger disconnected a rail and went home to his supper, leaving not so much as a warning flag.) Work trains blocked expresses, through freight was shunted to sidings and forgotten. Every railway operation seemed to be conducted in a casual and dangerous manner. As a result, in 1854 there were six times as many killled on the Great Western as on all Great Britain's railways, which carried three hundred times as many passengers. Following the Desjardins Canal disaster of March 12, 1857, in which sixty passengers perished, the London *Times* "in a scathing leader advocated the dismissal of the company directors and the immediate double-tracking of the line."

plowing operations and natural fall. A white warning signal light which, when lighted, indicates the fence is broken, had been disconnected for some time prior to the accident. In these circumstances, the Committee can only conclude that the derailment might have been prevented by the detector fence and warning signal" (CTC, 1972a).

Another pertinent case is that of an accident in which a CN *Rapido* train struck a maintenance-of-way motor car on August 7, 1970 killing one and seriously injuring the second crew member. The RTC concluded that "the methods of operating track motor cars and the procedures designed to ensure their safety leave much to be desired." The investigation suggested that there was no adequate communication between trains and maintenance motor cars, and that radio was not used for that purpose (CTC, 1972a).

Similarly, following an accident in which one crew member was killed, another injured and 26 passengers received minor injuries (on March 8, 1973, 35 miles from Montreal on the Toronto line), the RTC determined that CN's provisions for safe operation of insulated on-track equipment were lacking in many respects (CTC, 1974).

The unsatisfactory safety of railway operations in Canada is also apparent with respect to the maintenance of equipment. Every year CTC makes about 100,000 inspections of units of rail equipment – and every year it finds about 17% to be deficient (CTC, 1967R-72R). Would we tolerate such standards of maintenance in airline operations?

It appears that the condition of the track presents an even more serious situation. In the third report of the railway safety inquiry (CTC, 1973), the RTC found that it may be necessary to restrict the weight and speed of freight cars because of a generally poor state of the track (see p. 138 *et seq.*).

As uncalled-for accidents continue to interfere with rail services and take a heavy toll of human life, railway operations in Canada remain – in some areas – at a primitive level. Under these conditions, attempts to modernize are bound to be unsuccessful; events which accompanied CN's efforts to put the *Turbotrains* into service illustrate the point well. In December 1968, the inaugural press run of CN's *Turbotrain* was abruptly terminated when the train collided with a 40 ft trailer loaded with frozen meat at a level crossing near Kingston. On January 6, 1969, after 26 days of operation, *Turbotrains* had to be withdrawn from service due to a series of cold weather problems. It was expected that they would return shortly after suitable modifications had been completed, but when two trains were almost ready, a shunter inadvertently collided with one of the *Turbotrains* standing in a station and sent it into another just behind, causing extensive damage. A later episode involved a collision (on July 20, 1973, near Montreal) with a CN freight train. The result was a fire and total destruction of the *Turbotrain* which was on a test run before delivery to AMTRAK.

CHAPTER 11

THE MANNING PROBLEM

As already noted (Chapter 8 and Table 8.7), the manning of the U.S. and Canadian railways appears to be highly efficient in terms of "units of traffic." However, this is more a reflection of the much larger capacity of freight trains in North America than of economy in the use of manpower. In Western Europe, the annual train-miles per crewman exceed the North American values by a factor of about 3 (RGI, 1972a). Typically, on the 335 mile CN Montreal-Toronto line (the prime passenger run in Canada), the *Rapido* trains advertised as non-stop (5 hours scheduled trip time) come to a halt twice at the intermediate division points* to change the engine crew (engineer and fireman).

Even though Canadian and U.S. railways have been completely dieselized for more than 15 years (Fig. 9.1), the work rules and payment systems** of the "running trades" (engineers, firemen, conductors, brakemen and baggagemen) are still based on early steam locomotive technology. Since the steam locomotive required servicing (coal, water, etc.) about every 125 miles, railway "division points" were accordingly spaced and determined the length of normal crew runs. Although diesel locomotives can be operated for 6000 miles with little more than fuelling and minor servicing, they are manned on the basis of steam traction requirements. While railway companies wish to institute "run-throughs" across the too-frequent division points, the labour unions resist extended crew runs† The exercise of territorial seniority rights, with different seniority districts for various union groups, also impedes "run-throughs."

As would be expected, the payment system of the road ser-

---

* At Brockville, 127 miles from Montreal, and Belleville, 95 miles from Brockville, and 113 miles from Toronto. The train crew consisting of a conductor and two brakemen, continues through the whole journey.

** See Freedman (1965) and Flood (1968) for an extensive treatment of these aspects of manning of Canadian railways; detailed information on manning of U.S. railways is given in TRF (1972), p. 116.

† See Cottrell (1951) for comprehensive discussion of social and economic impact of "run-throughs."

vice employees reflects the antiquated work rules and, in its complexity, is unique in Canadian industry. The system is a dual one, based on (i) miles travelled, and (ii) time taken. In the passenger engine service, a day's work is defined as 100 miles or less, 5 hours or less, and approximates the duty typical of early steam operation, corresponding to a basic speed of 20 mph.[*] The extra mileage and overtime pay are computed as (i) the basic mile rate (= daily rate/100 miles) multiplied by the miles in excess of 100, plus (ii) the overtime pay based on hours on road in excess of miles run divided by the basic speed. In addition, the wage rates of road service employees differ by occupation, type of service, geographic region, and train size. Earnings also depend on additional compensation for delays (terminal time), extra services, and the like. To provide for distribution of earning opportunities, road service employees are subject to mileage limitations, which run from 3800 miles for freight engineers and firemen to over 6000 miles for conductors and trainmen (per month).

The existing system of road service personnel employment on Canadian railways, with a division determining the run of a crew and a 100 mile trip defining a day's work, bears no relationship to the performance of modern rail, which operates well in excess of the "basic speeds" of 20 and 12.5 mph. On other rail systems, more realistic work rules are observed. In the U.K., a day's work is defined as 350 miles or 6 hours on express (freight and passenger) trains, down to 125 miles and 7 hours on ordinary freight. In Switzerland, drivers work a 44-hour week spread over 5 or 6 days; 10 hours is the maximum for any one day (RGI, 1972a).

Another aspect of railway manning is the employment of redundant crewmen, governed by the so-called "crew consist" rules. In many countries, when diesel and electric traction were first introduced, steam practice was perpetuated by providing a second man in addition to the engineer. In Canada, a fireman is required on all locomotives in passenger service, but not in freight (Flood, 1968).[**] This is also the situation in the U.S., except where local state laws specify "full crews" (e.g. Indiana

---

[*] Freight service day's work is defined as 100 miles or less, 8 hours or less; hence the basic freight speed is 12.5 mph.

[**] See footnote, p. 81, re reduction in employment in Canada due to dieselization.

requires a crew of six per train, RGI, 1972a). In Switzerland, since 1959 only one man has been required to operate a loco-motive (diesel or electric). Moreover, the degree of versatility of Swiss locomotive drivers is very broad. They are expected to handle equipment which ranges from now-antiquated electric locomotives built in the 1920s, to the latest and fastest models, in freight as well as passenger service (Friedlander, 1974f). The requirement to carry a rear-end brakeman and a conductor on freight trains in Canada is another example of overmanning. The right to eliminate the rear brakeman (affecting about 5,000 jobs) was granted in an orbitration award in January, 1975, but was subsequently appealed by the union.

It is apparent that work and payment rules now in force in Canada are not geared to running fast trains over long dis-tances, a mode of operation particularly significant in this coun-try. On the contrary, overmanning of trains favours operation of very long and heavy (and necessarily slow) trains, a practice which results in excessive deterioration of track.

According to the 1967 legislation, the Canadian Transport Commission "may make orders and regulations ... (i) designat-ing the number of men to be employed upon trains ... (ii) limit-ing or regulating the hours of duty of any employees. ... " (Canada 1970b, Section 227). Although the CTC has not been active in exercizing these powers, experience shows that when there is determination, progress can be made. In February, 1967, CN was able to negotiate a special contract with its loco-motive engineers, which provided for non – stop operation of the ill – fated *Turbotrain* between Montreal and Toronto, with only two engineers on board. The maximum mileage permitted to be made by an engineer in the *Turbotrain* service was raised from 4800 miles to 6000 miles per month (Cann and Wilson, 1968).

CHAPTER 12

REGULATION AND SUBSIDIZATION OF RAIL OPERATIONS IN CANADA

Regulation and subsidization of railway operations in Canada reflect extensive government involvement in railway transportation, an involvement which has been expanding from the early days of railroading, as discussed in Part One. Over the years, a large number of measures has accumulated and many have been continued in spite of changed conditions. In 1967, the National Transportation Act (NTA) was passed, calling for development of "an economic, efficient and adequate transportation system involving the best use of all available modes of transportation at the lowest total cost" – but much of the older legislation, still on the books, was preserved.*

In this chapter the implementation of the 1967 Act and of the older legislation will be reviewed so that the success in meeting the postulated goals can be judged.** Control and subsidization of the freight rates and passenger services will be considered first, to be followed by an examination of subsidies for Canadian National, the rationalization of passenger train services and the regulation of safety in Canadian railway operations.

When examining the regulation of railways in Canada, it is

---

*The NTA (Canada, 1967) contains revisions of the Railway Act and other acts. The texts of this legislation, as amended, are given in the Revised Statutes of Canada (Canada, 1970a, b). The numbering of the sections here of interest is as follows:

	Canada (1967) Revisions of the Railway Act	Canada (1970b) Railway Act, Revised Statutes
Unprotected branch lines	314E	256
Guaranteed branch lines	314G	258
Passenger services	314J	261
Eastern rates	329	272
Compensatory rates	334-337	277,278
Normal payments	469	413

In referring to specific sections of the NTA (including the amended Railway Act), the designation as used in the Revised Statutes (Canada, 1970, a, b) is quoted (see Table 12.2).

** See Darling, 1974 for an up-to-date review of railroad subsidies in Canada.

pertinent to note in passing that Canadian railway regulations were written under the premise that railways are static, unchangeable technology. These regulations do not allow for technical progress as a factor affecting railway operations, and aren't concerned in the least with the quality of service (as discussed in Chapter 10). The rules of the Railway Act (Canada, 1970b, Section 366) on the use of blackboards, while pertaining to a matter of limited importance, are nevertheless quite typical of the technical sophistication of railway legislation. The Act states that "Whenever (a) any railway company . . . willfully neglects, omits or refuses to have a blackboard put upon the outside of the station house over the platform of the station, in some conspicuous place . . . (b) . . . the station agent . . . willfully neglects . . . to . . . write or cause to be written in white chalk on such blackboard a notice . . . stating . . . the time when such overdue train may be expected to reach such station; or (c) . . . such station agent . . . neglects to write or cause to be written on the blackboard, in like manner, a fresh notice stating . . . the time when such overdue train may then be expected to reach such station; such company is liable . . . to a penalty not exceeding five dollars . . ." Imagine such standards of information-handling technology being prescribed for the airlines!

Economic Aspects

Types of Rate Controls

From their very beginnings Canadian railways have been developed on the basis of extensive subsidies from public funds, or outright government ownership. Soon after completion of the first transcontinental line (Canadian Pacific in 1885), it was found that if the railways were to fulfill their objectives in the settlement and exploitation of undeveloped regions of Canada, the charges for carrying primary products would have to be below cost. Thus subsidization and regulation of railway operations – as opposed to railway construction – was introduced* with the Crowsnest Pass Agreement of 1897 (referred to in more detail below), has been continued and expanded over the ensuing 70 years, and is now part of the 1967 legislation. It is not our purpose here to review in detail the history of these developments – a subject of considerable complexity – but

---

*Starting in 1879, the maximum earnings or rail carriers were specified and thus an indirect control of freight rates was instituted (Purdy, 1972).

only to survey the present situation and to point out that, like the railway physical system, so too are the regulation and subsidization of railway operations in Canada a reflection of the past rather than of an overall transportation policy consistent with current technological and economic developments, and that, moreover, they are often incompatible with efficient and competitive allocation of transportation services.

The governmental control of railway rates and revenues falls into three categories:

(i) the maintenance of rates at below-cost levels without direct compensation;

(ii) the maintenance of rates at below-cost levels or of uneconomic operations (to achieve certain national or regional objectives), and compensation of railways for the losses thus incurred;

(iii) prescription of the minimum and maximum rates with the objective of precluding unfair competition through below-cost pricing, and exploitation through over-pricing.

Statutory Grain Rates

The first category usually referred to under the above heading is the oldest, having its origin in the 1897 Crowsnest Pass Agreement, through which Canadian Pacific obtained a Dominion subsidy of $3.4 million (and sizeable provincial land grants) for building a line from Lethbridge, Alta. over the Crowsnest Pass (see Map 1 (b)) to Nelson, B.C., and, in return, undertook to reduce its rates "hereafter" (i.e. in perpetuity) on two types of commodities important to the development of the Prairies: the settlers' effects, moving west from central Canada, and grain and flour, moving east to Fort William and Port Arthur. Effective in 1899, these rates were reduced by 3¢ per hundred pounds. By 1925, although in effect for less than 8 years, the rates were first reduced to meet lower rates negotiated by Manitoba and Saskatchewan with the Canadian Northern Railway, and later increased (under an Order-in-Council suspending the Crowsnest Agreement) to meet the inflation of World War I; in 1922 the rates returned to the 1899 level. In 1925 the Crowsnest Agreement was terminated and the special rates for settlers' effects were discontinued, but the 1899 flour and grain rates were made statutory. Today, the so-called Crowsnest Statutory Grain Rates apply in the western region (all lines west of Thunder Bay and Armstrong, Ont., see Map l(a)) to (i) grain and flour moving east to Thunder Bay and Armstrong, Ont., for export and domestic consumption, and (ii) grain and flour moving from Prairie points to Vancouver, to other Pacific ports and to Churchill, for export only. Provisions (i) and (ii) also include certain by-products of the milling, distilling, and brewing industries, and also certain feed products. In summary, the statutory rates apply to grain, flour and other products west of Thunder Bay; they cover both export and domestic shipments moving east, but only export shipments moving west and north (TRF, 1965, pp. 269-276).

TABLE 12.1 RELATIVE SIGNIFICANCE OF TRAFFIC UNDER STATUTORY GRAIN RATES IN 1972 (CTC, 1972c)

| | Percent of total freight traffic | |
	Canada	Western region
Ton-miles	28	43
Car-miles	22	40
Tons	18	35
Car-loads	16	34

| | Percent of revenue | |
	Canada	Western region
Revenue (total)	10	21
Revenue per ton-mile	35	48
Revenue per car-mile	46	53

(% Total revenue) / (% Total ton-miles): Canada — 36%; Western region — 49%

Note: Western region includes all lines west of Thunder Bay and Armstrong, Ontario see Map 1(a).

The significance of shipments under the statutory grain rates, as estimated for 1972 is indicated in Table 12.1. They account for some 28% of all rail freight traffic (ton-miles) in Canada, but bring only one-tenth of the revenue. In the Western region alone, the corrresponding figures are 43% and 21%. In terms of free-market, competitive economy, this is a highly anomalous situation: close to one-third of all railway traffic is priced today at a rate 3¢ per 100 lb below the 1897 figure. In 1948, CPR estimated that the statutory rates yielded only 50% of the total transportation costs and that the revenues earned by both railways on statutory rate shipments fell $35 million short of costs. The MacPherson Commission (Canada, 1961) suggested a deficiency of $22 million for 1958. Clearly, due to inflation alone, the disparity is much larger today. In June, 1975, CN's Vice-President for Marketing stated that "CN's annual loss on moving export grain under the Crowsnest Pass rates is about $100 million a year and is rising rapidly." In 1973, CP losses on hauling export grain were $68.6 million.

It has been estimated that the cost to the producer of moving grain by rail averaged 12.5¢ per bushel (60 lb), while the real transportation cost was close to 30¢, or 2.4 times the Crowsnest rate (Canada Grains Council, 1972, 1973). A recent study by the Canada Grains Council of the Brandon area (west of Winnipeg) showed that, if the grain originates on the main line, the costs of moving it to Thunder Bay (16¢ per bushel) are about twice the revenue the railway receives. Costs are twice as large (or four times the revenue) on grain originating in a branch line. Comparing revenues per ton-mile for various types of movements in Canada in 1972, the railways obtained 5.38¢ for agricultural machinery, 3.73¢ for fresh meat, 3.17¢ for live cattle, 2.11¢ for fertilizer, 2.38¢ for manufactures and miscellaneous, and 0.5¢ for grain under the Crowsnest Pass rates (TRF, 1975, p. 269).

The continued adherence to the unrealistically low export grain rates has led – as could have been expected – to indirect subsidization of grain traffic by the government. Since grain traffic is unprofitable, railways have not been interested in carrying grain and have refused to maintain, expand and modernize their fleet of grain-hauling cars. The number of boxcars available for grain transportation has been halved in the past ten years.* The volume of grain carried by CP has declined over this period by 6%. The railways have not been making any provision for the growth of economy – yet the economy, in fact, went through the greatest period of growth in Canadian

* In February, 1974, CP Rail's grain coordinator in Winnipeg stated that the railways were scrapping 1,800 grain-carrying cars a year, and that they don't intend to invest any more money in rolling stock for grain-handling if they

history in 1973.* (During the 1975-78 period, CN forecast a 7% annual traffic growth, while CP expects a 4.7% growth). Profitable shipments were being given higher priority than grains.

Faced with this situation, the government (through the Canadian Wheat Board) purchased two thousand, 100-ton hopper cars in 1972 (worth some $50 million). In March, 1974, at the height of the "wheat car crisis," Justice Minister Otto Lang (responsible for the Wheat Board) stated that additional 4,000 hopper cars, at a cost of $100 to $125 million, would be immediately ordered by the government, and that railways would be pressed to upgrade more lines to allow operation of these 100-ton cars (131.5t gross weight compared to 88.5t for the standard, 40-ft box cars). He also announced that the government had agreed to spend over a period of 5 years $3.43 million (the railways contributing an equal amount) for repair of 2,400 boxcars (CN: 1400 boxcars at $2 million; CP: 1000 boxcars at $1.43 million); this would add about 11% to the existing 22,000 car grain fleet. Commenting on these *ad hoc* measures, the Minister of Transport Jean Marchand observed: "But what happens when they [the railways] tell us they won't supply the locomotives to move them? Do we supply them too? We could have a third railway in Canada, it's not illogical."

Another hidden subsidy in connection with the new hopper cars – as pointed out by Darling (1974) – "is the inability of government to make any charge for lease of the cars which would be a normal procedure in a commercial transaction. Such lease payments could have aggregated to as much as $6 million annually for the 2,000 cars involved, constituting in part

can't make a profit on this section of their business (Frech, 1974). Speaking in the House of Commons on March 7, 1974, Minister of Transport J. Marchand said: "Railway companies are indeed not interested in carrying wheat. It is not profitable; they have been shaken by the present situation and do not want to buy cars to carry wheat. Even if they were paid, I doubt that they would do it." As one reader of *The Globe and Mail* (April 1, 1974) observed, "This is hardly perverse or anti-social behaviour. If the city of Toronto had frozen cab fares at 1899 rates, it's a safe bet that there would be remarkably few taxis on the streets today." Commenting on the shortage of wheat cars, J. Marchand stated later in the month: "But they [the railways] tell us they are following what we told them to do under the act [1967 National Transportation Act], which is to operate on business principles. And the first of these is to make a profit."

*In 1973, the gross national product increased 6.8% (in real terms, excluding inflation.)

interest and repayment of the government's original investment and in part payment for maintenance expenses.

A further subsidy that might be attributed to grain is a share of the branch line subsidization which covers many lines that are used almost entirely for this traffic."

As Darling noted, "only the appearances have been maintained that the grain rates are not subsidized."

The continued policy of subsidization of the Prairies through statutory grain rates—a mechanism first introduced over 75 years ago—has led to a number of undesirable, unintended and unexpected results. As pointed out by Purdy (1972), "the damage done to Canadian transportation arises out of the interference of the statutory rates with the normal function of prices and costs. With [today's costs] and the prices of 1899, the allocation of resources to . . . particular activities [is] distorted." On the one hand, overinvestment in branch lines is to some extent the product of the 1899 rate level, which made rail transportation artificially cheap and tended to eliminate competition from trucks; on the other hand, if realistic rates for grain traffic were instituted, many of the branch lines, today considered uneconomic, could earn their way. A further distortion results from railways attempting to recover the losses (except those compensated for under the branch line subsidies, see below) on statutory grain shipments through higher tariffs on other commodities. In effect, producers of grain on the Prairies are assisted by other users of railway transportation.

The discrimination between domestic rates for easterly versus westerly movement of grain in the western region results in railways charging two quite different rates for the same service. Because, as regards domestic traffic, the low statutory rates apply only to the easterly shipments, mile for mile the rate on western grain consumed in eastern Canada is less than the rate on domestic grain used in Vancouver; the discrepancy augments as the value of the dollar diminishes. At times, the maintenance of depressed grain rates, which enhances wheat production, appears to contradict other government policies, such as the 1970 measures to reduce the wheat acreage through direct federal aid to the farmer.

Although adherence to the statutory grain rates has been traditionally a cornerstone of Canada-Prairie relations, in recent years considerable concern has developed regarding the counterproductive effects of this arrangement. The low statutory

"I told you it was safe here. Nothing has moved since last year"

In the left bottom corner inset: "You're wasting your time, Mister—that's a CP track used for grain shipments".

The Edmonton Journal, April 1974

rates on raw, unprocessed products give a competitive edge to Ontario and Quebec and thus inhibit development of secondary industries in the Prairies. The case of the rapeseed processing industry illustrates this point (Chodos, 1973). When rapeseed first began to be grown in large quantities after the Second World War, it was made eligible for the Crowsnest Pass rates, whereas the rapeseed oil was not. Thus it became considerably cheaper to ship unprocessed rapeseed east and crush it there than to process it in the West and ship the oil and rapeseed meal (an animal feed) to the eastern markets. The difference in the transportation costs is quite large: to ship on CP Rail from Lethbridge, Alta. to Montreal, oil and meal obtained from 100 lb of rapeseed costs 103.1¢; to ship the same quantity of rapeseed for processing in Montreal costs only 68.5¢.*

It has been estimated (Harries, 1971; Chodos, 1973) that the four western provinces have an annual net deficit in manufactured goods of more than $2 billion. "This figure simply means that more than 100,000 jobs in the manufacturing industry are created in Ontario and Quebec to take care of the *net* western-Canadian demand. The manufacturing industry in the West is geared only to serving local markets except for the forestry industries of British Columbia. Railway freight rates combine with tariff policy and Canadian commercial policy to maintain the historic economic dependence of the West as a captive market for central Canadian industry" (Harries, 1971). The study also estimated the annual direct burden of freight-rate discrimination on Western shippers at $18.5 million.

It should be noted that just as in the previously discussed cases of political influence on railway construction, the maintenance of the statutory grain rates is largely the result of political rather than economic considerations. In 1922, when the expiration of the suspension of Crowsnest Pass Agreement was approaching, the Liberal government, lacking a clear majority and being dependent on Progressives from the West, restored the rates on grain and flour to the 1899 level, and extended their application to westerly shipments in 1925.

Many more inconsistencies and anomalies could be listed concerning the continued application of the Crowsnest Pass Agreement rates to a large fraction of railway traffic. But this

---

* As a result of representations of western rapeseed processors, the Canadian Transport Commission ordered a reduction of rates on rapeseed meal but not on rapeseed oil.

should not be necessary; it is inconceivable that the nineteenth century absolute (in current dollars) level of rates should be identical with the level which would be established today on the basis of rational economics and current politics. Obviously, many important factors affecting transportation have changed and new ones have appeared over the past 75 years. The transportation technology is drastically different, new modes have been introduced, the value of the dollar has declined, secondary industries have been developed, taxes and social benefits have escalated, per capita wealth has risen — yet the rail freight rate for a range of basic commodities has remained frozen. Evidently, even in a highly industrialized society, modernization is difficult to achieve.

*   *   *

Freight rates and uneconomic operations are supported through several specific subsidies, reviewed here in the order in which they have been established over the past several decades.

The Maritime Freight Subsidies
The subsidization of rail freight rates in the Maritimes has its origin in the 1927 Maritime Freight Rates Act (MFRA) which provided a 20% subsidy to certain traffic movements. The Act was extended to Newfoundland when it joined Canada in 1949. In 1957, the Act was revised by allowing a 30% reduction on outbound shipments, and subsequently became, virtually unchanged, a part of the 1967 National Transportation Act. MFRA applies to the "select territory," defined as lying east of Lévis and of Diamond Junction (located immediately east and south respectively of the Quebec City), and including part of Quebec, New Brunswick, Nova Scotia, Prince Edward Island and Newfoundland, and to the "preferred movements" within this territory. Thus a subsidy is paid to railways on (i) local traffic within the "select territory;" (ii) outward, westbound domestic traffic originating within the "select territory;" and (iii) export traffic (easterly or westerly) originating within the "select territory;" (in (ii) and (iii), the subsidy is applicable only to the portion of the through rate within the "select territory"). Since 1957, a 30% subsidy applies to the outward shipments ((ii) and (iii) above), while a 20% subsidy applies to the local traffic (item (i) above). In 1969, the 30% outward shipments subsidy was extended to truckers under the Atlantic Region Freight As-

sistance Act; in 1970, the subsidy for railways and truckers within the "select territory" was reduced to 17.5%, and again to 15% in 1974; the outbound benefits were increased to 50%. Significantly, the eastward domestic traffic (from the rest of Canada), the U.S.-Maritimes traffic and the import traffic were excluded from the "preferred movements."

As in the other instances of subsidization, the MFRA legislation has been inconsistent and ineffective, or even counterproductive. By excluding eastward domestic traffic, U.S. traffic and import traffic, the legislation helped only the export of products from the Maritimes (and therefore the producer in the Maritimes and the consumer in the rest of Canada and abroad), but not the Maritime consumer. Moreover, until 1969, or for some 40 years, the legislation did not recognize the competitive impact of highway transportation. As it turned out, by the late 1960s, "nearly one-half of the subsidized traffic carried by the Canadian National moved under rates controlled by the competition of highway or waterway carriers," so that the rail subsidy "offered no assistance to the shipper for whom it was intended" (Purdy, 1972). Even more serious, the truck competition in Quebec and Ontario caused rate reductions for rail traffic within central Canada that were not matched on traffic originating in the Maritimes, so that the intended advantage of the subsidy was lost to the Maritime producers competing for central Canada markets. To forbid low, competitive rail rates in central Canada would have only resulted in trucks taking over of a larger share of traffic without helping the Maritimes, while the rates in the "select territory" were by themselves reasonable and therefore could not be lowered. As observed by Purdy (1972), "There is a certain irony in the circumstances facing the Maritime interests. The twenty percent subsidy provided to their shippers inhibited the growth of trucking in the "select territory," and trucking competition elsewhere was destroying their ability to take advantage of the rail rate subsidy."

In the early years of the MFRA, the subsidy payments ranged from $2 million to $4 million per year; they now exceed $13 million per year. Between 1927 and 1972, over $376 million was paid under the MFRA. It has been suggested (Currie, 1967; Purdy, 1972) that the Atlantic provinces would have benefited more had the subsidy been used to increase the productivity of their economy instead of lowering the freight costs. Direct assistance with the modernization of fishing and other industries, highway construction, power generation and research into development of local resources have been mentioned as desirable programs which would have been more effective than subsidization of transportation.

The Feed Grain Rate Subsidy

This subsidy started in 1941 as a wartime food measure; it stipulated payment by the federal government of one-half of the rail freight costs on feed grain shipments from the Prairies to the eastern provinces, provided the eastern provinces paid the other half. The subsidy was eventually extended to cover both rail and water movements in eastern and western Canada. Between 1964 and 1968, the subsidy became applicable also to highway movements; it was continued in 1967 as part of the National Transportation Act. In 1971, the feed grain rate subsidy (all surface transportation modes) ran at about $20 million per annum (Purdy, 1972).

As in the other cases noted here, the feed grain subsidy has been continued far beyond the period to which the original premises applied. For example, the subsidy up until 1964 hindered the trucking industry. It's most important long-term effect, however, has been serious regional distortion of the economy. Because of the feed grain subsidy, it is cheaper to ship feed grain from the Prairies to Ontario, Quebec and the Maritimes, than it is to ship livestock; it is therefore in the East, rather than in the Prairies, that cattle-raising and meat-processing (as well as poultry products) industry is encouraged to develop. "In all of these instances, it would have been more favourable, under current rates [and in the absence of the feed grain subsidy], to ship the livestock products from the Prairies to the consuming areas...." (Canada, 1961). Clearly, the feed grain subsidy has the effect of arresting the development of processing industries in the Prairies—while the statutory grain rates are continued to assist the same provinces.

The "Bridge" Subsidy

Following recommendations of the 1951 Royal Commission (Canada, 1951), a so-called "bridge" subsidy was in effect between 1951 and 1966 (it was abolished under the 1967 legislation). The railways were paid $7 million per year for the maintenance of their tracks north of Lake Superior and, in return, reduced their rates on non-competitive traffic carried over the "bridge" (between Sudbury-Capreol and Thunder Bay). The subsidy discriminated against certain types of traffic and against British Columbia versus Eastern Canada.

Eastern Export Grain Subsidies

The movement by rail of bulk grain for export from points on the Great Lakes, Georgian Bay and St. Lawrence River to Canadian Atlantic ports has been subsidized since 1961 (so-called "At-and-East" grain rates), when the rates were frozen at the 1960 level. The subsidy has been continued under the 1967 National Transportation Act (Canada, 1970b, Section 272), which maintained the 1960 rate level for grain, the 1966 level for flour, and provided for payments to railways when the frozen rates fall below the compensatory level or exceed only the variable cost of service. Between 1967 and 1972, the payments amounted to $15.6 million.

These eastern export grain subsidies were considered necessary to provide protection to the Canadian Atlantic ports and to prevent the diversion of traffic to the U.S. However, the appropriateness of the particular selected rate levels has been questioned, as well as the rigidity of the statutory rate setting which makes it difficult to respond to varying competitive pressures (Purdy, 1972).

The General Freight Rate Subsidy and the 1967 National Transportation Act

The major mechanism of railway subsidization, continued in a modified form under the 1967 National Transportation Act, dates back to 1959, when the federal government, in order to prevent rate increases, provided $20 million to the railways. This "general freight rate subsidy" was continued and increased until the National Transportation Act authorized $110 million to be paid to the railways in 1967. The Act provided that in subsequent years, the subsidies (called "normal payments") would be gradually phased out, declining from $110 million in 1967 by $14 million a year and reaching $12 million in 1974, the final year (Canada, 1970b, Section 413). The spread of the reduction in the subsidy would allow the railways time to adjust freight rates from the frozen level of 1959. However, during the phase-out period (1968 to 1974) only a portion of the "normal payments" was made available for that purpose. First, the "normal payments" would provide funds for approved railway claims relating to the operation of uneconomic branch lines, uneconomic passenger services, and for the eastern export grain rate subsidy; the remainder, if allowed by the CTC, would compensate for uneconomic freight rates (See Table 12.2, p. 126). In view of the phasing out of the "normal payments," and the continuing claims for uneconomic (branch line and passenger) operations and eastern export grain subsidy, the margin available for the general rate subsidy quickly decreased; in fact, as early as 1970 the payments in the above three categories amounted to more than one-half of the "normal payment" for that year.

It could be presumed that, through their 1967 legislation, the government hoped to reduce railway losses through the elimination of uneconomic (branch line and passenger) services as direct rate subsidies were being reduced. This has not taken place: many branch lines were designated as "protected" from abandonment (see Chapter 6), and most of the passenger services, while compensated to the extent of 80% of losses, were continued.

Between 1970 and 1973, the railways received $105 million for operating branch lines; from $11.1 million in 1970, the subsidy has increased to $41.8 million in 1973 (Table 12.2). Since 1967, a total of $21.7 million was paid in eastern export grain subsidies; over $6 million was paid in 1972 and 1973 (Table 12.2).

Although the 1959 rate freeze was removed by the 1967 legislation, considerable damage was done in the intervening years through the maintenance of uneconomic rates. Harm was done to the growth of intermodal competition and to the achievement of the best allocation of traffic between highways and railways. If cost-determined prices had been allowed, the trucking industry's share would have been increased, and large sums of money paid in excessive prices and taxes would have been saved by the public.

Control of Freight Rates

Beyond the establishment of specific freight rates and subsidies, as reviewed above, the government under the 1967 National Transportation Act, controls the minimum and maximum levels of freight rates that railways can charge (Canada 1970b, Sections 277, 278). The rates must be at least compensatory, i.e. they must exceed the variable cost of the movement of the traffic concerned (as determined by the Canadian Transport Commission). As regards the maximum rates, these are prescribed when there is no competitive mode of transport; thus they apply only to "captive shippers," and cannot exceed the variable cost of the movement plus 150% of the variable cost (i.e. cannot exceed 2.5 times the variable cost).

The above pricing formula is designed, on the one hand, to prevent destructive and unfair rate cutting and – on the other – to prevent excessive charges in a monopoly situation. Unlike earlier regulations, which were designed to control the earnings of the carriers, the 1967 formula gives railway management considerable latitude in setting rates, depending on demand, competition and cost of service. Regretfully, since a large fraction of rail traffic is subject to statutory rates, direct rate subsidies and subsidies for uneconomic operations, the effectiveness of the 1967 formula in rendering transportation in Canada efficient and competitive is quite limited; the distortion which results from the application of a series of legislative acts dating back to 1897, and which today do not reflect a comprehensive policy but a sequence of unrelated and ancient measures, overshadows the advantages potentially offered by the 1967 liberal rate controls.

Furthermore, even within the rate extremes prescribed by the 1967 legislation, there appears to be much room for anomalous pricing of rail transportation. A major anomaly concerns the long-haul versus short-haul discrimination (Chodos, 1973). For example, it costs much less to ship steel products from Hamilton to Vancouver ($1.35 per 100 lb., to keep Canadian steel competitive with Japanese imports) than from Hamilton to Edmonton ($2.11 per 100 lb), a distance shorter by 760 miles. In fact, it is possible to ship many items from Ontario to Vancouver and back to Calgary or Edmonton for less than shipping them directly, adding in the process some 1500 miles of waste motion (Roseman, 1973). In general, on a per mile basis, rates between western points are higher than between eastern points.

Another type of discrimination relates to freight rate groupings: "The whole central Canadian region from Montreal to Windsor is considered one location in determining freight rates to or from the West, but western towns a few miles apart often pay different rates. In Alberta, the same rates apply to Calgary, Edmonton, Lethbridge and Medicine Hat, but Fort Saskatchewan, . . . Red Deer . . . and Grande Prairie pay . . . more

. . . . The rate per 100 lb for a minimum of 100,000 lb of iron or steel is $2.33 from central Canada to Calgary, . . . [but] $3.13 to Grande Prairie" (Chodos, 1973). The Harries (1971) study suggests that "In the absence of large rate groups it is likely to be futile for either the federal or provincial governments to spend money in attempts to diversify industry to all parts of Alberta. A few extra cents more on a freight rate can nullify a very large capital grant to encourage industry to go to a smaller center."

Another anomaly concerns container shipments in eastern Canada (APEC, 1973). Under present regulations, domestic traffic is denied the lower transportation costs possible through use of unit trains and containerization. At present, the railways will ship a minimum of twenty 20-ft containers a week, in any one direction, carrying exports or imports between Halifax and Toronto, for $207 each. For a minimum annual volume of 18,000 containers, the rate falls to $132. On the other hand, it costs $335 to send a domestically-originated and destined 20-ft container carrying only one-quarter of its maximum load. The rate is $1,340 for a maximum load domestic containers, or ten times as high as the minimum import/export container rate. For a fully loaded 20-ft container carrying 40,000 lb of domestic dry goods, the rail charge may rise to $1,656 — or 1255% of the minimum export/import container rate. It should be noted that these very large domestic/export-import rate ratios occur despite subsidies under the MFRA (see above) and exceed considerably (up to 7.7 times) the maximum permissible (150% of the minimum rate) differential under the 1967 legislation.

At present, it is impossible for import or export container traffic to break journey in the Atlantic region without losing its preferential rail freight rate. This is clearly discrimination in favor of export or import-related processing or manufacturing taking place in Central Canada or Europe rather than in the Atlantic region.* Unfortunately for domestic traffic, trucking costs as much as rail and does not offer an alternative as cheap as the import/export container rate. In effect, in eastern Canada there are two systems of transport: the cheap, efficient and fast, reserved for non-Canadians; the slower and much more expensive serving domestic needs. Overseas and central Cana-

---

*This is not how the railways view the situation. In February, 1974, CN ran center-fold advertisements in Canadian magazines extolling CN's role in the Atlantic provinces economy, and promoting CN's import-export facilities.

"If it's grain or lumber, we don't want it. If it's bigger than a bread box we don't want it, if it can be used about the house, leave it there, if. . . ."

The Vancouver Sun, March 1974

dian businesses are given preferential treatment compared to Atlantic region industries, which cannot take advantage of their proximity to the sea.

*　　*　　*

The above review of the rail freight regulations in Canada clearly indicates that the goals which the 1967 legislation set out to accomplish have not been attained. A large proportion of freight is rigidly priced and subsidized, thus eliminating the influence of free market competition, and preventing the efficient allocation of transportation services among various modes. Uneconomic, low density traffic branch lines are protected from abandonment. In many instances statutory and subsidized rail freight rates have resulted in an unbalanced development of secondary industries. Within the stipulated liberal controls of minimum and maximum rates, many anomalous pricing practices have developed. The competition between the modes has been lessened because both CN and CP own railways, trucks, airplanes and ships. It is apparent that the numerous controls and subsidies of freight rates do not add up to a consistent overall transportation policy, but are merely a collection of unrelated regulatory measures which have evolved since the end of the last century in a somewhat random fashion.

Losses in Passenger Operations

The 1967 Act reimburses railways for 80% of the approved (by CTC) claims for losses sustained in passenger operations (Canada, 1970b, Section 261); it also permits railways to apply for discontinuation of passenger services. This is the mechanism through which the CTC would "relieve the railways of the financial burden of uneconomic passenger-train services [and branch lines], thus placing them on an equal basis with competing modes of transport. Uneconomic services found to be necessary in the public interest would be ordered continued under specific compensation" (CTC, 1969R).

The new procedures established by the 1967 Act have been referred to by the CTC as the *railway rationalization program* "aimed at discontinuing those services no longer required by public need, ending unnecessary duplication and eliminating any over-capacity which may exist on services that are required to continue operating in the public interest" (CTC, 1971R).

Reviewing the developments since 1967 it is apparent that the 1967 Act did not produce the hoped-for competitive climate for railway transportation, and has not been effective in rationalizing rail services. Moreover, it has failed to acknowledge technological progress and service quality as factors influencing the economics of modern rail transportation.

The 1967 Act, by assuring the railways specific subsidies for uneconomic services, removes any incentive to render such services more efficient, and insures that, when judged "in the public good," they will continue to be operated while growing increasingly obsolescent.* This is, in fact, how the railways have interpreted the provisions of the 1967 Act.

By the end of 1971, the CTC had received 69 discontinuance applications covering virtually all passenger services in Canada. The corresponding losses reported by the railways amounted to $108 million for 1970. Prior to 1973, the CTC issued decisions on 61 applications; only in 11 cases was discontinuance approved. No passenger train services were discontinued in 1972. The parallel operation of CP's and CN's transcontinental trains has been continued (CTC, 1967R-1974R).

The significance of these developments is clear: the rail companies are not prepared to operate any passenger services whatsoever unless subsidized by the government, and the government considers operation of a large majority of the existing services to be "in the public interest." Thus the course for continuing support by the Canadian taxpayer of inefficient passenger rail services has been charted well into the future by the 1967 Act.

In order to fully appreciate the absurdity of the present system of passenger rail subsidization in Canada, it is worthwhile to consider in some detail the transcontinental services. In the late 1960s CP and CN transcontinental trains accounted for about 40% of the rail passengers in Canada. In 1969, the losses on *The Canadian* (CP) and on *The Super Continental* (CN) amounted to $29 million (as determined by the CTC; the railway estimates were higher), or about $1.05 for every dollar paid by users of the service. In other words, the cost of the transportation provided exceeded by 105% the fares paid; the railways

---

* Under the 1967 Act, reimbursement of losses is virtually automatic and is not tied to any standard of service. A graduated, incentive-type subsidy would be more effective to assure service quality. This approach has been used by AMTRAK in contracting with the railways for passenger operations (see p. 164).

received as subsidy 80% of the losses, or 84% of the collected fares.

Let us now consider the competition. A study of the air, bus and train fares in Canada has shown that in 1971, between cities on the transcontinental route, train coach fares and bus fares were about equal; Air Canada economy fares compared favourably to the train roomette fares. In both cases, CP fares were somewhat higher than CN fares, the air and bus fares lying in-between. The difference between the air and bus fares, and the train roomette and coach fares respectively, did not exceed plus or minus 10%. On the average, then, it is correct to assume that Air Canada fares equaled the train roomette fares, and intercity bus fares equaled the train coach fares (Transport Canada, 1975b, Fig. XV-2).

What do these figures mean? They mean that, if the trains were not subsidized, CN and CP transcontinental passengers (excepting pass holders) could travel at no extra cost to themselves by air and by bus, and at considerable savings to the taxpayer. At present, those passengers pay for only half what it costs to move them.

On the other hand, if the subsidy funds were given to Air Canada and the bus companies, 84% of the transcontinental train passengers could travel on free passes, at zero direct cost to themselves. If the subsidy were increased from 80% to 100% of the losses, all transcontinental train passengers (except those who now travel on passes, see p. 127) could be issued every year free air and bus tickets.*

The cost of subsidization of passenger rail in Canada has been quickly escalating, as indicated in Table 12.2: from $21 million in 1970, the payments have risen to $111 million in 1973. According to the Transport Minister they stood at $135 million in 1974, and "could rise to over $300 million by 1980 if no change is made." Between 1969 and 1974, a total of $426 million was paid to railways for the maintenance of passenger services.

The present system of passenger travel subsidization must be about the most expensive one could devise: not only does it offer no saving to the user, the rail fares being as high as the corresponding bus and air fares, but moreover it results in con-

---

*This was recognized in June, 1975 by Jean Marchand, the Minister of Transport, who said that "In many places in Canada, it would be cheaper to the taxpayer if passengers now travelling by rail were provided instead with free bus tickets."

TABLE 12.2 SUBSIDY PAYMENTS ($) UNDER THE 1967 NATIONAL TRANSPORTATION ACT (DARLING, 1974; CTC; 1973R, 1974R)

Year	Branch Lines Unprotected Section 256	Branch Lines Protected Section 258	Passenger Train Losses Section 261	Eastern Rates Section 272	Equalization Payments Section 413	Total
1967				1,641,294	108,358,706	110,000,000
1968				680,384	95,319,616	96,000,000
1969			121,438	1,218,639	80,776,660	82,116,737
1970	1,145,857	9,962,415	21,118,580	2,303,814	39,890,093	74,420,759
1971	2,848,093	22,299,522	66,461,503	3,758,323	1,172,768	96,540,209
1972	4,011,880	22,930,957	91,620,972	6,030,643	868,716	125,463,168
1973	4,302,351	37,536,562	111,924,559	6,070,101	564,666	160,398,239
TOTAL	12,308,181	92,729,456	291,247,052	21,703,198	326,951,225	744,939,112

NOTE: Payments are in respect to the years shown although actual transactions may have been made in later years. In addition, $26,000,000 was paid in 1973 on 1969-1972 claims (CTC, 1974R) and is not included in the above listings.

126

siderable expense to the taxpayer, who is asked to subsidize the rail passenger to the extent of almost 100%. Surely, a better use could be found for these funds; even the provision of free travel for the young and the old would be of more benefit to Canadian society.

"Privileged" (free) travel by rail

Passengers who travel free of charge (passholders and children under five) represent another form of passenger rail subsidization, seldom recognized or accounted for. The information on the magnitude of this subsidy is meagre, and even the railways do not seem to have it. Nevertheless, the available data indicates a surprisingly large proportion of passholders as opposed to revenue passengers use railway services.

A 1970 count has shown that on one conductor's run on the *Super Continental* over the entire year, 17% of the passengers were passholders, and 5% were children under the age of five. Another 1970 survey has indicated that during the peak summer months, non-revenue passengers account for about 20% of all passengers. On some local trains between Capreol and Nakina, fully 60% of all passengers were passholders in February and March 1971.*

In light of such numbers one must conclude that "privileged" traffic represents a significant amount (probably in the 10 to 20% range) of lost revenue and undoubtedly increases operating costs as a result of extra capacity requirements. Apparently, passholder travel is not regulated and is not considered when, for example, railways apply for fare increases.

Subsidization of Canadian National

In addition to the specific subsidies already reviewed, it has been the policy of the federal government to assist Canadian National by (i) retiring the publicly-held debt of CN at maturity by means of loans, (ii) allowing CN's deficit to become solely the balance of interest owed to the government, (iii) on loans from the government charging CN interest rates more favorable than could have been obtained in the open market,

---

* Free travel on the U.S. AMTRAK appears to be more restricted. In 1974, the value of free and reduced rate transportation amounted to 3.4% of the operating revenues (AMTRAK, 1974).

**TABLE 12.3 SUMMARY OF GOVERNMENT OF CANADA
ASSISTANCE TO THE RAILWAYS 1959-1972
(DARLING, 1974)**

Operating Subsidies	$ Million
The Maritime freight subsidies	
Maritime Freight Rates Act 1959-1972	193.9
Atlantic Region Freight Asst. Act, 1969-1972	16.9
Bridge subsidy, 1959-1966	54.1
Freight Rates Reduction Act, 1959-1968	506.5
At-and-East Rates, 1966-67	1.9
1967 National Transportation Act, 1967-1972	584.6
Sub-total	1.357.9

Capital Subsidies	
CN Preferred Stock, 1959-1972	392.9
CN Deficit, 1959-1972	528.6
Construction of the Great Slave Lake Railway, 1960-68	75.6
Purchase of grain cars, 1972	46.1
Sub-total	1,043.2

Total	2,401.1

NOTE: The Feed Grain Rate Subsidy (see p. 117), which applies
to all modes of surface transportation, is not included in
the above tabulation. In the years 1971-74, the subsidy
ranged from $19.5 to $21.5 million per annum.

(iv) permitting CN not to accumulate the deficits on its balance
sheet and not requiring CN to pay interest on interest owing,
and (v) subscribing each year to preferred stock (a policy in
effect since 1951). Between 1959 and 1972, these subsidies of
capital requirements amounted to $921.5 million (Table 12.3).
Over the six year period 1967-72, CN received $205.2 million
through preferred stock subscription, or 20% of the funds spent
on capital investment.

A Summary of Canadian Government's Aid to Railways, 1959-1972

Operating and capital railway subsidies, reviewed above, are summarized for the 14-year period 1959-1972 in Table 12.3 (as computed by Darling, 1974). They amount to $2.4 billion, ($1.36 billion for operations, and $1.04 billion for capital requirements). During the six year period 1967-1972, total subsidies averaged $168.7 million per year; they stood at $252.7 million in 1972, an increase of 42% or $74.5 million over 1971.

Passenger Services

In view of continuing and increasing subsidization of passenger rail services in Canada, the issue of so-called "rationalization" has arisen and has been of some concern to the CTC. "Rationalization" has for its objectives elimination of duplication of passenger trains operated by CN and CP, abolition of trains on routes that could be better served by other modes (e.g. by bus), integration of facilities which now belong to the two companies and amalgamation of their functions, etc.

The CTC's effectiveness in rationalizing passenger rail service has been limited, as indicated by its actions concerning the money-losing CN and CP transcontinental trains. While deciding, in early 1971, to continue transcontinental operation, the CTC advocated "elimination of needless duplication" and development of "a basic transcontinental passenger service," but did not specify deadlines for submission of rationalization proposals or for their implementation. Indeed, in June, 1971, the railways declined the CTC's invitation to submit such plans (CTC, 1971), and the transcontinental services have yet to be rationalized.

The need to eliminate uneconomic services is self-evident, and therefore the institutional framework which permitted duplication to develop must be judged inappropriate. Nevertheless, this has not been recognized by the CTC, which has rejected the option of setting up a single national passenger train-operating corporation (like the U.S. AMTRAK), but yet recommended a virtual amalgamation of CN's and CP's passenger services, including integration of ticketing, reservations, fares, terminals and equipment (CTC, 1971). How to achieve such functional and physical integration without a correspond-

129

ing institutionally-integrated organization has not been outlined by the CTC.

In recommending rationalization of passenger rail services, the CTC has been following the policy of inviting the public at large, and the principal users, to suggest improvements (CTC, 1972b). The CTC's reliance on "local inspiration" of a public which had never experienced high quality, modern rail transportation appears to be a somewhat naive approach to the solution of a highly complex problem for which much expertise is required. The complete lack of concern with the technical modernization of railways is painfully evident from the CTC's annual reports (CTC, 1967-1974R) which refer only to the regulatory activities; CN's *Turbotrain* is not even mentioned in these publications.

Passenger rail service is presumed to be uncompetitive, the railway having little control over the situation. The CTC suggests that there is little hope for passenger rail except in the areas in which "passenger traffic is captive to the rails" (CTC, 1972b) – a viewpoint that reflects an earlier era in which railway transport monopoly was a reality.

Standards of Service

In the examination of passenger services by the CTC the influence of service quality on traffic volume is not admitted or considered – in spite of the obviously important impact that the service quality must exert, and the telling evidence (see p. 94).* Railways are not requested to supply information on the punctuality of trains and on the actual trip time. The estimates of demand for passenger services are based entirely on past experience, and do not allow for changes which could result from the modernization of equipment and operational practice. There are no standards of service quality, and no re-

* But, it was appreciated already in 1849 by Keefer, who had this to say: "The importance of speed in the transport of goods is annually increasing; even now the more valuable descriptions of merchandize take the rail in preference to the slower and cheaper route by canal; and since the cost of transport upon a Railway varies in an inverse proportion with the business of the road, it is annually becoming less. . . . The superior speed and safety of Railway travel over the most expeditious water communications are scarcely more important than its extraordinary regularity. . . . Railways in the winter season have no competitors; . . . they . . . can compete with ordinary canals in price, while they can make two trips, to one on the canal, in less than half the time." (Keefer, 1972, pp. 12, 13).

quirements for railways to provide a service quality which could compete with the other transportation modes.

As would be expected, the performance of bureaucracy charged with the administration of the 1967 Act has been consistent with its purely regulatory character,* and thus devoid of any innovative initiative.

Faced with a deterioration of passenger rail services more drastic than in Canada, the American government – as is often the case – has been first to institute remedial measures. The rationalization of passenger trains was initiated through the formation, in 1971, of AMTRAK (see p. 163), which took over the responsibility for passenger operations throughout the U.S., including initiation of modern services between Washington, New York and Boston, and in the Chicago area. Significantly, the same legislation gave the Interstate Commerce Commission the authority to impose rules for the quality of service.

In December, 1973, the ICC issued its first decision regulating the quality of rail travel. This order, unprecedented in the 86 years of ICC's existence, must be regarded as an important breakthrough for passenger rail in the U.S. The new rules call for:

nationwide toll-free reservation service 24 hours a day
free meals and hotel rooms for passengers missing connections because of late trains
reserved seats in many coach and first class cars
food and drink on all trains travelling two hours or more
60 to 80°F mandatory temperature range in passenger cars
special help for the aged and handicapped
adequate facilities for handling and checking baggage
complaint forms readily available on all trains and stations
penalties, up to $500, that could be imposed for violation of any of the new regulations (actions would be initiated through complaints filed by passengers).

The new regulations which came into force on April 1, 1974, were designed – according to the ICC's chairman – to accelerate the growing trend in train travel, especially during the energy crisis. The ICC stated that "The emphasis is on making the trip a pleasant one even when things go wrong. Passenger comfort, for example, is the prime concern in a late-arrival

* As it has with the Parkinson's law: since 1967, the CTC's staff has grown at an average of 10% p.a. (CTC, 1967R-1974R).

situation, not exacting from the carrier a penalty which may not necessarily induce service improvement."

The initial reaction from AMTRAK has been positive. " . . . we feel the report is very constructive and will contribute to what we are committed to do – bring better service," stated an AMTRAK spokesman (Witkin, 1973).

In the context of the condition of passenger rail services in the U.S. over the past 25 years, the above developments in the regulation of railways are both revolutionary and promising. It is to be hoped that they will facilitate achievement of similar progress in Canada.

Safety Aspects

The CTC's previously mentioned railway safety inquiry, started in 1970, provides an excellent opportunity to examine the practical consequences of the existing regulatory legislation and its administration by the CTC and its predecessors. The most important aspects related to safety are noted below.

Unacceptable Safety Record

According to D. H. Jones, Chairman, Railway Transport Committee, CTC, "The Railway Act makes it abundantly clear that Parliament intended Canadian railways to operate safely, and it gave the Commission all the statutory tools necessary to carry out the job of insuring that they do" (Jones, 1973, p. 37). Under the existing legislation, the RTC "has the obligation of ensuring that all railway operations in Canada are carried out in maximum safety" (CTC, 1972a, p. 1).

As indicated previously, specific data (see Table 10.1, p. 96) on frequency of rail accidents on major railways indicates that minimal rather than maximal safety characterizes rail operations in Canada. This situation, and the inadequacy of the government in ensuring rail safety, have been acknowledged by the RTC, the body responsible for the regulation of railways. The RTC noted that "there is a long way to go before acceptable standards of operation and maintenance of railway trains are reached in Canada" (CTC, 1973, p. 6). The RTC "is not satisfied with the methods employed by CP Rail and CNR to detect and prevent journal failures" (CTC, 1972a, p. 7), and it condemns "the past practice on CN of taking slide detector fences out of service" (CTC, 1973, Appendix 2, p. 4). More significantly, the large scope and the vast number of measures RTC considers necessary to be carried out are a direct reflection of the present highly unsatisfactory situation.

Safety Not Enforced

In the past, institutional arrangements have been apparently inadequate to assure rail safety. In their on-going, routine "regulation" of railways the government bodies have largely neglected safety aspects. Although required by law (passed in 1879, see p. 134) to furnish every six months a detailed listing of all accidents (so-called "accident returns"), CN and CP were allowed not to file such returns for "about the last fifty years." Earlier reports "remained essentially a cryptic chronicle of mostly major, but sometimes minor, mishaps on the railways. It does not appear that any overt action was taken by the Board [of Railway Commissioners for Canada] as a result of these returns; the returns appear merely to have been received, marked and filed" (Jones, 1973, p. 25). Not surprisingly, the RTC's investigation of three 1970 accidents developed into "a complete examination of the operation and maintenance of the railway system of Canada by CNR and CP Rail" (CTC, 1973, p. 3). The RTC found it necessary to establish a more elaborate institutional structure in the area of safety. It announced in 1972 the formation of an Accident Investigation Team (stationed in Ottawa), of a Task Force on the Carriage by Rail of Dangerous Commodities, and of an Advisory Committee on Railway Safety.

Inevitably, the RTC also concluded that, "crucial to the successful undertaking of the large task involved in the realm of railway safety," "there was an immediate need for a very substantial increase in the strength of its Engineering and Operation Branches. . . . The necessary budgetary action has been taken. . . . " (CTC, 1972a, p. 25).

Lack of Information

It appears that the organizational shortcomings of the regulatory agency have been reflected in the inadequacy of the safety-related information at its disposal. The RTC's 1973 report (CTC, 1973) requests railways to report (file) on some additional 16 items, including: plans of major changes in signalling equipment, and functions of signals; failures of train crews to comply with signals; spare parts for signals; accidents at highway-railway crossings; plans of slide detector fences and their modifications; records of rock falls and accidents resulting from rock falls or slides; annual budgets, 5-year forecasts and annual reports of work accomplished for control of rock falls and slides; rail chart revisions; rail defects; progress in rail testing; detailed reports on each derailment. The references to accident-related information appear to merely reiterate railway's statutory obligations; other requests show that in the past the government did not seek information which it now judges necessary for control of railway safety.

The Secrecy of Accident Investigations

There can be little doubt that the legislation which allowed all information related to railway accidents to be treated as "privileged" and none of it to be disclosed to the public* has been a most significant factor in the maintenance of low safety on Canadian railways.

The first appearance of legislation concerned with railway accidents was in The Consolidated Railway Act of 1879, which stated that returns of all accidents, to be filed by railways semi-annually and giving detailed descriptions and analysis of accidents, "shall be privileged ccommunications, and shall not be evidence in any court whatsoever" (Section 34). Jones (1973, p. 27) comments that "as to the privilege Parliament attached to these returns, there has never been a discretionary power in the Commission (CTC) or its predecessors to give out or make these returns public." The cloak of privilege was extended in 1906 to " . . . the report or reports of any person or persons appointed by the Board to inquire into and report upon any accident or casualty occurring on any railway. . . . " (Board of Railway Commissioners General Order 2, made ex-parte, on the application of railway companies). In 1914, as a result of an application made by the Grand Trunk Railway Company, the privilege was extended to reports on fires burning off the right of way (General Order 126). Thus with the help of the railways, the veil of secrecy was fully drawn and, for close to 70 years, no attempts have been made to lift it. The rationale for preventing public disclosure of rail accident information is to be found in a 1908 Board of Railway Commissioners' decision on CPR's 1907 Moore Lake Accident, in which a locomotive engineer was killed, several passengers were injured and a large quantity of mail was destroyed. In discussing an application (made by the

* See Jones (1973) for detailed analysis of legislation on disclosure of railway accident information, here briefly summarized.

Post Office Department and the representatives of the deceased engineer) for a copy of the Board's inspector report on the accident, the Board stated that

> . . . the inquiries and reports of its accident inspectors are made for the purpose of informing the Board in the public interest only, and in order to enable the Board to judge of the causes of accidents and the rules and precautions to be made and taken for the purpose of avoiding them in the future, and not for the purpose of giving information to parties desirous of making claims against a railway company for injury to person or property; that this rule was adopted not only because the Board did not consider that its function was to obtain information for the purposes stated, but also because the Board did not desire that railway officials should be deterred from giving information to the Board's officials through fear that it would be used in support of claims against the companies.

Evidently, while the Board usurped the right of the public to protect its interests, it favored the interests of the railway companies over the protection of citizens.

Under the pressure of the evidence obtained since the railway safety inquiry was initiated in 1970, the era of the immunity of railways to open public enquiry may be nearing the end. It is apparent that railways have been negligent in maintaining desirable operational safety standards, and that freedom from public disclosure was a significant factor which enabled them to do so. In his 1973 Decision, D. H. Jones, Chairman, RTC, had this to say:

> The real issue involves the extent to which the causes of railway accidents, and their investigation, should be open to public scrutiny. In my view, the public has a right to know what is going on in this important area. The families of those involved in train wrecks, and who may be killed or injured, do not, at present, have any way of knowing what happened, beyond what they may be told by the railway company, or, in some cases, where there is a public inquiry, what they learn from these proceedings. Nor do railway employees, or the Unions representing them, have the full benefit, in terms of their own work habits or practices, of knowing all the results of a vigorous

and impartial investigation of train wrecks by the Commission. Furthermore, the public generally, particularly those who are users of the railways as passengers or shippers of freight, have a legitimate concern with the question whether the nation's railways are being operated safely. Finally, the managers of the railway companies do not now feel the additional spur that exposure of the causes of train wrecks to the cold light of day will bring to them, in their efforts to operate trains more safely.

In short, the public interest requires that the material circumstances, and causes, and the steps taken to remedy those causes, be freely available to the public (Jones, 1973).

Predictably, during the railway safety inquiry, the railways objected to public disclosure of any accident-related information, while the unions felt that everything should be disclosed.

Chairman Jones concluded that CTC had no power to declare the report of an accident enquiry to be privileged, and recommended that reports on railway accidents and on their investigations should be disclosed to the public (the regulations of the CTC to be revised accordingly), except "insofar as such disclosure would nullify substantive legal rights or immunities enjoyed by railway companies or their employees." Chairman Jones considered that only limited classes of information would fall into this category. As regards the suggestion (made in the Moore Lake Accident Decision, see above) that public disclosure would deter railways from giving information, Chairman Jones was satisfied that this would not happen and that "the Commission has ample power to compel disclosure of the truth, as any reluctant railway employee, whatever may be his rank, will learn to his dismay."

Minimum Standards Lacking

It is self-evident that in order to achieve the desired quality of any operation or service, suitable specific minimum standards have to be established as a yardstick against which an activity can be evaluated, and to which it can be forced to conform. As would be expected in the light of the poor service and safety records, such standards are apparently missing from the regulation of Canadian railways. This has been also established by the findings of the CTC's railway safety inquiry, which outlines a vast number of measures to be adopted by railways. Regretfully, instead of providing specific standards, such measures comprise a mixture of non-specific requirements, as well as requests for actions and approvals, or for specific technical solutions, which are the legitimate prerogatives of railways' managements. The examples quoted below (from CTC, 1973) amply illustrate the inadequacy of the above approaches.

In the matter of signals the railways are exhorted to "exercise proper inspection of this [signal] material as it is being manufactured to assure that the material does meet with all the specifications and requirements necessary to assure that it will function as intended under all types of conditions to which it may be exposed after installation." They are further requested to submit "a draft of proposed revised rules and instructions for the installation, inspection and maintenance of railway signal devices and equipment, sufficient . . . for the safe operation of trains," and another "draft of proposed instructions to those Maintenance-of-Way employees required to carry out weekly inspection of highway crossings protective devices. . . . " CN and CP "must re-examine their procedures of supervision and maintenance of signal equipment. . . . It is absolutely essential that more time be spent in direct supervision of the maintenance staff and in riding trains to observe the extent to which signal equipment is functioning in the manner intended for the safe operation of trains." A committee should be formed to . . . "develop a system of measuring units of maintenance and testing: that is, the average adequate number of man hours per year required to properly maintain each type of signal equipment. . . . " Railways should " . . . determine whether or not they have sufficient materials and replacement parts available . . . for proper maintenance of existing signal equipment . . . "

Regarding the detection of slides and rock falls, CN must re-examine and as necessary "supplement their existing staff, material and equipment resources to adequately repair and maintain all existing slide detector fence installations. . . . " CN should "connect the slide detector fences to the signal system . . . and . . . do away with the special signal consisting of a white light with the letter "T". . . . " CN and CP should "investigate the cost of and without delay . . . commence . . . replacing these older [slide detector fence] installations with the newer type using . . . series line wire design." "In the future all new installations or modification of existing installations of slide detector fences will require the approval of the RTC."

137

Concerning derailments due to poor track conditions, the railways "should review the existing program of inspection and detection of rail defects . . . and develop a revised and more frequent program of testing rail to detect defects using all ul-tra-sonic type equipment." However, the RTC is concerned with the costs and suggests that reduction of "costly derailments and the savings thus effected could offset the cost of more frequent testing." The railways should make "daily inspections, including Sundays, on all main line tracks and important branch lines where there are frequent train movements every day. . . . " The RTC warns that "it will be necessary to require the railways . . . to reduce the maximum net weight of car loads to 70 or 80 tons per car . . . , and . . . to reduce the speed of trains wherever the existing speeds are contributing to excessive stresses" [in the present track structure]. Finally, the RTC recommends formation of a committee "to study and de-velop adequate uniform specifications and minimum standards required for design and continued maintenance of all compo-nent parts of a track structure."*

The RTC is also concerned with the fire hazard of all timber or open deck timber tie bridges, and plans to examine all such structures and existing inspection procedures, and to establish new regulations " . . . which will eliminate all potential hazard as a result of possibility of fire in a structure."

In the matter of transportation of commodities which may damage the environment, the RTC stated that "the regulatory authority in Canada [is] being confronted with a new dimension in destructiveness and danger to life and limb," and felt that "action [was] needed to be taken urgently" to examine the ade-quacy of "railway practices and rules for dangerous commodi-ties, many of which date back twenty or thirty years. . . . "

The above representative sample of the RTC's findings con-tains many non-specific admonitions but no workable stan-dards. Indeed, it is clear that at present, adequate minimum standards do not exist for track performance and structure, for wooden track structures, and for transportation of hazardous materials. As for signalling equipment, even a basis for quanti-

---

*In the U.S., new national safety standards for track came into effect in October, 1973, and caused major difficulties in operation of some lines (see p. 77).

fication of maintenance and testing is not available. It is meaningless to require equipment to "function as intended under all types of conditions" without specifying them, or to call for rules "sufficient . . . for the safe operation of trains" without defining the safety level, or to request that "more time be spent to direct supervision of the maintenance staff" to insure that "equipment is functioning in the manner intended," without stating how much time should be spent and what is the "intended" performance. The railways are requested to make "daily inspections on all main line tracks" and where train movements are "frequent," but the minimum performance of the inspection equipment is not specified, and the frequency of inspections is not defined in terms of density and speed of traffic, the two major factors which determine the wear and tear of the track. Similarly, the speed of the trains is to be "reduced" by an unspecified amount pending amelioration of tracks.

In some cases, the railways are told what specific technical solutions they should adopt, such as connecting slide detector fences to the signal system, eliminating letter "T" signals, installing series line wire detector fences, using Sperry Car (Division of Automation Industries Inc.) ultra-sonic rail testing equipment, etc. Such approach presumes a static railway technology and does not allow for taking advantage of technological progress. Moreover, because it does not specify the performance of the specific techniques or equipment, it is not helpful in meeting specific standards.

In many instances, the RTC's findings concern not only the objectives, but also the actions railways should take to achieve them. In such cases regulation pre-empts the role of management and thus creates conditions which preclude responsible and dynamic management of an organization.* Railways are asked to "re-examine their procedures of supervision and maintenance of signal equipment . . . ," are told that they must spend more time "in direct supervision of the [signal] maintenance staff," "determine whether or not they have sufficient [signal] materials and replacement parts available . . . ," "supplement their existing staff, material and equipment resources to adequately repair and maintain" slide detector installations, investigate the cost "of replacing old detector installations," "re-

---

* It has been suggested that heavily regulated railway industry is unable to attract top notch managerial talent.

view the existing program of inspection and detection of rail defects . . . ." Railways "must revise their system of training train crews so that by means of model equipment or diagrams and drawings, these employees can receive adequate instruction . . . ," and "signal supervisory staff . . . must take a more active part in this training by attending classes . . . and by more frequently riding locomotives. . . . " It seems that if such instructions were truly necessary, the present management of railways must be highly incompetent, and therefore no amount of "regulation" could rectify the situation. On the other hand, a competent management is not likely to respond to that kind of interference with its legitimate functions.

This is also true in the cases in which the RTC considers that it should approve internal directives of railways' managements. This would apply, for example, to "all new installations or modifications of slide detector fences," to "changes in time-table speed or other changes . . . in signalled territory which might have an effect on the braking distance or other things [?!] in respect of the safe operation of trains," to "draft of proposed revised maintenance-of-way rules and instructions to meet present-day requirements . . . ," etc.

Finally, in some instances, rather than formulate performance standards, the RTC proposes to perform the work that is clearly the responsibility of the railways and that could be effectively accomplished only by them. For example, the RTC would "intensify their study of derailments on account of burnt-off journals" in order to determine "the most effective and efficient methods of reducing the number of such derailments. . . . "

Little Action Planned

From the information presented it is apparent that considerable effort would be required to develop equipment and standards adequate to assure a reasonable level of operational safety of railways. However, the findings of the railway safety inquiry do not go beyond the expression of a desire to see CN, CP, RTC, NRC, Association of American Railroads, American Railway Engineering Association, and the Canadian Institute of Guided Ground Transportation,* "carry on a continuing research program of possible improvements" in the design of signalling

---

*The Transportation Development Agency, the major government research organization in the field, has not been included in the RTC's list.

equipment and detector fences. It is of course unlikely that a mere continuation of past efforts would lead to significant improvements, particularly since the overall R & D effort in railways is negligibly small (see Chapter 18). Surprisingly, no consideration has been given by the RTC to funding of R & D activities through which specific problems could be solved. Evidently the safety of railway operations is not judged critical enough to merit such steps.

Rail Safety Control in the U.S.

As noted in Chapter 10, the U.S. railways' safety record is so poor that, on some lines, speed restrictions or even outright closure have been imposed by the Federal Railroad Administration. In a 1974 report, the Commerce Committee of the U.S. House of Representatives noted that the FRA was "not living up to either the spirit of the Federal Railroad Safety Act of 1970, or, in some cases, the letter of the law," and consistently "downgraded enforcement and inspections." The report stated that after three-and-a-half years of increasing numbers of accidents and injuries, the FRA "inspection of rail equipment and plant seems to be a stepchild of the department's low-key safety approach. By April of 1974 the FRA had only 12 track inspectors for over 300,000 miles of rail track, 16 signal and train control inspectors and only 50 inspectors for more than 1.7 million freight cars and 25,000 locomotives." There was only one bridge and tunnel expert in Washington, and 192,000 railroad bridges throughout the U.S. The Commerce Committee report demonstrated gross deficiencies in the control of rail safety in the U.S. and resulted in the introduction of a bill authorizing $18 million for 350 additional safety inspectors for the FRA.

It is evident that both in Canada and in the U.S. the railway regulatory agencies have been negligent in controlling safety, and have failed to develop resources adequate for the task. Interestingly, in both countries the attitude towards safety on highways has been quite different. A significant volume of research has been done, automobile safety legislation has been passed, and safer designs of highways and cars have been effectively enforced.

CHAPTER 13

THE ROLE OF THE RAILWAY COMPANIES*

As previously noted, the 1967 Act provides no incentive to update railway technology, and thus effectively encourages obsolescence. It is therefore not surprising that, in the area of passenger services, during the past twenty years neither CN nor CP has made a serious effort to modernize although both companies made attempts, during the 1950s and 1960s, to improve their equipment and services.

In 1962, CN founded a separate passenger department, introduced a market-oriented "Red, White and Blue" fare plan,** and embarked on an agressive advertizing and sales effort and a program of visual re-design. Starting with a new company symbol, a new colour scheme was applied to every piece of equipment and every building used by the railway; from letterheads to employees' uniforms, all items were redesigned. Some of the best cars from famous "name" trains which were discontinued in the U.S. were purchased, older equipment was refurbished and modernized in appearance.

In the mid-1950s, CP invested about $60 million on new passenger trains in an attempt to stimulate business. The scenic dome streamliner *The Canadian*, introduced in 1955, was the first passenger train in Canada to feature modern cars, finished in stainless steel with plastic panelled interiors. Since 1957, CP hasn't purchased any new passenger equipment.

Railways' attempts at improvements were largely superficial, limited to appearance, marketing, advertizing and public relations; almost all the 1400 passenger cars in Canada are at least 20 years old. CN and CP were not concerned with improving the basic quality (speed, punctuality, frequency and safety) of service. Their promotional activities have not resulted in long-term improvements: although the decline in passenger traffic volume was reversed between 1961 and 1967, the traffic has continued to decrease since 1967. In 1973, the revenue passen-

---

* See next chapter regarding research and development activities.

** CP adopted three-level fares in April, 1973.

ger-miles were at 62% of the 1966 level, and at 50% of the peak reached in 1967 (see also Chapter 16 and Figs. 16.3, 16.4).

The North American railways have a long tradition of negative attitudes towards passenger traffic. The big money has always been in freight, real estate, mining and other off-track ventures, and the railroad managements make no secret of their disdain for the passenger. In the classic words of James Hill, a 19th century President of the old U.S. Great Northern, "A passenger train is like a male teat – neither useful nor ornamental" (Southerland and McCleery, 1973).

In Canada, the CP in particular appears to have subscribed to this philosophy. When on September 1, 1965 the Board of Transport Commissioners ordered CP to continue operation of the *Dominion* transcontinental train, the *Dominion* that left Montreal for Vancouver on September 7, 1965, had no sleeping or dining cars, but consisted of an engine, a baggage car and two coaches. In its last days – before it was abolished on January 11, 1966 – the *Dominion* ran as a train of express or box cars with one coach attached (Chodos, 1971, pp. 32, 92).

In 1970, CTC refused E & N's (a CP subsidiary) application to abandon passenger service between Victoria and Courtenay, on Vancouver Island, and ordered the railway to improve its stations, trains, scheduling and publicity. It has been, at that time, E & N's practice to seat passengers (on an old unsecured waiting-room bench) in the baggage compartment when the passenger accommodation was full.* When the bench was full, the passengers had to stand in the baggage space. Some of the stations were in a state of unspeakable filth and in bad disrepair, with doors off, broken windows and rotted platforms. Trains were scheduled deliberately to miss the ferry connection from Victoria to Seattle (Chodos, 1971, pp. 42-43).

The desire of CN and CP to discontinue practically all passenger services (see p. 124) attests to their generally negative attitude towards passenger traffic. CN's reluctant handling of the *Turbotrains* has been another symptom of this approach (see p. 101 and p. 152).

In North America, railway managements often do not perceive any relationship between service quality and traffic volume. In January, 1974, I. Sinclair, Chairman of CP, felt that even though car travel was becoming increasingly expensive

---

* A practice still followed today, as reported in Appendix Two.

there will not be a resurgence of passenger rail traffic in Canada. Coincidentally, on the same day (23 January, 1974), newspapers carried a Canadian Press item on the success of the *Turbotrain* and the introduction of an additional *Rapido* train on the Montreal-Toronto line (to handle increased passenger loads). "The Turbo has been sold out almost every day" – said a CN spokesman – "and the real shortage is for coach accommodation."* On May 20, 1974, I. Sinclair stated that "the Montreal to Toronto run is not a train distance. It is too far for a train ride." The impact of rail modernization on passenger traffic volume, at last demonstrated also in Canada, has yet to be recognized by CP's management.

The same attitude prevails on American railroads; it has changed little from James Hill's day. A 1969 *New York Times* survey of railway executives revealed a general conviction that rail passenger service no longer serves a public need, and has to be reduced to cut losses. In 1972, the President of Southern Pacific predicted no increase in the passenger intercity rail traffic during the next decade except in the north-east corridor because "the demand is not there. . . . " "I think AMTRAK's function should be to preside over an orderly shrinkage of rail passenger service," he observed (AMTRAK's traffic increased 26% between 1972 and 73). He also predicted the failure of the Auto Train concept, which – as noted in Chapter 20 – has been totally successful (Southerland and McCleery, 1973).

Periodically, American and Canadian railways have been raising passenger fares to reduce losses, but also to discourage traffic and be permitted to abandon service. Reacting to a fare increase by Illinois Central, representative Mikva commented as follows:

> They are going to put up the fares so high that no one will ride . . . Then, like the guy who killed both his parents and pleaded for mercy because he was an orphan, they are going to come in and ask to discontinue the service. (Southerland and McCleery, 1973).

The safety of railway operations in Canada has been already discussed in some detail in Chapters 10 and 12 and was shown to be unacceptably poor. Although significant deficiencies in the legislation on safety-related aspects of railway operations

---

*The CN *Turbotrain* started operations in December, 1973, after over 5 years of unsuccessful attempts (see p. 152).

and in its enforcement exist, nevertheless the major share of responsibility for unsafe operations belongs to the railways. Apparently, they have neglected to establish and adhere to adequate standards, have allowed roadbeds to deteriorate beyond conditions necessary to safely carry the present traffic volume, and in some instances have adopted basically dangerous operating practices.* Predictably, CN reacted negatively to the findings of the RTC's railway safety inquiry (CTC, 1973). CN spokesman stated that the conclusions in the railway safety report (CTC, 1973) were based on outdated figures and did not reflect current conditions, and that the report's proposals have already been carried out with a 13% improvement in the accident record in 1973. (The RTC report stated that in 1972 the number of derailments caused by track conditions was almost double the number in 1969). N. J. MacMillan, CN's Chairman

---

*The disregard for law and safety in the early days of railroading in Canada was noted by Keefer (1972, pp. 164-5) in the following passage:

The evil effects of the past ascendency of railway influence are visible in the disregard paid by many of the companies to the law of the land. Every company chartered after the passing of the Railway Act of 30th August, 1851, is required to show a printed tariff in every passenger-car, and to submit all by-laws changing this tariff for the approval of the governor in council, and to publish the by-law and the order in council approving the same at least twice in the Canada Gazette before putting the same into operation; also to file in the registry office of each county traversed by the railway, a map and profile of the portion within that country; and one of the whole railway, in the office of the commissioner of public works; and to submit annually to the legislature *classified* statements of the passengers and goods transported by them. These provisions should either be enforced or expunged from the Statute-Book; for nothing can be more demoralizing in its example than long-continued disobedience by such conspicuous lawbreakers. An unnecessary tenderness has also been displayed toward companies which are exempt by the date of their charter from the wholesome provisions of the Railway Act. Almost all the early charters contain a clause declaring that subsequent enactments by the legislature in the public interest shall not be considered a breach of the privileges granted; and therefore those railways which, like the Great Western, do not exhibit notice-boards at level crossings, and do not remove timber which may fall across the track, should be required to do so as much as those chartered a few years later. The number of level crossings (at every one of which, sooner or later, loss of life may be counted on) has been reduced on the Great Western by the fact, that the contractors were paid in proportion to the work done, and not by the mile, and because frequent crossings of this description would increase the danger *to the trains*, with the high speed aimed at in the location of that work. On other roads, where the contractor's interest was supreme, or where the companies were very poor, these crossings are more numerous, as being the least expensive.

145

and President until 1974, noted that any blanket order reducing train speeds and car loads would be a backward step. The CN management appeared not to recognize the low safety level of their railway operations.

The above attitudes reflect railways' perception of their role. In North America, so-called railway companies do not necessarily consider railway transportation as their major mission and field of activity. Like the ordinary, unsubsidized corporations, the railways are also motivated – to the extent that the governmental regulation of their activities permits – to seek maximum profits or maximum net return on investment. In following this generally sound principle, they diversify through investing into fields more profitable than railway transportation, which, starved of capital and closely regulated, is allowed to deteriorate relative to the other transportation modes.

Canadian Pacific is one of the most diversified companies in North America, as evident from a study by Chodos (1973). It is involved in at least twenty industrial activities, which include, in addition to railway transportation, mining (metals, coal, oil and gas), smelting and refining, lumber and wood products, chemicals, electric and gas utilities, real estate, hotels and restaurants, telecommunications, business and credit services, road, water, air and pipeline transportation. The corporate components of Canadian Pacific, shown in Table 13.1, reflect these varied interests. In 1971, the original name, "Canadian Pacific Railway Company" was changed to "Canadian Pacific Ltd.," identifying the corporate parent (whose shares are traded on stock exchanges) of some ten major subsidiaries. In recent years, the railway operations contributed about one-half of the total profits of CP Ltd.

Quite naturally, diversification has been also espoused by the "peoples' railway," which, while burdened with operation of a basically inefficient, overextended railway system, has been eager to achieve "a profit position" through activities other than railroading. CN's 1971-1976 Corporate Plan calls for "developing and marketing new technological capabilities, such as pipelines," and "entering into other business arrangements, such as urban development projects, which are consistent with the best management of existing assets." CN System comprises over 40 companies and is affiliated with Air Canada, the national air carrier. In addition to involvement with numerous transportation enterprises, CN is also active in telecommunications, real

TABLE 13.1   DIVERSIFICATION OF CANADIAN PACIFIC LTD.
(Chodos, 1973)
Company names shown in CAPITAL letters

Transportation and
Communications

Rail	CP RAIL (includes CP and ownership or interest in 6 other railways)
Water	CP BERMUDA CP SHIPS PACIFIC COAST TERMINALS
Road	SMITH TRANSPORT CP TRANSPORT CP EXPRESS
Pipe	CASCADE PIPE LINE
Air	CP AIR
Communications	CP TELECOMMUNICATIONS

CP INVESTMENTS

Resource
Industries
	PAN CANADIAN PETROLEUM
	PAN ARCTIC OILS
	CP MINERALS
	PACIFIC LOGGING
	GREAT LAKES PAPER
	COMINCO
	  FORDING COAL
	  PINE POINT MINES
	  WESTERN CANADA STEEL
	  ABERFOYLE LTD.
	  MITSUBISHI COMINCO SMELTING
	  COMINCO BINANI ZINC
	  MAZAK LTD.

Real estate	MARATHON REALTY CP HOTELS
Other	CP CONSULTING SERVICES CP SECURITIES WEST KOOTENAY POWER & LIGHT

estate, hotels and consulting services. In 1971, CN's net railway operating income (before interest on debt, which amounted to $66.1 million) was $23.9 million, earned on $1,257 million of railway operating revenues; the "other income" was $24.4 million earned on $148.7 million of non-rail revenues. The high profitability of non-rail operations compared to rail is striking, and supports CN's corporate strategy of diversification.

Nevertheless, as noted by Darling (1974), this strategy must be questioned if it is recalled that CN received large subsidies from the government. While it has been claimed that money for such projects as a new hotel in Moncton and the CN Tower in Toronto "come from the Company's own funds without need to approach the government, this is only a manner of speaking so long as the annual subscriptions to preferred stock continue to be accepted as a matter of right, for which no specific capital use need be specified, and a capital deficit or depletion of working capital would have been incurred without them. Such non-rail projects in view of the massive assistance in one form or another that is being given to Canadian National, should probably be relegated to a low priority in the Company's budget so that in effect the government assistance can be directed to the more urgent needs of railway plant and equipment, and such projects left to the private enterprise."

As further observed by Darling (1974), government subsidies, which are an effective guarantee to Canadian National of freedom from the risk of bankruptcy, . . . "cannot fail to have some influence on corporate decisions and on the evaluation of the financial risk in any particular course of action."

The American railways have also been extending their business interests. The Penn Central, before it went bankrupt in 1971, owned or controlled 186 companies active mostly in real estate and hotels, from New York (including several Manhattan landmarks) to Florida and California (Southerland and Mc-Cleery, 1973).

In view of the original arrangements under which North American railways were developed, their propensity to diversify should have been expected. As noted earlier, profitability of railways was critically dependent on large subsidies, which often included generous land grants. To realize the benefits of the latter, the railways had to engage in the real estate business, so that their interests in this field at least must be regarded as quite legitimate, and of long standing.* However, the deterioration of railway transportation as the inevitable consequence of such diversification has not been foreseen by the governments and the society. With profitability of the railways running low, the business objectives of the railway industry no longer coincide with the social need of efficient railway transportation. The situation is not likely to change until the railways are viewed as a service in the first place, and as a business in the second.

* This is not always appreciated. For example, Senator Metcalf (Montana) noted that "The United States did not grant millions of acres to an oil company known as Northern Pacific, to a mining company known as Northern Pacific, to a timber company known as Northern Pacific. The lands were to construct a railroad and to keep it in working order" (Southerland and McCleery, 1973). And yet, how else could have Northern Pacific exploited its land subsidies?

CHAPTER 14

RESEARCH AND DEVELOPMENT ACTIVITIES

As would be expected in the light of the information reviewed so far, there has been a lack of significant R&D activity in the railway field in Canada. A study conducted for the Science Council (Lewis, 1971)* pointed out that in Canada, in 1968 (i) only 7% (or $40 million) of R&D funds were devoted to transportation, which accounted for almost 20% of the GNP, (ii) federal transportation research was lacking in cohesion, (iii) within the federal government, less than 10% of professionals engaged in the transportation R&D were concerned with the rail transportation, (iv) the aircraft industry accounted for 90% of industrial R&D in transportation.

The institutional framework within which marginal railway R&D is being conducted comprises the CTC, the Ministry of Transport, CN and CP; from time to time, various projects have been undertaken by the industry, by government laboratories and universities.

The 1967 National Transportation Act requires the CTC to "undertake studies and research into the economic aspects of all modes of transport within, into or from Canada" (Canada 1970a, Para. 22, (1), (b)). Significantly, only the economic studies and policies are mentioned throughout Para. 22 which deals with the duties of the CTC; technical aspects are altogether omitted. In order to carry out the R&D function specified by the 1967 Act, the CTC formed, in 1968, a Research Division. In 1970, a part of the Division's program was transferred to the newly-formed Transportation Development Agency (TDA) of the Ministry of Transport. The Canadian Surface Transportation Administration is another agency of the same ministry concerned with R&D.

In 1972, no R&D related to railway engineering was conducted by any of the agencies mentioned (Hanchet, 1972). The

---

*Curiously, Lewis' study omitted the activities of railways and airlines. "One obvious reason was the need to preserve commercial security and to respect other sensitivities" (Lewis, 1971, p. 9).

very modest technical R&D activities of CN* and CP (a total of 19 projects) were almost completely confined to operational problems of existing equipment. Such important aspects as electrification and track/train dynamics were addressed in only two (CP's) projects.

The lack of research activities confirms the previously noted indifference of CN and CP to rail modernization. The contrast with the situation in Western Europe and Japan couldn't be greater. In the U.K., France, West Germany, Switzerland and Japan railways are deeply involved in the development of new equipment and superior track, and operate extensive R&D facilities (such as British Rail's Technical Centre at Derby which employs 2500, or SNCF's and JNR's laboratories). In these countries the technical initiative rests with the state-owned railways, and leads to close cooperation with the industry in the development and production of new equipment. It is important to note that rail modernization is only possible if it is pursued by the railway operators (who may adopt equipment developed by others; more on this aspect below); clearly, unless the R&D is performed in their behalf, it can have no practical impact. In Canada, under the protection of government subsidies, the railways have largely excluded R&D into rail technology from the scope of their institutionalized activities. Once again, contrary to the declared intent, the 1967 Act has succeeded in eliminating technical competition in the railway field while allowing two independent systems to operate.

With railways showing negligible interest, no industrial initiative into rail modernization could be expected to result in significant changes. In recent years there have been only two industrial ventures into the improvement of passenger rail in Canada.

In 1964 CN had prepared rough specifications for an improved train to be used on the Montreal-Toronto run, but did not proceed towards development of a design (Cann and Wilson, 1968). In 1965 the United Aircraft Corporation (USA) approached CN with a proposal for a passenger train more advanced than that envisaged by the CN. This initiative resulted

*Supported by a large public relations campaign. In September, 1973, CN placed extensive advertisements in national magazines extolling the virtues of research carried out in its "8½ acre Technical Research Centre." It is certainly unorthodox to measure research effort by laboratory acreage; the size of the professional staff and the budget are more meaningful yardsticks.

in an order from CN to UAC's Canadian subsidiary (UACL)†
for the lease of five seven-car, 125 mph train sets; their construction started in the summer of 1966. In December, 1968,
CN introduced the UACL's *Turbotrain* on the Montreal-
Toronto run (originally intended to start operations in the 1967
Centennial). Characteristically, CN did not propose to exploit
the available performance, but intended to operate the 125 mph
trains at speeds below 95 mph. Because of cold weather problems, the service was discontinued after about one month, and
was again reinstated in May, 1970, only to be dropped eight
months later. In 1972, a new lease was signed by CN for 3
nine-car *Turbotrains*. The railway company agreed to give the
trains three more years of trial before deciding whether to purchase them. A test run made on January 25, 1973, ended in a
fiasco. On June 22, 1973, CN launched—for the third time—the
Montreal-Toronto *Turbotrain* service. Breakdowns occured on
June 22, 23 and 24. On June 25—the fourth day—CN cancelled
all *Turbotrain* services. As one reporter observed, "breakdowns
. . . were the only function the train could produce on schedule."* Launched again in December, 1973, the *Turbotrain* has
been operating successfully between Toronto and Montreal,
and, since August, 1974, also between Ottawa and Montreal.
On September 23, 1975, one of the *Turbotrains* was severely
damaged by fire while on the Montreal-Toronto run, leaving
only two *Turbos* in service; subsequently, the Ottawa-Montreal
Turbotrain service was discontinued.

UAC's *Turbotrains* have been operated more regularly by
AMTRAK between New York and Boston. AMTRAK was
planning to expand *Turbotrain* sets, to be used on the Milwau-
kee-Chicago-St. Louis run. As already noted, one of the trains
was demolished in July, 1973, when it collided on a pre-delivery
test run with a CN freight train.

In the summer of 1973, AMTRAK leased French RTG turbotrains (manufactured by ANF-Frangeco, S.A.) for operations
on the Chicago-St. Louis and Chicago-Milwaukee runs. Compared to the *Turbotrain* record, the French equipment has

---

† Now Pratt & Whitney of Canada, Ltd.

* *Turbotrain* became "Canada's longest running railroad joke except that most
of the time it wasn't running." Its misadventures have led it to be variously
known as "The Little Engine That Couldn't", or "Jonathan Livingston
Streamliner," or "The Great Distrubo" (*Time*, January 14, 1974).

"Well, we could try an ad in the paper—low mileage, like new, one owner...." (On June 22, 1973, CN launched—for the third time since 1968—the *Turbo* service between Montreal and Toronto. After a series of breakdowns, the service was cancelled three days later; it was reinstated in December, 1973).

Yardley Jones/Canada Wide June 1973

logged a far superior performance. Both in Canada and the U.S., the *Turbotrains* required extensive maintenance, which resulted in high costs and poor reliability. While the RTG trains racked up an availability record of 98% in 1973, and a perfect 100% in the spring of 1974, the Boston-New York *Turbotrains* were available only 46% of the time. Consequently, the on-time performance of the RTG trains was better than the *Turbotrains*. For the first three months of 1974, it was 48%, 74% and 80% respectively for the RTGs, compared to 34%, 54% and 66% for the *Turbotrains*. Furthermore, the RTG trains have amassed an impressive service record in France, and are about 30% cheaper to buy than the American *Turbotrains*.

153

Not surprisingly, when in 1974 AMTRAK was authorized to expand its fleet of modern trains, it opted for the French technology, in preference to the UAC's proposals of an improved *Turbotrain 2*. In June, 1974, AMTRAK placed an order for four RTG trains and decided to buy the two it had been leasing since 1973, for a total of $18 million for the six trains. In July, 1974, AMTRAK was authorized to procure seven new gas turbine trains for New York-Boston operations, at an estimated cost of $30 to $35 million. The 125 mph trains are to be produced in the U.S. by Rohr Corporation, under license from France's ANF- Frangeco.

Faced with the superior performance of the RTG trains and AMTRAK's choice of the French technology, United Aircraft Corporation announced in July, 1974 its intention to withdraw from the passenger train field. Thus, after almost a decade of activity and a $30 million investment, the only American effort in the development of modern passenger rail technology has been terminated in favor of construction of new equipment under a French license.

CN's and AMTRAK's experience with the *Turbotrain* operations has been significant in two respects. First, it has shown that the UAC's *Turbotrain* – the only advanced American train – is inferior to European designs, and, secondly, it has indicated that neither CN nor the American-Canadian train manufacturer were capable and willing to apply the resources required to ensure *Turbotrain's* success.

CN's and UACL's performance in the matter of the *Turbotrain* stands out in striking contrast to JNR's development of the New Tokaido Line. Following is a brief account of that undertaking.

By 1956, the old narrow gauge Tokaido Line was completely electrified; measuring only less than 3% of the total mileage of JNR, it carried about a quarter of the total JNR traffic. With freight and passenger traffic rising sharply, its capacity soon became saturated. "To resolve this difficulty, it was felt indispensable to build another double-track railway along this route. JNR started . . . research and studies for resolving the traffic difficulties on this route beginning in 1957, and came to the conclusion that it would be advantageous to build a completely new standard-gauge high-speed railway, not being bound by the technical details of the narrow gauge Tokaido Line. JNR conducted investigations and surveys for this proposal from 1958, and started construction work on the new railway, the "New Tokaido Line" (NTL) in April 1959. In 1962, it completed the trial section of the NTL and soon started test operations of a prototype NTL train – a multiple-unit electric railcar train – which registered a maximum speed of 160 mph on the trial section in 1963. Conquering many difficulties, the NTL was completed and opened for commercial passenger traffic in October 1964, five and a half years from the start of the construction work" (Kataoka, 1969).

Except for the CP's studies (Fisher, 1971, 1972) of electrification of the Calgary-Vancouver route (based on economics of freight), the only current activity related to modernization of Canadian railways is the LRC (Light, Rapid, Comfortable) train project,* a joint undertaking of Montreal Locomotive Works – Worthington Ltd., Alcan and Dofasco, with significant funding by the Department of Industry, Trade and Commerce.**

The design of the 120 mph LRC train could be described as a refinement of conventional diesel traction technology. Light alloys are used in the structure of locomotive and passenger cars. The shapes are streamlined and undersides are cowled to reduce aerodynamic drag. Speeds higher by up to 40% on curves can be permitted through active tilting of the passenger compartment. The LRC's performance, in terms of power and weight, is similar to the existing, standard European trains, such as the TEE (either diesel or electric), except for the permissible speed. The LRC is much heavier than the *Turbotrain*, or the more advanced British APT, or the Japanese NTL electric cars. The LRC coaches are nevertheless over 40% lighter than the standard, North American designs but somewhat heavier than the new European and Japanese equipment. The LRC's diesel locomotive is 75% lighter than the standard CN type, but 25% heavier than modern electrics; it has a loading of about 27 ton/axle compared with 10 to 17 ton/axle for modern gas turbine, diesel and electric traction.

*Early in 1975 development of *Futura*, a train concept similar to the LRC, was announced by Hawker Siddeley Canada and General Motors.

**The cost of a prototype locomotive and coach was estimated at $5 million, half of which to be paid by the Department of Industry, Trade and Commerce.

The LRC has been apparently conceived as a compromise solution which would conform to standard North American railway practice but allow somewhat higher speeds on existing tracks. The only departure from this approach, apart from greater structural efficiency, has been the inclusion of the tilt mechanism for passenger comfort. Conventional, non-articulated coach and locomotive configurations are used, to allow rapid changes in the consist and flexibility of use with standard equipment. Diesel-electric traction and other standard railway equipment are used so that conventional maintenance procedures can be followed.

In the light of developments elsewhere, the LRC train can be viewed only as an interim solution (indeed, it is similar to the BR's HST, see Chapter 21), to which however neither CN nor CP are committed. After 1976, when LRC will be ready to run, 125 mph gas turbine and electric trains will be operating in increasing numbers in the U.S. and Europe, and much more advanced equipment will be entering service.

Given the climate of institutionalized desinteressement on the part of the government and rail companies, the few federally-supported research projects at NRC and universities have not been significant. For example, in the 1950's McGill University engaged in research on a coal-burning gas turbine for rail traction. The project did not lead to any practical developments and was discontinued after several years. During the same period, the NRC started work on a gas turbine design for rail applications. After some 20 years, also this activity folded without producing a tangible result.

In the area of rail safety (see Chapters 10 and 12), there has also been a conspicuous lack of R&D activity in both Canada and the U.S., in spite of an alarming rise in the number of accidents, and a poor safety record in comparison with railways elsewhere.

CHAPTER 15

RAILWAY DEVELOPMENT
POLICIES ABROAD

The information thus far reviewed (especially in Chapter 12) shows that railway transportation in Canada has been rigidly institutionalized within the framework of both the 1967 National Transportation Act and earlier legislation. Bureaucratic regulation of supposedly competitive enterprises has been substituted for development of long-term policy and for dynamic planning.

An opposite situation has prevailed in recent years in Europe and Japan, where railway transportation has been viewed as an indispensable national activity worthy of public support, and where governments and railway state monopolies have been engaged in the formulation and implementation of long-range, national rail development and modernization policies. In the United States as well, since 1970 a vigorous policy to develop and modernize passenger rail has been implemented through government-supported AMTRAK organization and new regulatory initiatives. Freight operations in the Northeast are being nationalized and upgraded through consolidation of the bankrupt lines.

To appreciate the gap which has developed between Canada on the one hand, Europe, Japan and, to some extent, the U.S., on the other, it is useful to review recent railway policies and developments in some of these countries. Technological progress in Europe and Japan (see Chapters 9 and 10) has been concerned with (i) electrification of main lines (now largely completed on the leading European railways), (ii) exploitation of existing tracks with special high speed equipment, (iii) development of high speed equipment for use on upgraded and "dedicated" or specialized high speed links, and (vi) integration of railway operations across national boundaries in Europe. These activities have been financed through extensive subsidies and coordinated within long-term programs.

France
Since nationalization in 1938, the operation of French railways has been entrusted to one organization, the SNCF. After World

War II, the railway development in France became an integral part of the overall national economic policy; during the Fifth Plan (1966-1970), a program for railways was laid through 1985. Today, SNCF operates the fastest long-haul passenger service in Europe, with 11 expresses that average more than 80 mph. The electrification program of the main lines has been virtually completed, with 80% of passenger traffic relying on electric traction. France leads the world in the development of fast electric and gas turbine trains (see Chapter 21) and has supplied the latter to AMTRAK. A fast link (187 mph) is to be built between Paris and Lyon and all major intercity lines are being continuously upgraded for faster operation.

Great Britain

In the United Kingdom, the country which was the first to introduce railway transportation (in 1825), railway development in this century has paralleled the practices followed in continental Europe (Aldcroft, 1968). It was marked by consolidation (of some 130 companies, under the British Railways Act, 1921), and nationalization after the last war (on December 31, 1947). In 1962, the results of a detailed study of the entire British Rail System were published (Beeching's "Reshaping Report") and steps were taken to rationalize rail transport by eliminating marginal and duplicated services. Between 1957 and 1967, the BR passenger network declined from 14,622 miles to less than 10,000 miles, and the number of stations dropped from 5410 to 2750.

For a number of years, the BR has been vigorously pursuing modernization and research programs, including main line electrification and development of faster rolling stock (see Chapter 21) such as the HST (High Speed Train) and the APT (Advanced Passenger Train). In November, 1973, in a major policy statement,* the British government announced a 5-year commitment to develop railway transportation at the expense of urban road-building. The rail network would be maintained at its present size, while the investment over the next five years (£891 million) would be increased by 60% over the present level.** The strategy calls for 50% of all investment to go into

* Regarded by some as a reversal of Conservative government's policy and complete breakaway from the Beeching regime of big rail cuts.

** As of January, 1975, government estimates give BR's average annual capital expenditure between 1974 and 1979 as £230 million, up 77% from the previous 4-year period (RGI, p. 45, February 1975).

track, signalling, improvement of level crossings and telecommunications; 30% for high speed trains, commuter services and stations; 20% on electrification, freight and express services. East Coast main line electrification is planned after 1977. The government will also continue to provide substantial revenue support for the BR (Hunt, 1973).

These measures give long-term assurance for BR's development and indicate' acceptance of BR's point of view that the railways will never be commercially profitable – however much they are trimmed.

Western Europe

Concurrently with the modernization of major national railway systems, continental railway policies are being developed in Western Europe in the context of an expanding Common Market. Already the Trans-Europ Express (TEE), passenger and freight (TEE-M), and the European Freight Car Community provide integrated services. Twenty-one countries belong to the Intercontainer and Interfrigo organizations responsible for international movements of containers and refrigerated cars. Under the auspices of the International Union of Railways, a future "Europolitain" network is planned to secure top quality connections between the major conurbations in Europe (RGI, 1972c). Other objectives include common passenger and freight rolling stock and standardization of all aspects of railway operations and equipment (Fontgalland, 1972; Tessier, 1973).

The IUR's draft master plan (RGI, 1973b; Friedlander, 1974), announced in November 1973 envisages building 3750 miles of completely new track (including the now-postponed Channel Tunnel) and modernizing another 8,750 miles. The master plan lines are shown in Fig. 15.1; the new network could be completed by 1985. The plan establishes strict targets of service, including speed, frequency and reliability for passengers and guaranteed door-to-door times for freight. It calls for European standards on gradients, curves, and operating methods.

Ireland

In 1974 the Irish Government approved a major national modernization plan for the country's railway network at an estimated investment of more than $55 million. The plan envisages "the virtual creation of a new railway system," and proposes expansion of high speed passenger and freight services.

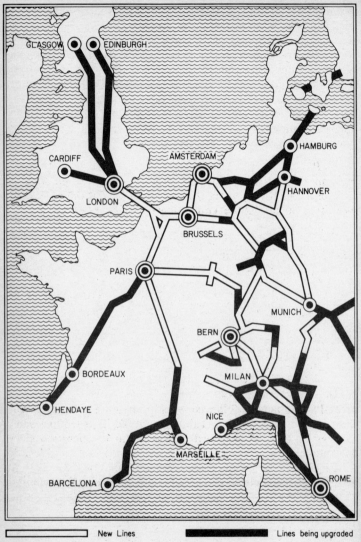

New Lines | Lines being upgraded

Map of Europe's proposed high-speed intercity rail network that is included in a plan formulated by the International Union of Railways.

FIG. 15-1

Poland

The Polish State Railways (PKP) are engaged in a long-range program of modernization and expansion. By 1985, over 40% of the network will be electrified (now 20%), and 80% of the traffic will move by electric traction. The track will be improved for operations up to 100 mph. By 1977, a new trunk line (double track, continuous welded rail, electrified, no level crossings) connecting Silesia to Warsaw and the Baltic will be completed. The program will result in a 50% increase in freight capacity by 1985, and in augmentation of average passenger train speeds from 60 to 100 mph.

Soviet Russia

Russian railways have been undergoing extensive modernization for about twenty years. Today, about 25% of the network is electrified (including the Trans-Siberian line west of Chita) and, since 1956, electrification progresses at over 1000 miles of lines per year (Fig. 15.2). Modern, high voltage (25 kv, 50 Hz) technology is being used, and new, faster and more powerful electric and diesel locomotives are being developed. On the Moscow-Leningrad line, 125 mph trains began running in 1975, cutting the trip time to 4 hours (100 mph average). In 1967, work was started on a second trans-Siberian, 2100 mile link, the Baikal-Amur (BAM) mainline (Fig. 15.2), which will open up exploitation of large mineral and coal deposits, and provide an alternative route to the Pacific; the line is to be completed in 1982.

Japan

Since 1949 Japan has followed a comprehensive plan of railway development (RGI, 1972b; Takiyama, 1974). This led to electrification by 1970 of one-third of track, and to operation since 1964 of the world's fastest train service on the New Tokaido Line (NTL) linking Tokyo with Osaka (322 miles). The latter is probably "the most profitable railway in the world, revenue in 1970 [and in subsequent years] amounting to more than double the total of operating expenses and capital charges" (Hope, 1972). Japan's long-range policy, announced in 1970, envisages extension of the Shinkansen* high speed (160 mph top speed) network by over 4400 miles by 1985. Improvement of passenger transport on existing normal speed and narrow gauge lines is

* *Shin* means "new superfast"; *kansen* means "main line."

161

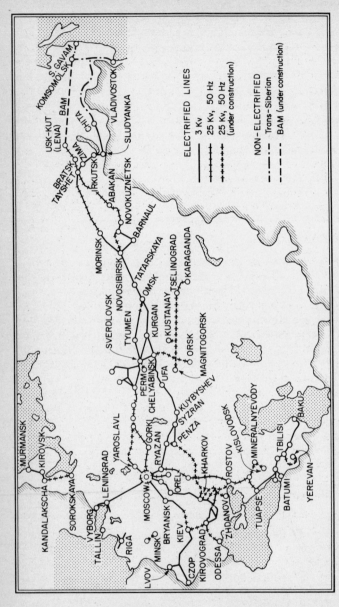

Electrification of railways and new lines in Soviet Russia. (Nouvion, 1972; Muraton and Feldman, 1972)

FIG. 15-2

also continued with diesel, electric and gas turbine traction, using articulated, body-tilt train designs.

Since March, 1973, the 100 miles of the Sanyo Shinkansen (extension of the NTL) came into operation (between Osaka and Okayama), and achieved load factors of 89% on weekdays to over 100% on weekends. In March, 1975, the remaining Sanyo section to Hakata (248 miles) was opened. The Sanyo line is built for operation at 163 mph maximum speed (compared to 130 mph on the NTL); new trains are being developed for this service. In October 1973, as the implications of the oil crisis were becoming apparent, construction of five more Shinkansen lines for completion in 1979, expanding the network to 2200 miles, was approved. Work on a further 10 lines (2100 miles) is to start in 1977. The feasibility of a second Tokaido Shinkansen line is being considered. In 1973, the Japanese diet approved a 10-year, $40 billion* program to upgrade JNR's equipment and tracks.

AMTRAK and Other Developments in the U.S.

In the 1960's, faced with a catastrophic decline of passenger rail travel*† and with increasing traffic congestion in the urban corridors, the U.S. proceeded to investigate new transportation technologies (1965 High Speed Ground Transportation Project) and to rationalize passenger rail operations. These initiatives resulted in introduction of modern equipment in the Northeast corridor (*Turbotrains* whose use is being expanded to other high traffic volume areas and *Metroliners*) and passage, in 1970, of the Rail Passenger Service Act which set as its goal the organization and maintenance of an efficient intercity railway passenger service. To carry out this task, the U.S. created the National Railroad Passenger Corporation (AMTRAK), designed to function on a profitable basis but initially extensively subsidized (see the end of this chapter re financing of AMTRAK).

AMTRAK** represents a novel concept in railroading: a semi-public corporation assuming responsibility for train opera-

---

* Comparable to the U.S. "man on the moon" Apollo project cost, estimated at about $25 billion.

*† Following the war peak of almost 100 billion passenger miles in 1945, the passenger rail traffic dropped from 35 billion passenger miles in 1950 to 10 billion in 1970.

** The information here summarized is based on Annual Reports and news releases by AMTRAK; see also Kizzia, 1974.

163

tions on an infrastructure (track and other permanent facilities) which is privately-owned by several (20 in 1974) companies. Through AMTRAK, passenger rail has been effectively integrated and rationalized in the U.S. (AMTRAK operates over 90% of all passenger route miles), and is being modernized and expanded.

In the beginning, AMTRAK contracted with the participating railroads for operating and servicing of trains and stations, for doing accounting and reservations, for maintaining and overhauling of the rolling stock, etc. It acquired and leased some 1600 passenger cars, and bought 275 locomotives. By 1975, AMTRAK has taken over all service functions on board of trains, all reservations and accounting functions, and most station service functions. It has also taken over one major overhaul facility and is operating an increasing number of day-to-day maintenance bases. On the equipment side, AMTRAK has on order 492 *Metroliner*-type (Budd Co.) passenger cars, 235 new bilevel cars (Pullman-Standard Mfrg. Co.), has acquired 150 General Motors Co., 3000 HP diesel-electric locomotives (25 additional ones are on order from the General Electric Co.), has bought 26 GE electric locomotives, 13 French gas-turbine trains (7 to be produced in the U.S.), 3 United Aircraft Co. *Turbotrains*, and 30 new high speed (125 mph), light-weight GM diesel-electric locomotives to be used to haul the new *Metroliner* cars – for a total of $540 million.

Initially, AMTRAK experienced considerable difficulties: it had little control over the priority of its trains versus profitable freights, over maintenance of its old passenger fleet, punctuality of services, cleanliness of cars, etc. (Loving, 1974; TRF, 1972, pp. 113-162). The situation was drastically improved in 1974, through negotiating new incentive-type contracts with the railroads which tie compensation to the quality of service provided. Performance requirements comply with the standards set by the Interstate Commerce Commission; most importantly, the railroads make no profit unless they reach or exceed the specified performance level. For example, there are incentives for on-time performance in excess of 65% (90% on-time performance earns 21% of initial costs) and equipment availability (85% for cars and 90% for locomotives), and there are penalties for excessive delays, failure to clean cars, failure to maintain equipment in operable condition for 95% of the time, etc. According to Roger Lewis, the Chairman of the Board and first President of AMTRAK, "This change in contractual relationship is undoubtedly one of the most encouraging milestones of progress in AMTRAK's short history" (AMTRAK, 1974).

The effectiveness of AMTRAK, developed under the leadership of an aerospace industry executive, is evident from comparison of its operating results over the years. AMTRAK began operations on May 1, 1971, by discontinuing almost half of the U.S. passenger rail services. In 1974, it operated 240 trains per day on 24,315 route miles, served 457 stations and carried 18.5 million passengers (compared to 15.8 million in the first year of operations; its average on-time performance was 75.3% (up from 61.7% in 1973).

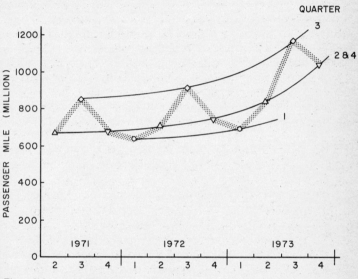

Fig. 15.3   AMTRAK's progress.

The steady expansion of AMTRAK's patronage is shown in Fig. 15.3, for each quarter starting with the 2nd quarter of 1971, the first year of operations. In the peak 3rd quarter, the travel increased by 37% between 1971 and 1973. On some runs, the increases have been truly spectacular. Between August 1971 and August 1972, the northeast corridor traffic (on fast *Metroliners* and *Turbotrains*) between Washington-New York and New York-Boston jumped 60% and 78% respectively. The increase has continued: 24% more passengers were carried on the New

York-Washington run in the first quarter in 1974 than in the same period in 1973; a 61% increase occured on the Boston-New York line. There was substantial augmentation on many other runs; for example, New York-Buffalo, 97%; Chicago-St. Louis, 48%; Chicago-Detroit, 88%; Los Angeles-San Diego, 57%. The same trend prevailed on the long haul routes: New York-Florida, 80%; Chicago-Florida, 52%; Chicago-Oakland, 78%; New Orleans-Los Angeles, 52%; Los Angeles-Seattle, 74%; Washington-Montreal (via New England)74%. All told, the AMTRAK system carried 41% more passengers in the first quarter of 1974 than in the same period in 1973; its revenues were up 40%.*

As a result of AMTRAK initiatives, a long-term policy of passenger rail modernization and development in the U.S. is emerging. In September, 1974, AMTRAK sent Congress a 5-year, $2.1 billion capital acquisition plan, calling for $1.2 billion for improvements of 12 major intercity routes (to allow speeds up to 110 mph average) and $263 million for new equipment, doubling the capacity by 1979. An expenditure of $700 million is planned for segregating, upgrading and electrifying the Penn Central's Washington-New York-Boston 450-mile route for use by AMTRAK fast trains. In May, 1975, $1.118 billion was authorized to finance AMTRAK to October, 1977; included was $245 million for capital improvements.

Under the 1970 Rail Passenger Service Act, which permits states to request AMTRAK to operate a service provided the State pays at least two-thirds of any losses incurred, five states are sponsoring AMTRAK trains and more intend to do so. In 1974 New York State voted $250 million for a 5-year rail improvement program in the New York-Albany-Buffalo corridor. 125 mph French trains are to eventually provide a 4½ hour service from New York to Buffalo.

As noted by Mertins (1972, p. 58), a remarkable aspect of the 1970 Act was the exemption of AMTRAK from the quagmire of Interstate Commerce Commission (ICC) regulatory provisions governing rates, fares and charges, abandonments and extensions, routes and services. Paradoxically, virtually all of the railroads that are participating in the AMTRAK network have been seeking precisely this kind of freedom for many decades.

* However, in 1975 (January to August), the number of passengers carried by AMTRAK decreased by 10% compared to the same period in 1974.

The other unprecedented implication of the 1970 Act was the abolition of the sacred principle of intramodal competition in railway transportation. AMTRAK has been given exclusive passenger traffic rights on the routes it chose to operate and, as virtually the only organization responsible for passenger services, became a subsidized national monopoly. The impracticability of providing passenger rail service on supposedly competitive, profit basis has been at long last tacitly admitted, and a decision has been made in favour of social rather than commercial benefits.

The same motives may prevail in resolving the problem of the bankrupt lines in the Northeast and Midwest (Penn Central and seven other railroads).* Under the Regional Rail Reorganization Act, the U.S. Railway Association was created in January, 1975 to develop a plan for transforming the bankrupt lines into a viable system. Under USRA proposal (filed with Congress in July, 1975), a semi-public company called Consolidated Railway Corporation (Conrail) would operate only 15,000 miles of the consolidated lines (leaving 5100 miles which now carry only 2.1% of traffic), and would require $1.8 billion of government financing. USRA recommended 16 new and improved passenger routes; between New York and Washington, freight traffic would be transferred from Penn Central tracks to a parallel line, allowing faster and more frequent passenger service. The implementation of the USRA Conrail plan would amount to a major rationalization of U.S. railways and provision of substantial capital for their upgrading, developments which must be viewed as significant, new departures in American railroading.

Three other recent American initiatives should also be mentioned. In 1973, for the first time in the U.S. the road construction funds became available for spending on other forms of transport. The 1973 Federal Highway Act authorized the use of up to $800 million a year from the sacrosanct Highway Trust Fund for bus and rail transit; it also allowed cities and states to substitute mass transit projects for urban roads already authorized. A further dilution of the Highway Trust Fund was proposed in 1975 by President Ford: it would divert 75% of the federal gasoline tax into general revenues (federal and state).

---

* When the Chicago, Rock Island & Pacific Railroad filed for bankruptcy in March, 1975, the "Northeast railroad problem" was extended to New Mexico.

Another important step in the process of upgrading U.S. railways is the proposed (in May, 1975) Railroad Revitalization Act. Its aims are to encourage elimination of duplicate tracks and facilities, to provide up to $2 billion in guaranteed loans for reconstruction, and to reduce the power of government to fix tariffs.

Financial results
The picture of progress in railway transportation in Europe, Japan and the U.S., sketched above must be matched with the costs which railway operations entail. Because the financing of railway construction and operation has always been highly complex (involving government loans and grants, regulation of tariffs and different accounting procedures), extensive research would be required to establish true and consistent revenue and

TABLE 15.1 OPERATING CHARGES AND REVENUES, 1971 (IUR, 1971)

	MILLION DOLLARS		(LOSS) GAIN	
	Charges	Revenues	(Loss) Gain	% Revenues
UK	1,550	1,470	(80)	(5.5)
Switzerland	485	448	(37)	(8.3)
W. Germany	4,950	4,230	(720)	(17)
Italy	1,950	990	(960)	(96)
Japan	4,120	3,420	(700)	(20.5)
CN (Canada)	1,120	1,096	(24)	(2.2)
CP (Canada)	613	637	24	3.8
USA	11,993	12,688	695	5.5
AMTRAK 1972-74	1,201	622	(579)	(93)

expenditure figures. Such a task cannot be undertaken here; instead, the review of costs of operations will be based on the information listed in *International Railway Statistics*.

Although the exact numbers may be subject to interpretation, a review of the balances of railway operations (Table 15.1) reveals that Japanese and West European nationalized railways operate at considerable deficits, while the U.S. railroads as a whole and the privately-owned CP are unique in showing profits.

In absolute terms, the losses of Western European and Japanese railways have been huge. In 1971, the aggregate deficit of the six Common Market railways amounted to $1.6 billion; Germany's share alone was $720 million. From 1972 to 1974, German railways received $11 billion from the government. Japanese railways have been running in the red since 1964, and had accumulated, by 1972, a deficit of $2.5 billion; their deficit in 1972 was almost $1 billion, in spite of phenomenal profits on the NTL Shinkansen.* AMTRAK, the U.S. passenger service, received $559 million in government grants and $900 million in loan guarantees up to December 31, 1974. Over the three-year period, AMTRAK ran up a deficit of $579 million (calculated as excess of operating expenses over revenues). By comparison, the average total subsidies of $169 million per year granted Canadian railways from 1967 to 1972 (see Chapter 12) appear as a small figure.

In relative terms, the losses experienced by the major Western European railways in 1971 ranged from 5.5% (BR) to 17% (DB) of the revenues.** JNR showed a loss of 20.5%, AM-TRAK, a loss of 93%, while CN showed a loss of only 2.2%. On the other hand, the U.S. railroads and CP showed gains of 5.5% and 3.8% respectively.

It is tempting to conclude (and, in North America, it is indeed often concluded) that such figures indicate higher productivity under private than public management, and that therefore nationalization of railroads would be undesirable on grounds of economic efficiency. Such judgement should not be accepted uncritically without examining the nature of the services performed.

A major difference is the distribution of passenger versus

---

* In 1974, JNR's gross annual deficit stood at $5.3 billion.

** Except for Italy which showed an almost 100% loss.

freight traffic (the data quoted below is for 1970-71; see Tables 8.5 and 15.1). Passenger service provides from 33% of rail revenue in West Germany to 76% in Japan; it is close to 100% for AMTRAK. The operating losses amount to 17% of all rail revenues (exclusive of subsidies) in West Germany to 20.5% in Japan; AMTRAK stands at 93%. CN, with 6% of its revenue from passenger service, runs at a 2% loss. On the other hand, the U.S. railways derive only 3.5% of their revenue from passenger movements and show a 5.5% profit. For CP, the corresponding figures are 3.2% and 3.8%. Clearly, the nationalized railways in Europe and Japan, and AMTRAK, are largely engaged in passenger service, which is much more expensive to run than freight. Moreover, they carry passengers cheaply. Of course, there are many other factors (such as overmanning and operation of lightly-loaded lines, as in Japan) which affect financial results of operations. Nevertheless, the deficits of nationalized railways do not necessarily attest to their poor efficiency, but may indicate different priorities (as in Europe and Japan). "The deficits reflect a deliberate choice to provide, at low cost, the most labor-intensive form of rail service: passenger traffic," observed B. Commoner (1973).

PART THREE
FUTURE DIRECTIONS

Some people see things as they are and say, "Why?"
I see things as they ought to be and say, "Why not?"
            – ROBERT F. KENNEDY

CHAPTER 16

THE REASONS FOR CONCERN

The material presented in Parts One and Two indicates some of the current deficiencies and inconsistencies of railway operations in North America, problems often rooted in the distant past. In light of historical record one would not expect fundamental changes and improvements to occur in the near future: on the contrary, one would predict the "institutionalized obsolescence" of railway transportation to carry on along well-established lines, resulting in a continued decrease of the railway's share of both freight and passenger traffic. In fact, this is what historical traffic trends and predictions based on a traditional static environment show (Fig. 16.1 to 16.4). The 1980, 1990 and year 2000 estimates are those given by Munro and Constable (TRF, 1974, pp. 591-592), who based their data on *Canada: Transportation Projections to the Year 2000* study by Systems Research Group, Toronto, 1970. Specifically, they have assumed that (i) relative prices within transportation and between transportation and other sectors of economy remain constant, and (ii) there will be no major innovation in transportation technology.

Fig. 16.1 shows the growth of intercity transportation in Canada (by all modes) as predicted (or, in effect, extrapolated on the basis of past trends) until the year 2000. The freight volume is estimated to double every 14 years (or grow at 5% per year) until the end of this century; the passenger traffic is expected to grow at the present rate of about 5.5% until 1980, and then to slow down to a 3% yearly growth.

The modal distribution of freight traffic is illustrated in Fig.

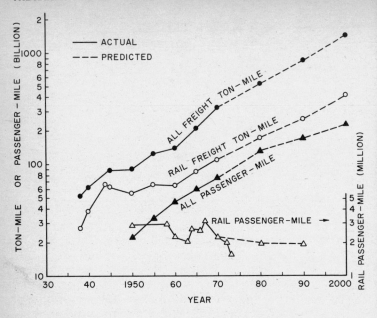

Fig. 16.1   Growth of intercity transportation in Canada (all
modes).
(Statistics Canada 1969, 1970a; TRF. 1974, pp.591,
592.)
Passenger-miles: See Note, Fig. 16.4
Ton-miles: See Note, Fig 16.2

16.2. The water and road modes are predicted to maintain their
present status (about 28% and 6% respectively); the pipelines'
(gas and oil) share is expected to grow, while the railways' is to
continue to diminish (from a peak of 74% in 1944 to 29% in the
year 2000).

The situation in the intercity passenger sector is analyzed in
Figs. 16.3 and 16.4. For the past twenty years, the private car
accounted for about 85% of intercity passenger traffic, leaving
15% to the public carriers (Fig. 16.3). The public carriers' share
is predicted to grow after 1980, reaching some 38% in the year
2000. The modal distribution within the public carriers sector
(Fig. 16.3), shows fast growth of the air mode's share, and a

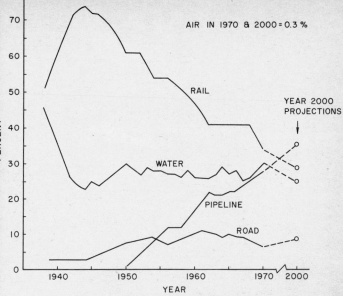

AIR IN 1970 & 2000 = 0.3 %

RAIL

YEAR 2000
PROJECTIONS

WATER

PIPELINE

ROAD

Fig. 16.2   Distribution of intercity freight traffic among modes
in Canada (Statistics Canada , 1970a; TRF, 1974, p.
591).
Note: Intercity ton-miles include domestic traffic plus
the ton-miles within Canada of traffic between Canada and the U.S. Pipeline ton-miles include only oil
and gas, trunk pipelines.

continuing decrease in rail's share (down to a mere 2% in 2000,
from 20% in 1970).*

The diminishing role of the railway is also apparent from Fig.
16.4, which compares the volume of railway traffic with the
total of all public carriers: while the latter has doubled between
1960 and 1970, that of the railways, after a modest and short-
lived increase, has returned exactly to the same level.

* Between 1980-2000, the rail passenger traffic volume was taken as constant
at 2 billion passenger-miles, "assuming that government policy . . . will
maintain overall rail passenger output at current levels" (TRF, 1974, p. 592).
In the light of only 1.6 billion passenger-miles logged in 1973, even this
might have been an optimistic assumption, as evident from the downward
trend since 1967 (Fig. 16.4).

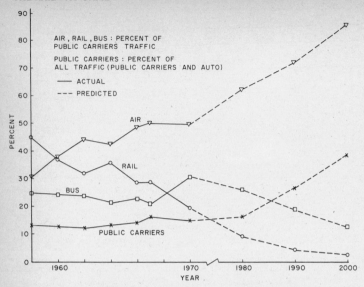

Fig. 16.3   Distribution of intercity passenger traffic among modes in Canada (Passenger-miles: See Note, Fig. 16.4)
Statistics Canada 1969; TRF 1974, p. 592).

Summarizing, the future of railway transportation in Canada (and, presumably, also in the U.S.) – as extrapolated from the current trends – is not bright. More significantly, this is not a desirable future from the point of view of national well-being, for a number of reasons.

The railway has two attributes which make it more attractive today than any other transportation mode, whether for freight or passenger traffic: it consumes relatively little energy (it is energy efficient) and does not have to rely on oil: it can run on electricity, generated from any kind of fuel. In view of the diminishing availability of cheap oil and general difficulties in meeting the energy demand, these are most important, long-term advantages offered by rail traction. For intercity freight and short to medium-haul intercity passenger travel, electric rail is the only available alternative which reduces the dependence of transportation on oil.* The railway is also attractive in environmental terms: it uses little land in relation to the traffic

* This is also true for the urban rapid mass transit sector.

174

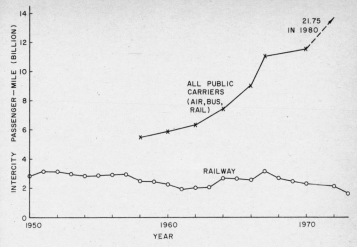

FIG 16.4   Decay of passenger rail travel in Canada (Statistics
            Canada, 1969; 1970, Pt. IV; 1973, Pt. IV; TRF 1974, p.
            592).

            Note: Intercity passenger-miles include domestic
            passenger traffic plus the passenger-miles within
            Canada of traffic between Canada and the U.S. (by
            residents of Canada and visitors from the U.S.) Over-
            seas air traffic not included. Rail traffic includes
            commuter rail (11% and 14.4% of rail passenger-
            miles in 1972 and 1973 respectively).

volume it can handle, and its pollution impact (air and acoustic) is relatively small.

In addition to the energy aspect, there is a second, equally
compelling reason to be concerned with the future of railways
in Canada and the U.S. Although, as already noted, rail's share
of freight traffic has been steadily diminishing in Canada since
1944 (Fig. 16.2), the rail freight volume has been growing at an
appreciable rate (Fig. 16.1): at about 6% per year between 1960
and 1973, and it has been predicted to increase 3.7-fold between 1970 and 2000 (4.5% per year). The capacity of the existing network of Canadian railways, with some lines already operating at near maximum volume, is inadequate to accommodate the future traffic growth. Thus capital investment for modernization and expansion of Canadian railways will be required

– an investment which cannot be envisaged under the present system of railway financing in Canada.

The oil-energy crisis and traffic growth are the two pressures which will increasingly influence the transportation situation in Canada and the U.S., and – most likely – enhance the development of railways. The analysis of factors which led to the present predicament of railways in North America, and the determination of initiatives which would facilitate their development will occupy the remaining chapters of this study.

CHAPTER 17

THE ONE-DIMENSIONALITY
OF THE RAILWAY MODE AND ITS
CONSEQUENCES

In this chapter the basic and unique, physical characteristics of the railway mode are considered. A clear understanding of these characteristics goes a long way towards explaining the present situation of railways in North America, and is helpful in formulating desirable directions for future development of railways.

The air, space and underwater transportation modes exhibit three translational degrees of freedom: an aircraft, a spacecraft or a submarine can move forward and sideways as well as in altitude or depth. Movement on roads (assuming an adequate road width) and on water is restricted to a surface, and therefore to two dimensions (in translation). In all of these cases the vehicles are capable of overtaking those which move in the same direction, and avoiding the on-coming traffic. The railway, on the other hand, guided by tracks, can move only along one, predetermined path. Moreover, the railway vehicle - track system is essentially unidirectional: unless passing loops are provided, it requires all vehicles to move in the same sense, at compatible speeds. It follows that in the multidimensional transportation modes the vehicles can operate independently of each other (can pass) while in the one-dimensional railway mode their movements are mutually constrained and must be therefore closely coordinated. Thus several carriers can operate at different speeds without interfering with each other on airways, waterways and roads, but not on railroad tracks.* With the multidimensional modes, the interference – if any – need arise only at the terminals (air and water ports, and parking facilities) and, at least in principle, is easily overcome.

These basic physical limitations of the transportation modes affect their organizational structure and competitive standing. The multidimensional, non-interfering modes can function effi-

---

*A pipeline is also a one-dimensional mode but, unlike railway, because it moves bulk materials in one-direction only, it can serve, it turn, several shippers.

ciently with each mode comprising several carriers (e.g. airlines or trucking firms), organized independently of each other and of the infrastructure (e.g. airports and highways) used by all of them. With the one-dimensional railways, this type of organization cannot result in efficient operation. Since movements of all vehicles on a track are highly interdependent, efficiency requires close coordination, which can be best attained through completely integrated organization, in which a single carrier controls both the vehicles and the infrastructure (tracks, stations, etc.). To be of maximum benefit, such integration must extend over the whole territory served by railways, otherwise frequent transfer of shipments between various systems becomes necessary and reduces the speed and efficiency of transportation. The highest efficiency is achieved through integration of shipments as well, as with unit trains, which do not require complex car sorting operations and extensive marshalling yards.

The physical characteristics of the various transportation modes, by determining their desirable, efficient organizational structure, also define the scope for competition within each mode. In the multidimensional modes competition between different, independent carriers within the same mode, as well as competition with the other modes, is possible and may be desirable. On the other hand, since efficient rail operation calls for a single, integrated organization, the competition within the railway mode is not viable, and only competition between the railway and the other modes is in general desirable.

These organizational and competitive limitations of the railway mode have not been generally recognized in the first century of railroading, and, as this study demonstrates, have yet to be appreciated in North America. There have been significant reasons for such lack of perception. Until the 1920s, for close to a hundred years railways had monopolized fast overland passenger and freight transportation. Only where waterways were available, and the speed was not critical, could the supremacy of railways be challenged. In the majority of cases, due to the absence of other transportation modes, the only possible competition was between alternative services offered by different railway companies. Because of the one-dimensional nature of the railway mode, and the resulting integration of track and vehicles, competitive railway operations inevitably required construction of parallel roadbeds between major centers as well as competing fleets of cars. Thus the basic paradox of railway development: free enterprise and competition – the well-proven guarantees of efficiency – have resulted in duplication and overcapacity. Railways had to rely increasingly on public subsidies and, having lost their monopoly status, could not compete effectively with the newer air and road transportation modes.

CHAPTER 18

FINANCING RAILWAYS

Counterproductive Results of Subsidized Competition

As noted in Part One of this study (Chapters 2 and 7), the development of railways in Canada was governed by political – national and partisan – goals rather than by the demands of the market place. Governments insisted on private ownership of railroads, but enough private capital could not be attracted to enterprises based on political – as opposed to profit – considerations. Special incentives, in the form of cash and land grants, loan guarantees, tax write-offs, and even monopoly clauses had to be provided. As it turned out, the huge public subsidies, while supporting the expansion of railways, have financed construction of competing lines, causing overcapacity and maintenance of traffic at uneconomic levels. Subsidization of competition by public funds reflected the previously-noted misconceptions about the fundamental nature of the railway mode, and – ironically – reduced the efficiency of operations of privately owned, profit-oriented railroads.* This led eventually to takeovers of the bankrupt lines by the state, a process which was accelerated by the appearance of new, competitive transportation modes.

There is no doubt that the free market, competitive economy

---

*It is interesting to note that a similar situation has now developed in the heavily subsidized airline industry: intramodal competition has led to overcapacity and reduction of profits (O'Hanlon, 1974) which have been also adversely affected by rising fuel costs. Most of the over 200 international airlines are financially ailing. In 1973, the losses on transatlantic routes reached $490 million. Total losses of the world's scheduled airlines in 1974 were in excess of $1 billion; seven major Canadian airlines lost $1.9 million. (In 1973, they made $19 million profit). TWA was losing money at a rate of $2 million per month in 1974. In the first quarter of 1975, scheduled U.S. airlines posted a record loss of $190 million. The North Atlantic route, accounting for 30% of scheduled air traffic, is the principal source of airlines' financial troubles. Thirty scheduled carriers and some 20 charter airlines compete in the transatlantic market. An equivalent of 27 jumbo jets have been flying empty across the Atlantic every day. For an informative discussion of excessive growth see Watt (1974).

has served the industrialized West well, particularly in the U.S. and Canada, at least in terms of material wealth and technical progress. That the same economic and political philosophy should have misfired when applied to railway transportation is an unexpected result. In fact, it is a major example of failure of a regulated and subsidized private enterprise in a free society, a failure which so far has been only marginally recognized in the U.S., and has yet to be acknowledged in Canada.** Today, there are many examples of such – to use J. Forrester's (1971) term – "counter-intuitive behaviour of socio-economic systems".† Thus, contrary to the expectations of Canadian and U.S. legislators, it is the state monopolies of Western Europe and Japan which conduct some of the most modern railway operations; although heavily subsidized by the taxpayer, they efficiently deliver the services which are accorded high priority by European and Japanese societies, while the privately-owned North American railways continue to lag in technological progress. Moreover, a closer inspection (see Chapter 15) reveals that the only railways that bring profits (several U.S. railroads and CP) derive their revenues almost entirely from freight and operate under particularly favorable conditions. It is evident that, except in very special circumstances (such as prevail in the high density Tokyo-Osaka corridor), even the most efficient passenger rail cannot rely on fares set at a profit level, but requires a broad tax support base.

Lack of Capital

The possibility of railway development and modernization in North America critically hinges on provision of adequate financing: the traditional reliance on the private sector and on government subsidies, which merely compensate deficits and maintain unprofitable services, cannot provide the required new capital.*

** Although in 1923 the deficit-producing railways were taken over by the government-owned CN, the emphasis has been on operating CN as a profit-oriented, competitive enterprise.

† For example, the fiasco of urban renewal and welfare programs which often aggravate the ills they were designed to cure.

* CN President Bandeen (1974) estimated the capital investment required to meet rail freight requirements in Canada at $5 billion over the next six years.

181

The ability to attract private capital is governed by the magnitude of return on investment: in the railroad industry, it is among the lowest. Since 1955, the average rate of return for U.S. railways never exceeded 4%. In 1968 U.S. railroads yielded a 2.4% return on the investors' equity; by comparison, truck lines yielded 12.2%, bus lines 12.4%, and oil pipelines 10%. The rate of return for AT&T was 8.9%, for General Motors Corporation, 18.2%. In 1969, the average of Class I U.S. railroads (73 companies) was 2.4%, or less than half the rate available in a savings bank. Only 5 railroads exceeded 8% (10.6% was the maximum return); 19 showed deficits. For the first six months of 1975, the U.S. railroads recorded a deficit of $243.5 million. Compared with trucks operating on publicly-owned highways, U.S. railways require 10 times more capital to generate a dollar of revenue (5 times more than buses, 3 times more than airlines, ASTRO, 1970). Faced with generally small profits, North American railways practice "deferred maintenance" and tend to diversify their activities and invest in more profitable enterprises. The situation in Canada, as discussed in Chapters 12 and 13, has been similar.

The other major causes of financial plight of railways in Canada and the U.S. are the inequities in railway subsidization compared to other modes, and in the pricing of railway transportation.

The Cost of Infrastructure

A basic anomaly in railway financing concerns the allocation of the infrastructure costs, or the expenditures which are not directly related to the vehicles. Such costs are of two types: capital and current. Capital costs include depreciation (or the capital lost through finite life of assets), the cost of the remaining net capital (i.e. the interest which could be realized through alternative use of the net capital), and the opportunity cost of land (or right of way). The latter is based on the current market value and takes into account the continuing appreciation of land.

For example, in the case of the air mode, capital costs include expenditures on airport construction (runways, buildings, roads, utilities), acquisition of equipment (vehicles, telecommunications, navigation, office), and the opportunity cost of land. The current costs include control, regulation and general administration of civil aviation, operation of airports, communications, meteorological services, search and rescue operations. In Canada, the Ministry of Transport, the Department of National Defence, and the Department of the Environment are responsible for civil aviation expenditures.

The infrastructure costs borne by the government (i.e. the taxpayer) are recovered in varying degrees (depending on the mode) through revenues obtained from the users of the facilities and services provided. Direct government subsidies, as in the case of railways, are not included in thus defined revenues. In the case of civil aviation, the revenues include landing fees, gas and oil fees, aircraft parking fees, mobile equipment registration fees, space rentals and shop concessions, terminal facilities charges, observation turn-stiles, sale of utilities, aviation fuel taxes, and others.

The difference between the revenues and the costs determines the profitability of the infrastructure operations, or – since the costs usually exceed the revenues – the indirect, hidden subsidy received by the particular transportation mode.

The magnitude of the transportation infrastructure costs and revenues in Canada has been the object of a recent study (Haritos, 1973b); its results indicate the extent of inequitable allocation of these costs between the various modes. In the case of railways, which operate as both carriers and owners of the infrastructure, there is a difficulty in separating revenues into infrastructure and rolling stock sectors (although no such difficulty is present on the cost side). Complete data for both are given in Table 18.1, for 1968. Using a 6% annual rate for the cost of the capital, the total railway costs amount of $1,832 million, of which $477 million is allocated to the infrastructure; the total revenues come to $1,349 million. Since in all other modes the costs of vehicles – i.e., cars, trucks, aircraft and boats, are fully recovered – it has been assumed that the rail rolling stock costs would be also fully recovered given a similar institutional structure. Application of this principle to rail shows that the revenues don't even pay fully for the vehicle costs, which result in $6 million deficit; no infrastructure costs are recovered.

This is not the situation in the other modes, as evident from Table 18.2 comparisons. Regarding water and air modes, 21% and 27% respectively of the infrastructure costs are recovered; 72% is recovered in the road mode. However, in absolute terms

TABLE 18.1   COSTS AND REVENUES (MILLION OF 1968 DOLLARS) OF RAILWAYS IN CANADA IN 1968 (HARITOS, 1973b)

	Infrastructure (road and land)	Vehicles	Total
Depreciation	136	122	258
Opportunity cost of land	8	–	8
Capital cost (at 6% p.a.)	158	117	275
Operations and maintenance	175	1116*	1291
Total costs	477	1355	1832
Total revenues	–	–	1349
Deficit	477	6	483

* Includes $79 million in corporate taxes and regulating costs

Amount of capital stock: Infrastructure .... $2,619 million
Amount of capital stock: Vehicles .... $1,955 million

Value of land stock .... $136 million

Total .... $4,710 million

the road mode shows the highest deficit ($528 million), comparable to the infrastructure costs of $477 million which railways have to bear. A more detailed study (Haritos, 1973a) of the road infrastructure costs in Ontario in 1968 shows that the revenues obtained from the users of private automobiles pay for only 67% of their share of the road costs; trucks pay about 79%, and buses about 88% of their respective shares. Applying these percentages to the road costs in all Canada (as given in Table 18.2), we find that the use of highways by private motorists was subsidized to the extent of about $369 million; by trucks $150 million, and by buses $9 million (in 1968).

The inequitability of financing of the transportation infrastructure costs is clear: while water, air and road infrastructures are subsidized to the extent of 79%, 73% and 28% respectively, the rail infrastructure receives no subsidies. The direct subsi-

TABLE 18.2   INFRASTRUCTURE COSTS AND REVENUES (MILLION OF 1968 DOLLARS), ALL MODES, CANADA, 1968 (HARITOS, 1973b)

Mode	Rail	Water	Air	Road	Total
Capital and land stock	2,755	2,641	646	9,476	15,518
Annual costs					
Depreciation	136	102	40	649	927
Cost of capital* (at 6% p.a.)	166	158	39	568	931
Operations and maintenance	175	133	129	658	1,095
Total costs	477	393	208	1,875	2,953
Total revenues	0	83	56	1,347	1,486
Deficit	477	310	152	528	1,467
Revenues as % of costs	0	21	27	72	50
Deficit as % of costs	100	79	73	28	50

*Includes opportunity cost of land

dies which the railways receive under the 1967 Act and other legislation (see Chapter 12), and which in 1968 amounted to some $96 million, do not begin to pay for the $477 million infrastructure deficit. Obviously, had the railway infrastructure costs been offset to the extent of water and air modes (for railways, these levels of subsidy would have generated $377 million and $348 million respectively in 1968), the capital needs of the railways would have been largely met.

The unequal extent of infrastructure subsidies among the different transportation modes is not generally recognized by the public or by the government. The 1967 National Transportation Act, while solemnly declaring that all modes of transport should bear "a fair proportion of the real costs of the resources, facilities and services provided . . . at public expense," makes no provision whatsoever for reimbursing railways for the infrastructure costs whose deficit the government defrays for the other modes.

Also, it is sometimes argued that extensive land grants and other capital aid, which the railways originally received, should provide them—in perpetuity—with adequate capital resources. Such views do not allow for the growth of investments needed to accommodate increasing traffic and to modernize technology. Neither are they borne out by the history of expansion of infrastructures of the other modes. Could we have today satisfactory water and air transportation if the government support of canal, harbour and airport construction was arrested several decades ago?

Research and Development

This is the second critical area of inequity in the allocation of transportation costs. Since the Second World War, the United States has been engaged in a very extensive aerospace R&D activity. The magnitude of the U.S. effort in this area can be judged from the listing of industrial R&D expenditures in 1971 and 1966 (Table 18.3). In 1966, at the peak of the aerospace effort, a total of some $5.5 billion was spent on aerospace, or 35% of the industrial R&D effort in all fields. The federal government was the major source, providing $4.7 billion. All other transportation modes received only $1.3 billion, or 24% of the aerospace R&D funding, of which industry contributed about $1 billion. Although the aerospace expenditures have been mostly related to military and spaceflight developments, they have nevertheless largely underwritten the costs of civil aviation R&D in all major areas, such as structures, propulsion, and electronics. Aviation is also benefiting from continued funding by the Federal Aviation Administration, which inaugurated in 1972 a five-year, $530 million annual program ($2.65 billion total) of improvements to airports and air-navigation facilities.

While the aerospace effort in other countries has been much smaller, it has nevertheless contributed significantly to civil aviation. In some cases, such as with the Anglo-French *Concorde* supersonic transport, the total development costs of about $2.5 billion have been absorbed by the taxpayer. There can be no doubt that the commercial jetliner – the workhorse of every major air carrier – has been made possible through generous public support of aircraft technology.

TABLE 18.3 INDUSTRIAL R & D EXPENDITURES ($ MILLION) ON TRANSPORTATION IN THE U.S. IN 1971 AND 1966 (STATISTICAL ABSTRACT OF THE UNITED STATES, 1968 AND 1973)

		Source of Funds		
	Year	Government	Private	Total
Aerospace	1971	3,938	1,012	4,940
	1966	4,690	756	5,446
Other transportation modes	1971	301	1,458	1,759
	1966	345	976	1,321
Aerospace as % of total industrial R & D (all fields)	1971	51	9.5	27
	1966	57	10	35

The pattern of R&D in transportation in Canada is evident from Table 18.4. The total industrial effort in 1973-74 amounted to only about $84 million, of which the aircraft industry share was 85%, leaving only $12 million for R&D in the other transportation modes. Transportation accounted for only about 8% of the total (industry, government, universities, etc.) R&D effort. In 1972-73, the Department of Transport spent only $4.4 million on R&D. In spite of this relatively low level, Canada has supported from time to time large R&D projects in the general area of transportation, such as the AVRO *Arrow* supersonic fighter (cancelled in 1969 after expenditures of over $250 million) and the *Bras d'Or* hydrofoil craft (cancelled in 1971, after some $54 million). In 1974, the government announced plans for the takeover of the two major aircraft manufacturers, deHavilland (Toronto) and Canadair (Montreal)*. The government has also funded the STOL demonstration project (flights started in July, 1974) between Ottawa and Montreal, at a cost of $25 million, in the hope of stimulating orders for the ailing deHavilland company. Regarding other transportation fields, federal funds are used in support of some new and

---

*In May, 1974, the government acquired de Havilland Aircraft of Canada, Ltd. from the Hawker Siddeley Group of Britain for $38.8 million. The purchase of Canadair Ltd. for $38 million was to be completed in January, 1976.

TABLE 18.4 INDUSTRIAL R & D EXPENDITURES ($ MILLION) ON TRANSPORTATION IN CANADA IN 1973-74

| | Performed By | | | |
	Government, Universities, etc.	Private Industry	Other	Total
Aircraft	*	71.6	*	*
Other transportation modes	*	12	*	*
All transportation	11	83.6	*	*
Industrial R & D (all fields)	355	561	159	1075

*Data not available

Sources: *Federal government expenditure on science, 1972-74*, Statistics Canada, 13-202, October 1973, Ottawa.

Industrial research and development expenditures in Canada, 1971, Statistics Canada, 13-203, January 1974, Ottawa.

Scientific activities, MOSST, September 1972, Ottawa

Federal Scientific Resources, 1972-74, MOSST, December 1973, Ottawa.

unproven technologies such as air cushion and magnetically-supported vehicles (see Chapters 21 and 23). The only R&D activity of any significance in the railway field is the LRC train, which is being developed at a cost of $2.5 million (see Chapter 14) to the taxpayer.

It is apparent from this review that the newer competing modes, particularly air, have been receiving enormous public funds for research and development, while the railways have received virtually none. The heavily regulated railway technology – one of the oldest in our industrial age – has been taken for granted in North America, operating on a level of traditional, static performance. One could well question the priorities chosen in funding of the R&D effort. Would not modernization of railways benefit Canada more than the unsuccessful attempts to tackle more glamorous projects? Will the investment in the space shuttle contribute more to the U.S. economy than if it were applied to the upgrading of railway transportation?

The Pricing of Railway Transportation

As discussed extensively in Chapter 12, the pricing of moving freight by rail in Canada is heavily regulated and, in many cases, is not related to the actual costs. The statutory Crowsnest Pass rates alone, which apply to almost one-third of the rail freight in Canada, produce close to $200 million in annual, uncompensated losses. Other controls and subsidies tend to distort the allocation of traffic between the modes and the thrust of regional industrial development, and hence of traffic patterns. In the light of past experience, the use of transportation pricing as a tool for achieving regional economic objectives is to be discouraged, in favour of more direct subsidization of specific economic regional sectors.

*　　*　　*

As indicated above, the current financing of railways in North America is both inadequate and inequitable. The governments, the legislators and the public are under the delusion that transportation is and should be operating on a straightforward profit basis, that this is how modes other than the railway operate, and that therefore direct, highly visible subsidies of the rail mode are undesirable and should be, in as much as possible, denied. The fact that railways, as well as other transportation modes, would have never attracted private capital without extensive government subsidies, is also forgotten. These fundamental differences in the financing of transportation versus manufacturing and other industries have been often neglected. In Canada, this was true in the case of no lesser a person than J. W. Pickersgill, who, as Minister of Transport in the years 1964-1967, fathered the 1967 National Transportation Act and became, in 1967, the first Chairman of the Canadian Transport Commission. Pickersgill said in 1970 (Chodos, 1971): "The public generally, and businessmen specifically, must come to realize that it is just as moral and just as praiseworthy to operate a railway, an airline, or trucking firm at a profit as it is to make a profit manufacturing motor cars or packing meat or making steel." Regretfully, this is not a matter of morality, but of straightforward profitability: why would anybody today invest in a railroad?

189

CHAPTER 19

THE IMPERATIVES OF
INTEGRATION AND PUBLIC OWNERSHIP

The analysis presented in the two preceding chapters has served to identify those fundamental characteristics of the railway transportation mode which determine the desirable organizational structure of railways and their ownership. Summarizing, it is apparent that:

(i) Because of the one-dimensional nature of the railway mode and competition from the newer transportation modes, the competition between railway companies operating in the same territory is in general not viable. It follows that, in order to assure efficiency and effective competition between railways and the other modes, a completely integrated, unified operation of railways (all track and all vehicles) under a single management is required.

(ii) Railways in North America, as in the other countries, have shown low (compared to other enterprises) or negative return on investment. Because of this situation, and with subsidies that do not go beyond compensation of operating deficits, railways have been unable to attract private capital needed to modernize, or even to maintain the infrastructure and equipment. The operating subsidies, while enabling railways to maintain services, have in fact removed any incentive to render them more efficient and have thus encouraged obsolescence. In these circumstances, the capital necessary for modernization and maintenance of railways (which, as already seen, have become – in some aspects – highly obsolete in North America) can come only from the public sector.

We are thus led to conclude that integration of railways into one, publicly-owned system is the only alternative which would result in an efficient structure and would provide the required financial resources. This is the solution that has been adopted for all major railway systems outside of North America (see Chapter 15).

It should be noted that industrialized societies have been increasingly relying on coordinated services in many areas, not necessarily operated for profit. We would not think of water

Plate 17. From their very beginnings, railway operations in Canada have been a hazardous business. ABOVE: On July 9, 1895, one Grand Trunk Railway special train (carrying pilgrims to Ste. Anne de Beaupré) rammed another at Craig's Road Station near Lévis, Quebec killing 12 and injuring 36. The driver and fireman of the moving train were killed; the accident was attributed to their negligence. (*From a railwayman's scrapbook, lent by A. Leeson*). BELOW: Grand Trunk Railway snow clearing operations at Haliburton, Ontario resulted in this unusual accident in which a grain train engine rode up the nose of the snow plow and came to rest on top of the plow engine. Grand Trunk crews proudly posed for the photographer (about 1890, *The Public Archives of Canada*).

Plate 18. Inadequate engineering design and equipment failures have often led to mishaps. ABOVE: A train on a partially collapsed bridge on the National Transcontinental Railway line near Hearst, Ontario in 1914 (*The Public Archives of Canada*). BELOW: Uneven application of brakes caused these two freight cars, which were in between coal cars, to telescope each other and come to rest, less wheels, in this unusual configuration in Rahway, N.J., 1930 (*Wide World Photos*).

Plate 19. Level crossings—too numerous and poorly protected—are the curse of Canadian railroading, and the cause of many deaths and injuries, and extensive property losses. Until level crossings on the main lines are largely eliminated, and the remaining ones effectively protected, the operation of fast trains in Canada will not be possible. ABOVE: Wreckage of a school bus is wrapped around the front of a CN diesel locomotive following a level crossing collision that killed 16 high school students near LaMont, Alberta, on November 29, 1960 (*Wide World Photos*). BELOW: In Canada, even the superhighways are not free of level crossings. The one shown here in 1975 is on the Macdonald-Cartier (401) four lane freeway, east of Toronto (*J. Lukasiewicz*).

Plate 20. Traditionally, the railways have had "the right of way."
ABOVE: Canadian Pacific carries on freight operations on the Gran
River Railway tracks in the streets of Waterloo, Ontario, in Septembe
1973 (*K.A.W. Gansel, KAG Photographic Services Ltd.*) BELOW: The ab
sence of a level crossing did not prevent a CP freight car from blockin
traffic for several hours on Montreal's Metropolitan expressway (Octobe
22, 1974). (*Canada Wide Feature Service Ltd.*).

Plate 21. The effectiveness of rail traffic control is not adequate and head-on collisions occur frequently. They usually result in death and injury to train crews and passengers, and cost millions of dollars in equipment losses and track repairs. In accidents, the safety of passengers depends on the solidity of the rolling stock. LEFT: On September 28, 1974, CN *Super Continental* and a freight train collided head-on near Blue River in British Columbia. Two crewmen died in the accident. The wrecked locomotives can be seen in the centre, with passenger cars towards the top and the freight cars below (*Canadian Press*). BELOW: The inside of a coach was strewn with seats which tore loose from metal bases when a CN Toronto-to-Barrie commuter train derailed on October 9, 1975. Many of the 31 injured passengers believed that they were injured because seats "went flying". Canadian railways have not purchased new passenger equipment for over 20 years (*Toronto Star Syndicate*).

Plate 22. Derailments are common in North America, and are usually caused by the poor condition of track and rolling stock. Deprived of capital and subsidies for infrastructure, North American railways have been practicing "deferred maintenance" and have allowed their plant to deteriorate dangerously. ABOVE: In a typical view of a major derailment aftermath, freight cars are scattered like matchsticks over the right-of-way. CP main line between London and Windsor, Ontario was closed after 33 freight cars left track on January 19, 1976 (*London Free Press*).

BELOW: AMTRAK passengers, returning from Christmas Holidays, sit on their luggage awaiting transportation following the derailment of *Broadway Limited* on December 27, 1974, enroute from Chicago to New York (*Wide World Photos*).

Plate 23. Much Canadian and American track is in poor condition. Wooden ties and simple fasteners are almost exclusively used to anchor the rails. ABOVE: Penn Central tracks on deteriorated wooden ties in 1974 (*B. Welling, Business Week*). In 1973, Penn Central declared 6,900 miles of its track substandard. In 1974, "slow orders" prevailed on 8000 miles of Penn Central lines. During the first four months of 1974, there were 2,149 derailments on Penn Central. Freight cars have been known to "derail" while standing still. BELOW: Tracks west of Ottawa, Ontario, 1975. *(J. Lukasiewicz)*. In 1972, the number of derailments in Canada was three times that in 1959.

Plate 24. ABOVE: Condition of track on a main line west of Ottawa 1975. (*J. Lukasiewicz*). Cut spikes, generally used in N. America, held in place by friction only, work their way out of wooden ties. BELOW: In Eurpoe and Japan improved rail fasteners are being used. The *Pandrol* system, here shown, is simple, effective, maintenance free and economic it is standard on British Rail (*Pandrol Ltd.*).

Plate 25. In Canada, some railway lines and stations, still in use, are poorly maintained. Vegetation overtakes railroading in many locations. ABOVE: A local freight train winds its way in August 1971 towards its terminus in Tignish, Prince Edward Island. (*W. R. Linley, Ottawa*). LEFT: Weeds find their way into signalling equipment on a main line west of Ottawa, Ontario, 1975. (*J. Lukasiewicz*).

Plate 26. In many places in N. America (even on main lines) railway operations are conducted as they were years ago. ABOVE: A station agent's office on a main line west of Ottawa, Ont. in 1975 (*J. Lukasiewicz*). Orders are passed to trains with hoops (top left). Information on train movements is transmitted by telephone. Semaphores are operated with mechanical levers (by the window). Lights (right) indicate the approach of trains. Not shown: an antiquated typewriter, a pendulum clock, a radio to receive time signal to set the old clock. BELOW: According to the Railway Act, each station in Canada must be equipped with a blackboard on which arrival times of overdue trains should be written with white chalk (failure to do so is subject to a penalty not exceeding five dollars). (1975, *J. Lukasiewicz*).

Plate 27. The marriage of railway technology and electronics has been awkward and slow. ABOVE: Radiotelephone equipment was installed in the cab of this diesel locomotive for communication with train dispatchers at a major terminal (in 1950s; *Canadian National*). BELOW: The engineer, leaning out from the leading diesel, has just caught the hoop with train orders attached (on a main line in 1975; *J. Lukasiewicz*).

Plate 28. The caboose is symbolic of the traditional character of railway operations in Canada. The men who ride in the caboose monitor the progress of their train. Today, remote sensing techniques could perform this function. RIGHT: a CN caboose, complete with oil lamps and hand brake. Here it is being used behind a rail grinding crew for dousing the railbed to extinguish sparks and prevent fires. Evidently, this wasn't a highly automated operation (1974, *The Globe and Mail, Toronto*). BELOW: The caboose tradition has been continued with the introduction of a new design (1970, *Canadian National*). The new caboose features comfortable crew quarters equipped with built-in beds, modern cooking and washroom facilities, and oil furnace heating. Electric lighting has replaced oil lamps, and track inspection lights have been added. Safety has been improved with seat belts in the cupola.

Plate 29. The problems of winter operations have yet to be overcome by Canadian railways. Little progress has been made in this century with the snow clearance techniques, and low temperatures continue to adversely affect equipment. LEFT: Canada's most important contribution to world railroading is probably the rotary snowplow, here shown in action in British Columbia in 1910. It was invented by a Toronto dentist in 1869, and developed for practical use in the 1880s (*The Public Archives of Canada*). BELOW: How to beat the snowdrifts? CN track supervisor and snowplow crew ponder the next move at Mile 55.5, Miami Subdivision, Prairie Region, 1974. The wedge snowplow, here shown, is a simple outgrowth of the cow catcher and dates to the very early days of railroading. Although ineffective in deep snow, it is still extensively used (*Canadian National*).

Plate 30. Inadequate equipment necessitates the use of much hand labour in snow-clearing operations. ABOVE: Men with shovels and several locomotives were needed to clear snow bound CN tracks near Saskatoon in April, 1974 (*Canadian National*). BELOW: An ex-CP wedge snowplow awaits the clearing of tracks at a level crossing, 1972. *(W. R. Linley, Ottawa).*

Plate 31. Switches are not designed for operation in snow and cold. LEFT: Just as today, a yardman clears switches in Montreal's Outremont freight yard during a blizzard in March, 1948. Hand operated switches, equipped with oil lamps – like the one shown here – are still used in Canada (*Information Canada Photothèque*). BELOW: In 1963, CN was experimenting with portable switch-defrosting equipment (*Canadian National*).

Plate 32. Railway operations are not only capital-intensive, but continue to be labour intensive as well. ABOVE: The five men clear the ice from the Upper Spiral Tunnel near Yoho (1973; *CP Rail*). BELOW: Repairing track using rail tongs and pinch bars after a derailment in Almonte, Ontario in 1974. (*Peter Lukasiewicz*).

and sewage being offered in one metropolitan area by two or more *competing* companies; the same is true of other utilities (e.g. electric, gas or telephone) even though they may be privately-owned. Neither would we consider development of a network of freeways, such as the 42,500 mile U.S. interstate highway system, on the basis of competitive, privately-owned routes. In spite of their long history, railways belong today to the same category of services, and require similar organization and similar financing.

One of the basic objections to railway nationalization is a deep-seated conviction that nationalization means inefficiency and waste. Who would want to see railway services deteriorate to the extent the post office services have declined in recent decades? While the apprehension is in general both genuine and valid, nevertheless it is not necessarily supported by the experience on some modern nationalized railway systems, which provide excellent service at reasonable cost. On the other hand, there is ample evidence of catastrophic deterioration of some large, privately-owned systems, such as the Penn Central in the U.S.

In North American society, attuned to the principle of "exacting as much profit as possible from whatever the traffic will bear" (Commoner, 1973), the notion of railway nationalization has been, and still is, strongly resisted. As Commoner (1973, p. 79) noted, "The question of social ownership of the railroads has seemed to be as firmly protected from public discussion in the U.S. as was the question of sex in Victorian England." Nevertheless, railway nationalization has been making inroads in both Canada and the U.S. as the only measure which allows unprofitable operations to be maintained. This was the rationale for the formation of the CN system in the early 1920s, for the recent purchases of the wheat cars by the Canadian government, and for the 1974 Canadian election promises of a public passenger rail corporation. For the same reasons the AMTRAK passenger rail monopoly was formed in the U.S. in 1971, and now consolidation and subsidization of the Penn Central and the other bankrupt railways in the American Northeast is being undertaken.

The editorial writers and the politicians reflect the changing attitude towards railways. "The public has invested tens of billions of dollars in subsidizing the competitors of railroads – in building interstate highways for the truckers, airports and sophisticated traffic control systems for the air lines, and canals for the barge operators. Why must it now adopt the myopic criterion of profitability when it comes to subsidizing the railroads? They are indispensable public utilities, not merely public ventures" (editorial, *The New York Times*, May 19, 1975). "Today, with the Federal Government taking a more active role in railroading, the thought of nationalization still may not have much appeal, but it does not seem to hold the same terror as before. Indeed, Senator Vance Hartke, Indiana Democrat and Chairman of a Senate Commerce Transportation subcommittee, said last month: 'The mood of the floor [of the Senate] is for nationalization. I could get a vote for it if I asked for it" (*The New York Times*, June 2, 1975).

The need to restructure the U.S. railways is being increasingly recognized, and several proposals are under discussion (Ford, 1973). They range from consolidation into a small number of systems (four nation-wide systems have been proposed) that can better compete with the interstate highway system (in the U.S., 70% of railroad ton-miles are interline, i.e. over two or more lines), to integration into one privately or publicly-owned company. It is generally agreed that a large measure of consolidation is necessary to reduce the size of the railway plant and fleet, and to render railways competitive with the other modes.

It is likely that eventually, also on this Continent, railways will become largely nationalized and subsidized as heavily as the other modes of transportation have been to date. By then, we would have come full circle, the railways being again viewed – as they have been by Keefer in the early days of development – as indispensable to national well-being rather than as opportunities for profitable investment. The still pertinent views of T. C. Keefer are contained in his famous 1849 essay, in which he was promoting western rail connections to Montreal, when there were less than 60 miles of track in all of British North America. Keefer asked: "If the liberal provisions of our Railroad law prove inefficient to produce association and corporate effort, shall we allow it to drop? Shall we not rather as a people, through our Government, take it up, '*coute qui coute*'? We cannot any longer *afford* to do without Railroads. Their want is an actual tax upon the industry and labour of the country. Men may talk, says an eminent New Englander, about the burden of taxes to build Railroads, but the tax which *the people pay* to be without them is a hundred fold more oppressive." Keefer concluded by addressing " . . . the generous and patriotic consideration of every intelligent merchant, manufacturer, farmer, and mechanic – . . . every Canadian, native or adopted," and asking "Shall we have Railroads in Canada?" (Keefer, 1972, pp. 35, 36, 38).

CHAPTER 20

RATIONALIZING RAILWAYS

As indicated on many occasions in this study, the process of railway development has often been poorly understood and has frequently led to the establishment (on this Continent and elsewhere) of highly irrational railway networks and operations. In recognition of the need to correct this situation, the term "rationalization" has been coined. As used here, rationalization will encompass mainly two aspects: the elimination of duplication which results from organizational fragmentation and intra-modal competition, and – except in cases of "natural monopoly" – operation of only those services which are truly competitive vis-à-vis the other modes.

In light of historical record, railway organizational integration and nationalization do not automatically assure their rationalization. For example, the integrated and nationalized (in 1923) CN system has not been rationalized, as an overextended network of lightly-loaded lines is still being operated. Had a rationalization policy been implemented, it is likely that trucks would have taken over many of the Prairie branch lines, and that the network of grain elevators would undergo a corresponding consolidation.

If railways in Canada were integrated into one organization, further gains could be realized through operation of some lines as unidirectional tracks. As shown earlier, at present Canadian network contains only a negligible length of double track (see Chapter 6). The proposed unidirectional operation of one-track CN and CP lines, which – although sometimes separated by a distance – connect the same end points, would be an effective substitute for regular double track lines: it would allow a considerable increase in traffic throughput as well as faster and safer operations.* In such cases, provided the traffic volume is sufficiently high, advantage could be taken of the duplication of lines.

* Long overdue study of unidirectional operation of the transcontinental CN and CP lines has been initiated in 1975. Transport Department estimated that joint use of tracks could increase capacity up to five or six times where opposing flows on a single track were replaced by a one-way scheme.

With respect to competition, rationalization should reflect the relative superiority of the railway mode in various parts of the transportation spectrum.

In the freight sector, the share of traffic handled by rail has been decreasing while trucks' share has remained at a more or less constant level (Fig. 16.2). Compared to railways, trucks have been providing a faster, more reliable, more frequent and safer service. By improving performance in these areas railways could enhance their relative position. (As noted before, long, slow and infrequent trains, which necessitate extensive sorting operations in classification yards, cause shipments to move in the U.S. at an effective speed of only 3 mph!) Railway freight would be also improved by yet more extensive and more auto-mated application of containers and, as noted below, through further integration with the road mode.

In the passenger sector, as discussed at length in Part Two, North American railways have been highly obsolete, and, partly as a result of this condition, the competitive potential of passen-ger rail has not been appreciated. The situation is changing, at least in the U.S., where AMTRAK shows an understanding of the relationship between service quality and travel demand. In the 1974 Annual Report, AMTRAK's President stated that "Demand does not arise full-blown when a service is first initi-ated. The services must first be provided at a level of quality sufficient to attract demand. Because of the inherent advan-tages of rail travel in the areas of speed and comfort, we are confident that a significant number of travelers now using auto-mobiles for intercity travel would utilize good rail service were it available. While the extent of this traveler diversion may be difficult to project, its potential impact must be considered."

Experience gained in recent years in Europe and Japan shows that modern rail can compete successfully with aircraft and automobile for travel between major cities (where traffic volume is sufficiently large) over distances of several hundreds of miles (see Chapters 10 and 15). In planning the future "Eu-ropolitain" network of fast railways, it is considered that, to compete with private cars running at an average of 56 mph, the railways need to average 84 mph, or to cruise at 100 mph. On some routes higher speeds will be necessary, so that return journeys could be made in a day between cities 300 miles apart.

As faster and more comfortable trains are introduced, the competitive edge held by railways sharpens and extends to larger distances. Already over distances up to about 250 miles, modern railways can match aircraft total trip time, are much faster and more comfortable than bus or car, and should be unaffected by weather. They are even superior to a STOL (short take-off and landing airplane) air service, which is no faster than rail but less reliable, less comfortable and more expensive (see Chapter 23). Moreover, social costs of railways as a mass transportation mode are low compared, for example, to a private car, with its requirements for space, need of regulation, low safety level, high fuel consumption and production of pollution.

Regarding long distance travel, it is unlikely that, for reasons of capital cost, energy consumption and safety, the speed of surface transportation of any kind could surpass in the foreseeable future the speed of high altitude jet aircraft. Where distance is large (over, say, 500 miles) or where travel over water or other obstacles is involved, and when time is at a premium, the airplane has no competition. For transoceanic travel, the aircraft is still cheaper and faster than the liner. For transcontinental travel, if economy rather than speed governs, the bus offers a service much cheaper and faster than the long-haul train. Transcontinental trains, just like the ocean liners, represent obsolete and vanishing technologies which have been maintained only because governments were prepared to absorb the losses. In the case of trans-Atlantic liners, reason and social responsibility have already prevailed and the fleet of boats has been substantially reduced: most countries have decided not to continue the heavy subsidization of luxurious travel that only those having plenty of time and cash could afford. *La France*, the world's largest liner, is a recent victim of this policy: it was withdrawn from service in October, 1974, after running up a deficit of $24 million in its last year of operations. In March, 1975, Italy announced plans to lay up its fifteen ocean liners (representing most of Italy's passenger fleet) over the next few years, including *Michelangelo* and *Raffaello*, the trans-Atlantic flagships of the Italian Line. It is likely that conventional long-haul trains* will follow the fate of the liners: as the folly of subsidizing a most expensive mode of travel is realized, other and better uses will be found for public funds.

Competitiveness can be extended to the railway mode

---

* As discussed below, it is only through integration with the road mode that long-haul passenger train can become competitive.

through imaginative combination with other modes. This was done for freight by the "piggy-back" system, introduced in the 1920s and quickly expanded in the 1950s. The system involves moving highway trailers to special railway ramps, loading trailers on flat cars (TOFC) for hauling by rail, and finally unloading and connecting with another tractor-trailer for delivery by road to destination. Thus "piggy-back" combines the economy of rail movement over long distances with the flexibility of truck pick-up and delivery. The use of containers offers similar advantages in water/rail shipments.

In the passenger sector, the "piggy-back" system was first used in the early days of steam railways, when land owners in England and Nova Scotia had their carriages loaded on flatcars, hauled by a steam locomotive, unloaded and pulled by their own horses along the highways to destination (Currie, 1967). Later, the use of a taxi or auto rental in conjunction with rail or air travel served a similar purpose. When car ownership became popular in Western Europe, the railways again offered "piggy-back" passenger service, the motor car substituting for the horse carriage. This development was not perfected in North America until 1971: it is particularly significant because it fills the need for a special type of long-haul passenger service.

The Auto Train Corporation was organized in the U.S. in 1971 by Eugene Garfield, a Florida lawyer, who got the idea from a Department of Transportation study which concluded that the concept would be profitable. The dual mode Auto Train transportation can be thought of as a "mobile motel" (Collins, 1973). The auto driver and his passengers stop at a point en route to their destination, the car is garaged (on an auto-rack rail car) and after dining and sleeping in transit by rail, they awake the next morning to find themselves and their "garaged" automobile hundreds of miles closer to their destination. During the trip, they are served by attractive stewardesses rather than by car porters and waiters. After breakfast enroute the guests "check out" to claim their car and continue their journey.

The Auto Train Corporation owns the locomotives, the auto carriers (purchased from CN), and the passenger cars. Its operation was made possible by a 15-year agreement with Seaboard Coast Line and the Richmond, Fredericksburg & Potomac for the use of their tracks.

The Auto Train service was introduced in December, 1971,

between Lorton, Va. (15 miles south of Washington, D.C.) to Sanford, Fla. (37 miles from Disney World). Every night trains leave Lorton and Sanford and cover 856 miles in 15½ hours, at an average of 55 mph. Each train hauls bi-level auto-rack cars (each holding 8 cars), bi-level coaches with reclining seats upstairs and lounges below, sleeping cars, lounge-restaurant cars, night club cars, etc. The line charges $198 to transport one car and two passengers, meals included (one way, coach). Additional passengers are charged $20 each and staterooms cost extra $40 to $65 depending on size.

The Auto Train has been a remarkable success: in the 1974 fiscal year, it earned $1.6 million on revenues of $20 million. In the 3rd quarter of 1972 the Auto Train logged a gross profit of $750,263; in the same period, the AMTRAK trains (between New York and Miami) operating on the same routes produced a deficit of $485,129. The Auto Train is the only long distance passenger train in North America which has operated profitably in many years. The train has been running full, solidly booked for weeks and months ahead: during the prime southbound (December, 1973) and northbound (January, 1974) travel periods, space was sold out 11 months in advance.

In May, 1974, a second Auto Train service was inaugurated between Louisville, Ky., and Florida; a similar service is being planned between Chicago and the Colorado ski resorts. These expansions of the Auto Train services were first fought by AMTRAK unsuccessfully; rather than lose the market, AMTRAK decided in the summer of 1974 to start its own "Auto Track" service from Indianapolis to Florida.

The Auto Train service is a compromise between the high cost of the air - rental car combination requiring only about 3 hours travel time and the much slower, less comfortable, low-cost automobile mode. To the potential Florida-bound traveler the price of Auto Train is slightly higher than driving the entire distance but far below the air - rental car combination. By exploiting the infinite flexibility of the automobile for ultimate origin and destination pick-up and delivery, the Auto Train serves wide areas around both end-point terminals.

From the railroad's perspective, the Auto Train is similar to a unit train, except that it carries passengers and their automobiles in lieu of coal or grain. It is a non-stop service with only two low-cost end-point terminals, which can be located in a semi-rural environment, remote from urban congestion. The

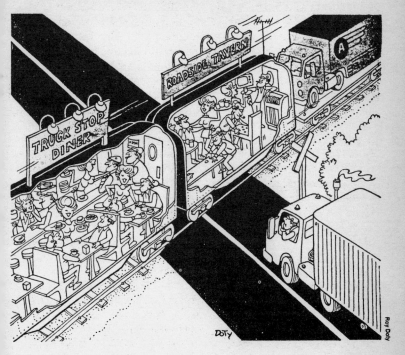

Truck—Train will offer drivers sleepers, a club car, and entertainment to their taste.

Business Week, 9 November, 1974

Auto Train Corporation is considering initiation of a "truck-train" service, to carry trucks and their drivers between Florida and northeast destinations.

The Auto Train story is important because it demonstrates that an imaginative combination of existing transportation modes can result in a service that is both needed and profitable. Predictably, the Auto Train was not initiated by a railway company but by a lawyer, who saw the potential in combining the convenience of a car with the comfort and economy of rail – a concept that, particularly in North America, with its large distances and record car ownership, is likely to expand and provide a viable, new, long haul intercity travel mode. This is possibly also the only viable application of rail to long-distance passenger travel in North America,* a development which will gain popularity as the price of gasoline increases.

*The Auto Train makes the world's longest non-stop runs (856 miles from Lorton, Va., and 988 miles, from Louisville, Ky., to Sanford, Fl.).

CHAPTER 21

TECHNICAL
MODERNIZATION

The comparison of current railway technologies and quality of
service, presented in Chapters 9 and 10, indicates the major
areas in need of modernization in Canada and the U.S.; they
include traction (electrification), track and traffic control, and
passenger trains, and are considered in this order below. In the
last section, the desirable scope and direction of the research
and development efforts are discussed.

Is Railway Electrification Viable in North America?

The technical superiority of electric traction, as outlined in
Chapter 9, coupled with its non-dependence on oil, leaves little
doubt that electrification of railways is desirable. However, in
view of the large capital investment required, a significant traffic density (measured in gross ton-mile/mile-year, i.e. in

**TABLE 21.1   ELECTRIFICATION OF RAILWAYS IN 1968
(IUR, 1968)**

	Electrified Track, %	Electric Traction Traffic, %	Mean Traffic Density Million Ton/Year	Electric Traction Traffic Density Million Ton/Year
Canada	0	0	4.5	0
U.S.A.	0	0	7	0
S. Africa	23	49	5.8	12.4
Sweden	62	94	3.4	5.2
Japan	39	66	10.3	17.4
France	32	75	4.5	10.8
W. Germany	38	66	5.7	9.9
Switzerland	100	100	7.9	7.9
Italy	60	89	5	7.4

Data based on running track length; traffic in gross ton-mile per
year; density in gross ton per year

gross-ton/year; equivalent to traction energy density, kwh/ mile-year) is needed to render electrification economical. Therefore, in order to assess the basic viability of railway electrification in North America, it is necessary to compare the traffic densities on electrified systems abroad with those on the major lines in Canada and the U.S. This is done in Table 21.1 which gives the average traffic densities (based on the running track length) on some of the major railway systems, and on their electrified portions. The average densities (for all types of traction) in Canada (4.5 million gross-ton/year) and in the U.S. (7 million) are comparable to the densities on the South African (5.8 million), Swedish (3.4), Italian (5), French (4.5) and West German (5.7) systems; the same is true in terms of total (including industrial, yard, etc.) track length. The traffic densities generated by electric traction are higher, and range from 5.2 million (Sweden) to 17.4 million (Japan) based on the running track length; about 70% of these densities are attained when referred to the total electrified track length. Typically, French, West German and South African systems indicate the viability of electric traction at densities of about 10 million based on the running track length.

Although little data has been published on the USSR experience, a recent paper (Muratov and Feldman, 1972) states that on Soviet railways "electric traction is economically effective where freight traffic has reached a level of 10 to 13 million net tonnes per year for single lines, and 27 to 30 million for double track lines." To obtain gross tonnage, in terms of North American experience these numbers should be increased by a factor of about two (see Table 8.3), giving some 20 to 26 million gross tons per year for single track lines.

An alternative method of assessing the viability of railway electrification is to consider the rate of energy consumption per unit track length (energy density), instead of traffic density. In France it was suggested that electrification was economical at traffic levels which result in consumption of 150,000 to 400,000 kwh/mile-year (Nouvion, 1971, 1972). This criterion is corroborated by the actual consumption on major railways; for example, French and German electrified systems operate in the 350,000 to 400,000 range.

With the average traffic density in the U.S. and Canada as high as in other countries, and assuming a similar distribution of traffic between the main and secondary lines, considerable scope for rail electrification would be expected to exist in North America. Lacking data on traffic densities between specific city-pairs in the U.S., an estimate of the traffic density on main lines can be made on the basis of experiences of other systems. For example, assuming that about one-third of the running track carries two-thirds of the traffic (as on the French and West German electrified systems, Table 21.1), the corresponding traffic density would amount to double the average value, or to 14 million, a level exceeded only on Japan's electrified rail, and presumably on the Soviet system.

The viability of railway electrification in the U.S. has been in fact indicated by a number of recent studies. A 1970 report by The Edison Electric Institute concluded that about 22,000 track miles (or 9% of total trackage) of U.S. railroads, which carried about one-half of the ton-miles, operated at a traffic density sufficient to make electrification viable. The corresponding traffic density was estimated at about 35 million gross ton per year on single track. In terms of energy, the electrification would result in consumption of 600,000 kwh/mile-year. (RSMA, 1974, p. A36; Middleton, 1975).

Electrification was also advocated by the U.S. Task Force on Railroad Electrification in a report prepared in 1974 for the Federal Railroad Administration (FRA, 1974), "as the only available alternative to diesel-electric operations on high density, long-haul railroad lines." A General Electric Co. paper of the same year (RSMA, 1974, p. A36) stated that:

> Careful railroad studies show that . . . there is a substantial investment [in electrification], yet high volume railroads can expect a 12-25% discounted rate of return on the investment because of the electric locomotives' higher horsepower and speed capacities, lower initial cost, lower maintenance costs, more efficient use of energy, longer economic life, and higher availability . . . . We confidently predict that it is only a very short time before key North American railroads start the electrification era on this continent.

A 1975 study by Middleton, while pointing out some of the major difficulties, considered electrification to be

> a rare opportunity. . . . Despite the high level of current interest in electrification, no one can say with any cer-

tainty at this juncture that significant new electrification will actually take place. Representing as it does a very fundamental change in the way railroads are operated, as well as an extremely costly, long-term commitment, a decision for electrification can be an extraordinarily difficult one for the railroad management. Government, too, must act boldly to create conditions under which the necessary investment can be financed. But in their consideration of electrification, railroad management and government are confronted with a rare opportunity to simultaneously advance the productivity of the nation's rail system and the national interest. If they are able to bring it off, American railroading may be on the verge of a new era of enhanced efficiency and productivity through electrification that could well approach that produced by the conversion to diesel-electric motive power a quarter century ago.

Middleton (1975) identified 16 U.S. and Canadian railways which have been involved in electrification studies (six have been considered serious candidates for an early start), and several U.S. industrial suppliers.

TABLE 21.2   DISTRIBUTION OF RAIL TRAFFIC DENSITY IN CANADA IN 1970 (For CN and CP systems taken together)

Note: Density, based on running track length, given in million gross ton per year

Density Exceeding	% Running Track	% Traffic	Mean Density
5	28	83	13.7
10	20	72	16.7
15	14.8	56	18.2
Density less than			
5	72	17	1.1

The possibility of railway electrification in Canada can be judged on the basis of detailed information (Lukasiewicz, 1973b) on the traffic density distribution on CP (Fisher, 1973) and CN (Gratwick, 1973) systems, summarized in Table 21.2. In 1970, on 28% of the running track a density of 5 million gross tons per year was exceeded; 83% of all traffic was carried at a mean denisty of 13.7 million. On 15% of the track, a density of 18 million was attained (56% of the traffic). The highest density (29 million) was recorded by CP between Vancouver and Golden. The high density lines are shown in Map 6; more detailed distribution of traffic on the CN and CP systems is indicated in Maps 7 and 8, Appendix One.

Regarding energy density, in 1970 Canadian railways consumed diesel fuel at a rate equivalent to 31 kwh/1000 gross ton-mile (assuming a 35% efficiency of diesel locomotives). For a mean traffic density of 13.7 million gross tons per year on the high density portion of the Canadian system. (Table 21.2), this gives a consumption of 425,000 kwh/mile-year, i.e. a level typical of electrified systems.

As previously noted, the traffic density typical of electrified systems varies depending on local conditions: in Europe it is around 10 million gross tons per year, in Russia, 20 to 26 million, in the U.S. it has been estimated at 35 million. In light of these figures, detailed studies would be required to determine the exact extent to which railway electrification should be carried out in Canada, taking into account present levels of traffic and future growth. If a density of 15 million gross tons per year were regarded as the electrification threshold, over 20% of track could be electrified, carrying more than 70% of traffic (Table 21.2). To date, the only specific electrification study in Canada was completed by Canadian Pacific for the Calgary-Vancouver line (Fisher, 1971, 1972; see also Chapter 9). It indicated the desirability of electrification, but the project was shelved in favor of more profitable (higher priority) investments (Klein, 1974). As noted by Fisher (1971), "the ultimate question on electrification is probably not 'if' but 'when'". The prospects for railway electrification in Canada were appraised by K. Campbell, senior executive of CP Rail (RSMA, 1974, p. A5), as follows:

The traffic density on some of our main lines now bears comparison with many that, in the past, have been considered in Europe to justify electrification. By 1980, we expect the tonnage on CP Rail's single track through the mountains of British Columbia will rise to at least 35 million gross tons and, at the higher estimates one sometimes hears concerning coal and grain, even 45 million is possible. This is possibly a greater gross tonnage of traffic than that moved on the electrified 4-track route between

London, Liverpool and Manchester. These are indeed impressive reasons for electrification.

Curiously enough, the electrification of railways in Canada was advocated as early as 1899 by T. C. Keefer, who even then envisaged pollution-free electric railways travelling at speeds over 100 mph, and correctly assumed the basic difficulties in converting to electric traction. This is what he had to say in addressing the Royal Society of Canada (Keefer, 1899):

> The substitution of electricity for steam, as the motive power for railways, is regarded as inevitable sooner or later on many roads. It has already taken place as regards suburban railways, notably in the case of the Charlevoix road and Hull and Aylmer railway, where water is doing the work which has heretofore been done by coal. The chief obstacles to an early change on the larger roads are the hundreds of millions invested in locomotives, and the very large outlay required to equip existing steam roads with the electric system. The principal inducement would be the passenger service, owing to the increased speed possible, – it being confidently stated that, with electricity, a speed considerably over one hundred miles per hour could be attained. Moreover there would be entire abolition of the poisonous smoke which drops upon the Pullman in preference to any coach ahead of it.
>
> While the conversion of trunk lines would be attended with a cost which is for the present prohibitory, this objection does not apply to new lines which may be worked independently, or in connection with electric ones. When the time arrives for such railways, water power will have a field of usefulness of which we can at present form little conception. Water wheels and wires would displace the coal docks, the coal laden vessels, the huge coal yards, and the trains required for distributing their contents over hundreds of miles of lines.

Circumstances Which Influence Rail Electrification

The trend towards rail electrification, as discussed above, is quite general outside of the North American continent,* and is

* The electrification of U.S. railways reached its peak in the 1930s with some 2500 electrified route miles; in 1966, only about 1000 miles were in full

evident on railway systems which operate within a wide spectrum of topographic, demographic, economic and climatic conditions. This would indicate that the expansion of rail electrification is due to the inherently favorable characteristics of electric traction (see Chapter 9), rather than to advantages that can be realized only in special circumstances, and that different factors must have influenced electrification in various countries.

In Switzerland, it was the availability of hydroelectric power coupled with the absence of fossil fuels which caused the railways to switch, after about 1920, to electric traction; by 1928, traffic moved by electricity grew to 80%, and reached 99% in 1959 (SBB, 1971a). The abundance of coal and lack of oil in France, Germany and South Africa favored electrification over dieselization. On the contrary, the availability of oil in the U.S. and Canada encouraged the general conversion of their economies to liquid fuel, with railways switching completely to diesel traction. In Europe and South Africa, electrification has been steadily expanding over several decades, and has been extensively developed for suburban services and fast passenger trains. In the U.S. and Canada, because of much larger distances between population centers and the construction of superhighways, private cars, aircraft and trucks absorbed much of the traffic volume which in other countries has been handled by rail; the oil fuel-fired internal combustion engine became the major prime mover of transportation in North America.

The proliferation of railroad companies in the U.S. also discouraged electrification, which – to be efficient – must be carried out over an integrated network of lines and thus requires extensive coordination of diverse corporate policies.

The large distances characteristic of the U.S. and Canadian transportation network were another serious obstacle to rail electrification, which – until recently – required special, expensive distribution systems. As discussed in Chapter 9, with the introduction of solid-state devices this is no longer an important factor, as modern electric traction operates at high tension at commercial frequency.

---

service. The largest electrified system in full service is that of Penn Central, between Washington D.C., New York, Harrisburg and Enola, with 656 route-miles (Friedlander, 1968). This is less than one-third percent of a total of about 226,000 route miles operated by the U.S. railways in 1966. Canada has only two electric railways: an 8-mile long iron-ore train at Carol Lake, operated by the Quebec North Shore and Labrador railway, and a passenger commuter line through Montreal's Mount Royal tunnel.

The Cost of Electrification

Large capital costs have been a deterrent to railway electrification, particularly in North America, where straight profit is the major criterion in the operations of railway industry. As discussed in Chapter 18, the return on investments in railways had been small (compared with other sectors) or negative so that railways could not attract the necessary capital, even where electrification could have been economically justified in the long term.

Railway electrification involves installing overhead wire equipment for supplying electrical energy, constructing feeder sub-stations at intervals along the line and connections to the power grid, providing electric locomotives and train sets, and compatible signalling. Because electrification is often accompanied by improvements in overall railway performance (including an increase in speed) and an increase in traffic, it usually encompasses other aspects, such as modernization of signalling and upgrading of track (e.g., the elimination of excessive curves, the improvement of track quality, etc.). The costs of all these items depend on the initial characteristics of the line and the intended scope of work. Therefore, cost estimates for electrification of a given line must be based on detailed engineering analysis. In North America, only very few rail electrification studies have been completed to date, and little information is available on costs. Nevertheless, "guesstimates" of the required expenditure can be made on the basis of the available figures. Four sets of data will be considered.

(i) Canadian Pacific investigated the cost of electrifying the Calgary-Vancouver line and branches (Klein, 1974; Middleton, 1975). Although detailed cost estimates have not been published, a figure of $200 million could be taken as representative of the electrification cost of some 630 route miles of mostly single track line, giving an average of about $320,000 per mile. It should be noted that the Calgary-Vancouver route crosses difficult mountain terrain (the line includes some 47 tunnels and 23 through-truss bridges) and requires long feeder lines, conditions which escalate the costs over the levels typical of flatter and more industrialized regions.

(ii) Detailed estimates of electrification of the northern section of the U.K. West Coast line, from Crewe to Glasgow (236 route miles, 630 miles of track), put the total cost at $285,000 per mile of track. This includes about $130,000 for overhead equipment and feeder substations, and $155,000 for signalling and track rationalization (RGI, 1974a).

(iii) In a recent U.S. study (FRA, 1974) the costs of electrification alone were estimated at $50,000 to $70,000 per mile of track for overhead equipment, and $5,000 to $7,500 per mile for feeder substations (spaced at 40 miles).

(iv) Several American railroads are engaged in cost studies of 50 kV, 60 Hz electrification (Middleton, 1975). Union Pacific estimated $70,000 per track mile for catenary installation, and $41,000 per track mile for signalling and communications, for a total of $111,000 per track mile.

The above estimates range from $55,000 to $130,000 per track mile for catenary and feeder substations installation. Additional costs would be involved in upgrading the track and signalling for faster electric traction operations: based on the CP and U.K. data, such costs may range from $150,000 to $200,000 per track mile. As reported below, AMTRAK's estimate for modernization of track and signalling on 12 major intercity routes averaged $200,000 per track mile, a figure which probably reflects poor condition of many lines in the Northeast and Midwest.

In order to arrive at a very rough guess of railway electrification costs in Canada, we shall take the conservative figures of $125,000/mile for catenary and substations, and $175,000/mile

TABLE 21.3   ROUGH COST ESTIMATES OF RAILWAY ELECTRIFICATION IN CANADA

Density Exceeding (million gross ton per year per track)	Miles of Track	Mean Density (million gross ton per year per track)	Cost at $300,000/mile ($ billion)
5	12,400	13.7	3.7
10	8,750	16.7	2.6
15	6,500	18.2	2.0

for track and signalling improvement, for a total average of $300,000 per track mile. The corresponding total electrification and improvement costs for high density track in Canada are indicated in Table 21.3. The figures range from $2 to $3.7 billion, depending on the length of the track. Thus it appears that a ten-year program of rail electrification in Canada would require yearly expenditures on the order of $200 to $370 million, i.e. of a magnitude which roughly corresponds to the infrastructure costs now borne by the railways (see Chapter 18 and Tables 18.1, 18.2).

Track and Traffic Control

The second area of fundamental significance in railway modernization is that of the infrastructure, particularly of the track and traffic control portions. The major tasks, already mentioned in Chapter 9, include (i) reconstruction of existing tracks (and road crossings) to enable faster, safer and more comfortable travel; (ii) development of traffic controls compatible with higher speeds and safer operations, and (iii) consideration of incompatibility of freight and fast passenger operations, and desirability of separate lines, "dedicated" to fast passenger service or to freight.

The acuteness of these infrastructure deficiencies, and the corresponding resources and costs required to overcome them, vary between different railway lines and can be determined only on the basis of detailed studies of local conditions. They are also, of course, a function of the specified performance levels.

Some indication of the costs can be gained from the AMTRAK 5-year plan (see Chapter 15) estimates for right-of-way capital improvements on 12 intercity routes. AMTRAK's ambitious proposals include upgrading the majority of lines from the present maximum speeds of 50-60 mph (30 mph on the Chicago-Cincinnati line) to 90-110 mph, often by a factor of two; the average maximum speed is to be increased from 51.9 to 91.4 mph, i.e. by 76%. With one exception, the costs per track mile range from $0.1 to $0.5 million, and correspond to a $0.2 million average.

In Canada, the only estimates of track improvement costs have been published by the CTC (1970) for the Toronto-Montreal line. They amounted to $200 million, or $300,000 per track mile for 3.5 hour service (96 mph average), and increased to $500 million or $750,000 per track mile for 3 hour service (110 mph average, with the track reconstructed to 135 mph maximum speed standard). In view of the relatively good quality of the existing lines, and the above-quoted AMTRAK figures, the CTC estimates appear to be excessively high.

It should be also noted that, in the light of French experience, conventional ballasted track can be used for speeds up to 187 mph. In fact, research in France has been concentrated on limiting the stresses exerted on the track by the rolling stock rather than on development of tracks with a solid bed, which keep their geometry with minimum maintenance (Prud'homme, 1975).

As mentioned in Chapters 9 and 10, railway traffic control in North America is geared to low train speeds and, even on some of the major lines, has yet to be centralized; the control of trains relies essentially on visual observation of signals by the train crews, a procedure which is subject to human error and contributes to a low safety record.

Modernization of traffic control will result not only in improved performance, but also in considerable long-term savings. Their magnitude is indicated by British Rail's progress in traffic control modernization. British Rail's National Signalling Plan envisages control of all important intercity and commuter routes from about 75 signalling centers. As of 1975, 6000 manual signal boxes have been eliminated and 39 centers established. The rest of the system continues to be controlled from over 3,300 signal boxes, operated by some 20,000 men. Clearly, the productivity of railways can be significantly improved through application of improved traffic controls (I. Mech. E., 1975).

In fact, in terms of technological development, the status of railway traffic control is paradoxical. The railway mode of transportation is unique in that the movements of all vehicles are rigidly guided and completely pre-determined by the track configuration (only one degree of freedom is available with respect to the track). Therefore, it is the railway mode which is most easily amenable to completely remote and automatic operation. The technical capability to monitor the position and speed of trains on tracks, to project their movements in time and space, and to control them as desired to achieve an optimal operation, has existed for many years, but has been only marginally exploited so far. On the other hand, fully remote and highly automated controls have been developed for space flight, a task technically much more difficult but also too complex to be handled by human operators.

Looking into the future of railway operations, progress towards complete automation of train movements can be envisaged: it is already being adopted on urban transit systems, suburban lines and industrial railways (as noted in Chapter 9).

Passenger Trains

Since the 1960s, faster and more comfortable passenger trains are being intensively developed in Western Europe and Japan and are being introduced into service. The inventory of new passenger equipment includes:

Japan: Shinkansen electric train sets, introduced on the NTL in 1964, 130 mph max. speed; Series 961 Shinkansen electric train sets, 163 mph max. speed, now being developed (a prototype tested in 1972 established a speed record of 179 mph for electric rail cars); fast (81 mph top speed) articulated trains with tilting bodies (electric and gas turbine-driven) are being developed for Japan's narrow gauge lines; the electric ones (type 591/381) entered service in the fall of 1973.

France: The first generation, ETG (*Eléments Turbine à Gas*) 100 mph top speed trains have been operating since 1970 on the Paris-Caen-Cherbourg line. The second generation RTG (*Rame Turbine à Gas)* series, 125 mph train sets are now in service in France and the U.S., and are being produced under license in the U.S. Experimental TGV (*Train Grande Vitesse*) train sets for operation at 162 mph starting in the 1980s, on new lines (Paris-Lyon, Paris-Brussels), are being developed. The TGV-001 gas-turbine driven prototype attained 198 mph on a test run in 1972; the electric version Z-7001 (Zebulon) was tested at 190 mph in 1974.

U.K.: Passenger equipment for operations at speeds up to 163 mph is being developed. The High Speed Train (HST), whose prototype was completed in 1972, established in 1973 a world record for diesel traction of 141 mph. A total of 59 HST sets have been ordered, and will start service in 1976. The HST is to be eventually displaced to secondary services (on non-electrified lines) by the Advanced Passenger Train (APT), under development since 1969 for speeds up to 163 mph. The experimental, gas-turbine version (APT-E) was tested at 152 mph in 1975. Three prototype electric APTs for service between London and Glasgow in 1978, at an average speed of 101 mph, were ordered in 1974.

West Germany: A 125 mph electric train (ET 403) is being developed for intercity service. An 88 mph diesel (VT 614) will serve secondary lines in mountainous regions. Both trains feature tilting bodies.

Research and Development

It has been noted in Chapter 18 that R&D in surface transportation has been at a low level in the U.S. and Canada. Moreover, particularly in North America, it has been largely directed towards radically new approaches, such as air-cushion and magnetically-levitated (maglev) designs. There has been a tendency – perhaps reflecting the style of successful space and weapon R&D programs – to seek exotic solutions rather than to fully exploit more conventional designs, such as steel-wheel-on-steel-rail. The emphasis on technical newness for the sake of newness* has not been productive either here or in Europe: by 1975, several of the major R&D projects of this kind have been terminated.

The development of tracked air cushion vehicles (TACV) was abandoned in 1973 in the U.K. (*Tracked Hovercraft* project), in 1974 in France (Bertin's *Aérotrain*) and in 1975 in the U.S. (Grumman and Rohr vehicles). In 1974, a major West German maglev urban transit project (by Krauss-Maffei) lost government support, and cancellation of the $25 million Ontario GO-Urban demonstration line in Toronto (to have been built by Krauss-Maffei) followed. Trials of the Krauss-Maffei *Trans-*

---

*This kind of approach has been also noted in the area of urban transit: in North America, new techniques rather than higher standards of service are often sought. The European approach is different, as described by Hoel (1973): "We must remember that the passenger regards transit service not in terms of mode or technology but in terms of attributes. He doesn't care if the vehicle is a bus, tram, or train, or if it runs on steel wheels, rubber tires, or air. He cares about comfort and quiet, frequent service, reasonable travel times, reasonable costs, and convenience of access. European systems are based largely on conventional technology, primarily rail rapid transit, tram cars, and buses. European planners view technology as the least important variable in transit; service counts more."

B.C. *by* Johnny Hart

rapid 04 intercity maglev vehicle were also suspended. The funding of maglev projects in the U.S. has been tapering off.

These "advanced" concepts have failed because they offered no advantages and were found, in many respects, to be impractical. For example, switching of tracks and turning – straightforward maneuvers on a railway – represent unresolved difficulties for TACV and maglev designs. As development of exotic surface transportation modes is being abandoned, conventional (steel-wheel-on-steel-rail) railway technology is progressing towards higher speeds. The current rail speed records are listed in Table 21.4. In the future, one can envisage rail travel at 150 to 200 mph, i.e. at speeds competitive with aircraft on intercity distances up to about 500 miles. Higher surface speeds appear impractical on at least two counts: excessive energy consumption due to high drag at ground level (high air density) and safety. In fact, jet aircraft, operating at high altitude, is the most practical mode for fast travel over large distances.* In economic terms, both the energy costs *and* the maintenance costs of track and rolling stock escalate with speed. For these reasons, 150 to 200 mph are now considered (in U.K. and France respectively) to be the maximum *economic* speeds for rail.

Unlike the efforts on exotic surface transportation devices, the progress in railway engineering, evident from the information reviewed in this chapter and in Chapters 9 and 14, reflects extensive and productive research and development activity in Western Europe and Japan during the past fifteen years. It is only common sense to suggest that railway modernization on this continent should take advantage, to the fullest possible extent, of the modern technology developed abroad, and that the R&D effort in the U.S. and Canada should be focussed on special problems characteristic of the North American conditions, and on solutions which go beyond the current "state of the art." As already noted (see Chapter 15), AMTRAK has followed the former course by acquiring French turbine-driven, fast passenger trains through purchase in France and production under license in the U.S., in preference to American-

---

* Short-haul air transportation is expensive. In spite of large subsidies for the infrastructure (see Chapter 18), in 1974 Air Canada lost $19 million on its operations linking Toronto, Ottawa and Montreal. This represented 91% of the losses suffered on all domestic operations. Surveys show that 56% of travellers using Toronto International Airport are on journeys of less than 500 miles.

TABLE 21.4 HIGHEST SPEEDS ON RAILS

Maximum Speed mph	km/h	Year	Country	Equipment
				Traction: Steel-wheel-to-steel-rail
206	332	1955	FRANCE	Electric locomotive, SNCF Co-Co Nr. 7107
206	332	1955	FRANCE	Electric locomotive, SNCF Bo-Bo Nr. 9004
198	318	1972	FRANCE	TGV 001 gas turbine-electric prototype train
190	306	1974	FRANCE	TGV electric power car, Z-7001 Zebulon
179	286	1972	JAPAN	Shinkansen electric train set prototype Series 961
152	244	1975	U.K.	APT-E (Advanced Passenger Train—Experimental), gas turbine-electric drive
141	227	1973	U.K.	High Speed Train (diesel-electric) prototype
130	210	1965	JAPAN	NTL Shinkansen electric train set; fastest train in regular service
126	202	1938	U.K.	"Mallard" LNER steam locomotive
				Traction: not through wheels
255	410	1974	U.S.A.	LIM Research Vehicle, Dept. of Transport. Propulsion: linear induction motor and jet engines

designed equipment of inferior performance (discontinued since 1974). This has not been the case in Canada, where equipment of the type rejected by AMTRAK has been in limited service since 1973. Moreover, in Canada there has been as yet no long-term commitment to introduce modern passenger trains; only limited support has been given to the development of an improved diesel train (the LRC, see Chapter 14), which nevertheless conforms to the conventional North American practice. A concept similar to the LRC, named *Futura*, was announced by the industry in 1975.

Concerning areas in need of vigorous R&D effort on this continent, winter operations – in view of the data presented in Chapter 10 – should rank high on the list. There can be but little doubt that decisive application of modern engineering techniques would render the reliability of trains independent of weather.

CHAPTER 22

RAILWAYS
AND ENERGY

The energy aspect is the most recent newcomer to the transportation and railway scene. In spite of the early predictions of eventual oil depletion (Hubbert, 1956, 1962, 1973), it is only since the Middle East crisis in the fall of 1973 that the United States, Canada (North, 1975) and Europe have begun to appreciate the coming scarcity of the fuel* which powers most of the transportation.

As the energy crisis develops, the augmentation of rail's share of traffic and the modernization of rail traction through electrification gain in pertinence, attractiveness and economic viability, for three reasons.

First, rail is a relatively energy-efficient mode of land transportation. Thus, as oil is depleted, one may expect freight and passenger traffic to shift from highways to railways, making the expansion of electrification even more desirable and economical.** Moreover, electric (as opposed to diesel) railway can be made even more energy efficient through application of so-called regenerative or dynamic braking, a system which slows down the train by converting kinetic energy into electricity and feeding it back into the grid. Tests conducted on a typical line (which included 1% gradients) in France have shown that energy savings of 10 to 20% can be realized through regenerative braking (Nouvion, 1974).

Secondly, electrification allows a wide range of options regarding the primary energy source (from coal to nuclear, geothermal, solar, etc. generation) and thus eliminates dependence on oil. Indeed, the electrification of railways and an increase in

---

*This wasn't apparent in the U.S. Department of Transport proposal for salvaging the bankrupt Penn Central and other railroads in the Northeast. The DOT plan would result in a 25% increase in regional truck freight (transferred from the abandoned railways) and a 3.5% increase in the consumption of oil used in freight haulage in the U.S. (Commoner, 1973).

**In the U.S. and Canada intercity freight ton-miles generated by trucks amount to about 53% and 18% respectively of the rail freight volume. (Statistics Canada, 1970a; Hirst, 1973a; see also Fig. 16.2).

the rail share of traffic would help to conserve oil for uses for which its unique characteristics of portability and high energy density are essential, as for aircraft propulsion.*

Thirdly, the generation of electricity in central power plants allows maximum utilization of the primary fuel energy through the use of "low grade" or waste heat for district heating and industrial applications.

TABLE 22.1   OIL AND ENERGY USE IN TRANSPORTATION IN THE LATE 1960's IN CANADA AND U.S.

	Canada[1] %	U.S.[2] %
Oil energy as % of total energy used by the country	48	42
Transportation energy as % of total energy consumed	18	24
Oil used in transportation as % of total oil used	37.5	57

[1] Winter and MacNabb (1974)
[2] Rice (1972)

In Canada and the U.S., close to one-half of all consumed energy is obtained from oil (48 and 42% respectively, Table 22.1). The transportation sector is one of its major users and accounts for 18% in Canada and 24% in the U.S. Moreover, since the completion of railway dieselization (see Fig. 9.1) and in the absence of rail electrification, all transportation (road, rail, air and water) on the North American continent is totally dependent on oil.

The consumption of oil varies greatly between different transportation modes. Typical energy efficiencies of passenger and freight transportation are compared in Tables 22.2 and 22.3. The efficiency of passenger transportation is given in passenger-miles per (U.S.) gallon of fuel; the assumed number of passengers is indicated for each vehicle. The latter reflects the actual average use in the U.S. rather than the number of avail-

* It should be noted that there are no significant differences in the energy efficiency (in terms of primary fuel) between diesel and electric traction (except for regenerative braking, see above). However, diesel locomotives would be expected to produce electricity at a higher cost than central power stations, which can attain high utilization and use less expensive fuels.

219

TABLE 22.2 ENERGY EFFICIENCY OF TRANSPORTATION (RICE 1970, 1972)

Passenger Transportation (number of persons carried given in brackets)		Freight Transportation	
Mode	Passenger-Miles Per U.S. gallon	Mode	Cargo Ton-Miles Per U.S. gallon
automobile (urban use, 1)	6	20 ton helicopter	3
executive jet (8)	10	cargo jet (B-707)	8
SST airplane (150)	14	cargo jumbo jet (B-747)	12
Pullman night train (100)*	18	40 ton truck	50
DC-8 jet (78)	20	fast freight train (90 mph)	100
CN passenger trains in 1970	25	15,000t container ship	150
B-747 jumbo jet (210)	26	inland barge	220
automobile (average use, 2)	30	freight train (40 mph)	250
DC-10, airbus (180)	32	freight train (25 mph)	400
urban bus (12)	40	large pipeline	500
VW "beetle" (2)	60	100,000 t supertanker	1000
London-Manchester electric train (400)	110**		
two-level commuter train (1200)	120		
highway bus (22)	140		
VW microbus (7)	180		

* the old standard American 10-sleeping car, 2 diesel locomotive Pullman train with 160 berths (1150 ton gross weight)

able seats (e.g., although most American cars can accommodate 5 persons, the passenger-miles per gallon are based on the average occupancy of 2 per car), so that the listed efficiencies correspond to the actual practice. A modern passenger train achieves more than 100 passenger-miles per gallon, and is only bettered by highway bus (140) and the VW Microbus (180). It is ten times as efficient as an executive jet, almost four times as efficient as an automobile and an airbus, and twice as economical as a VW beetle. However, obsolete passenger trains, of the type traditionally used in North America, show poor energy efficiency, due to excess weight and small seat occupancy. For example, a standard American Pullman train (Table 22.2), consisting of 10 sleeper cars, 1 diner, 1 baggage car, and 2 diesel locomotives (for a total of 1150 ton, or 11.5 ton/passenger) achieved only 18 passenger miles per gallon, a performance inferior to the commercial jet airplanes. With all passenger space occupied, its efficiency would increase to a maximum of 33 passenger miles per gallon, at par with a jet airbus but three times below the level of a modern train.

Regarding freight, the energy efficiency of trains is exceeded only by supertankers and pipelines. Large trucks achieve only one-eighth to one-quarter of the ton miles (per gallon of fuel) produced by freight trains.

Another way to look at the efficiency of various transportation modes is to compare the share of traffic and the corresponding fraction of energy consumed. This information is shown in Table 22.3 for the U.S. in 1970. Under the American conditions, passenger rail is only slightly more efficient than the automobile. In freight, railways match within 23% the waterways and pipelines, and exceed by a factor of four the truck efficiency; they are sixty times more economical than the airplane.

The development of new transportation techniques, such as air-cushion and magnetically-levitated vehicles, has been advocated in recent years (see Chapter 21). It is pertinent to observe here that all such systems require considerable energy not only for propulsion of the payload, but also for its support, and are therefore inherently less efficient than the conventional (steel-wheel-on-steel-rail) railway technique. Rail freight requires only about 0.5% of the energy needed by an air-cushion vehicle (Cockshutt, 1973); it has been estimated that a magnetically-levitated electric train would consume two to three times

The New York Times, 27 March 1974.

the energy required by a conventional electric train (at 200 mph).

The railway is an energy efficient transportation mode also for other reasons. It has been calculated (Bezdek and Hannon, 1974) that highway construction (per mile of a two-lane highway) requires about twice as much energy as a mile of single-track railroad. The energy consumed in the manufacture of an average American car is equivalent to 1000 U.S. gallons of gasoline, or to a distance of 16,000 miles covered by a car in intercity travel (Berry and Fels, 1973). Because of lower weight per passenger and longer life, the corresponding energy consumed in the manufacture of passenger rail equipment is much smaller.

The energy and oil savings which would result from shift of traffic to rail, and from rail electrification, have been estimated for Canada (Lukasiewicz, 1975) and the U.S. (Hirst, 1973b). The consequences of the scenario developed for Canada (based on 1970 data) are summarized in Table 22.4 for intercity traffic. The shift of one-half of auto, air and truck traffic to rail results in a saving of 14.5% of the energy used in intercity transporta-

**TABLE 22.3   RELATIVE TRANSPORTATION OUTPUT AND
ENERGY CONSUMPTION IN THE U.S. IN 1970
(HIRST, 1973)**

Intercity Passenger Transportation

Mode	a % passenger mile	b % energy	Relative energy efficiency a/b*
bus	2	0.8	1.8
rail	1	0.7	1.0
automobile	87	76.8	0.85
airplane	10	21.7	0.35

Intercity Freight Transportation

Mode	c % ton-mile	d % energy	Relative energy efficiency c/d*
waterway & pipeline	46	23.3	1.23
rail	35	21.7	1.0
truck	19	49.2	0.24
air	0.15	5.8	0.016

*Assuming a value of one for rail.

tion; the electrification of 75% of the intercity rail traffic saves another 21.5% of oil, for a total of 36% of oil used in intercity transportation. In terms of the total (for all purposes) oil consumption, the saving is over 7%.*

In connection with the above scenario, it is also of interest to consider the extra electrical energy production which would be required to provide the electrical energy for transportation. This has been estimated assuming (i) a 4% p.a. growth in the energy used in transportation (NEB, 1969), (ii) a 7% p.a. growth in the production of electrical energy (Statistics Canada, 1972), and

*If the urban traffic sector is also included, additional savings (due to shifts of traffic, the use of more economical cars and electrification of urban cars, trucks and transit) of 14% in the total use of oil (for all purposes) have been estimated (Lukasiewicz, 1975).

223

TABLE 22.4 SAVINGS OF ENERGY AND OIL IN INTERCITY TRANSPORTATION IN CANADA RESULTING FROM SHIFT OF TRAFFIC TO RAIL AND RAIL ELECTRIFICATION

Traffic Shift	Energy and Oil Savings, %	Electrification	Oil Savings, %
Shift one-half of intercity auto passenger traffic to rail (50% rail load factor)	6.6	Electrify 75% of passenger traffic	12
Shift one-half of passenger air traffic to rail (50 % rail load factor)	3.3	Electrify 75% of freight traffic	9.5
Assume existing passenger rail traffic at 50% load factor	0.9		
Shift one-half of intercity truck freight to rail	3.7		
Sub-total	**14.5**		**21.5**

Total saving of oil in intercity transportation: 36%
Total saving of oil in all transportation (intercity and urban): 19.4%
Total saving of all oil used (all purposes): 7.3%

(iii) an initial (in the first year of the period considered) ratio of the electric traction energy to the total electrical energy produced in Canada based on 1970 data (Statistics Canada, 1972). The intercity rail electrification, as stipulated in Table 22.4, requires the electrical energy production growth rate to be increased from 7% p.a. to 7.3% p.a. for completion in 10 years, and to 7.1% p.a. for completion in 20 years. At the end of these periods, rail electric traction would account for 3.1% and 2.6% respectively of all electrical energy consumption.

The above estimates indicate that electrification of intercity rail would require small but significant increases in the forecast growth rates of electrical energy production in Canada.

CHAPTER 23

THE
POLICY VOID

This is a really fortunate country. We have everything in Canada. We have water, air, surface – we have ice, we have snow and we have distance – we have everything to have fun in transportation. Something we do not have is a real policy and I hope that sooner, rather than later, it will be possible to have such a policy.

> Hon. Jean Marchand, Minister of Transport,
> House of Commons, March 7, 1974

I can't manage transportation in Canada. If you ask who is managing transportation policy, I say to you I don't know.
If the transportation situation continues in the mess it is now, I don't want to stay in this job.

> – Hon. Jean Marchand, Minister of Transport,
> in an address to the Canadian Railway Labor
> Association, Ottawa, March 19, 1974.

Under heavy questioning from the Progressive Conservatives the Transport Minister conceded that there was "no overall policy" in his department to cope with transport problems which he described as "in a mess" (*The Ottawa Journal*, January 23, 1975). Opposition Leader Robert Stanfield said Mr. Marchand's comment that there is no overall policy "is an extraordinary statement on transport policy from a government that has been in power for 10 years" (*The Ottawa Journal*, January 25, 1975.)

The lack of an effective transportation policy in Canada has been admitted on several occasions in 1974 and 1975 in remarkably candid statements by the Minister of Transport. Regarding railways, the Minister's perception is amply supported by the material already reviewed in this study and covering such aspects as technology, service quality, manning, regulation and subsidization, research and development. In recent years the government has continued to rely on ad hoc measures to cope with current problems and has avoided tackling the underlying causes of railway transportation deficiencies. This approach has been demonstrated through several specific actions taken by the government, as well as by government's proposals for a "new policy."

Ad hoc Measures

Export Grain Traffic

In the first half of 1974, serious difficulties which were experienced in Canada with export wheat traffic led to the so-called "wheat car crisis." Starting in February, 1974, the rail shipments of grain were found to lag badly behind schedule, threatening Canada's export obligations and Prairie growers' income. By April, according to the Wheat Board, the railways have fallen 26,515 boxcars or 56 million bushels behind their own minimum delivery targets. As rail service improved in May and June, bottlenecks developed in the ports so that for the first time western wheat was being moved directly by rail to eastern Canada during the Lake Superior shipping season. The failure of railways to keep the grain deliveries on schedule from February to May, 1974 was attributed to many reasons, including unusually severe winter weather, backlogs resulting from the 1973 railway strike and increased demand for rail transportation. But, as mentioned in Chapter 12, at the root of the problem lay the fact that grain traffic was not profitable under the unrealistically low statutory rates, and consequent reluctance on the part of the railways to provide the necessary capacity. Rather than tackling the fundamental issue, the government has been buying fleets of wheat cars for the railways. The inability of the government to deal with the situation has been admitted by the Minister when he observed that, while the railways have a legal commitment for delivery of grain, "there is no time limit;" railway would deliver grain "in due course and in due time. . . . "

Freight Rate Freeze

The general commodity rail freight rates, which affect about 22% of rail freight traffic and 52,000 shippers in Canada, were frozen by the government from February, 1972 to the end of 1974. The freeze was ordered initially as an anti-inflation mea-

227

sure, and was later (in July, 1973) extended to meet the wishes of the western provinces. The railways complied, but protested against such restrictive government policies. In March, 1974, the government included in supplementary estimates for 1973-74 a $41 million subsidy to compensate railways for the losses resulting from the freight rate freeze. Effective January 1, 1975, the rate freeze was lifted and a 25% increase started coming into effect.

The 1972-1974 rate freeze and subsidy have in effect compromised one of the essential provisions of the 1967 National Transportation Act, which was to insure competitive and equitable pricing of transportation. While acknowledging inadequacy of the 1967 Act, the government has opted for short-term, politically expedient measures in preference to formulation of a long term solution.

Railway Costs
Although under the 1967 Act the government has the power to control the maximum and minimum freight rate levels (see Chapter 12), it has no power to compel railways to disclose their operating costs, on which basis compensatory levels can be determined. At the 1973 Western Economic Opportunities Conference held in Calgary, the federal government promised to provide the provinces (which accused the railways of charging regionally discriminatory rates) with details of the railway costs; railways were given until December 21, 1973 to open their books but have failed to comply fully with this request. In December, 1974, a bill (the Cost Disclosure Act) to amend the Railway Act to force costs disclosure by the railways was introduced in the House of Commons. Introduction of a more comprehensive Information Act "at an appropriate time" was envisaged by the Minister of Transport in June, 1975.

As would be expected, the railways have opposed costs disclosure; they regard the data on costs as proprietory information whose disclosure would be detrimental to good management and competitiveness. The problem of costs disclosure highlights the basic incompatibility of strict regulation and commercial competition, a conflict that the government has not resolved.

Intercity Passenger Transportation
In this sector there is ample evidence of a penchant for ad hoc, sometimes contradictory measures. Following on the U.S. 1965

High Speed Ground Transportation (HSGT) program, an analogous but very much more modest government-funded and short-lived effort was undertaken in Canada by the CTC and Canadair Ltd. The U.S. study resulted in the North-Eastern Corridor Project, an intercity transportation study which was submitted to Congress in 1971. It recommended upgrading of the rail services to provide 119 mph and 83 mph speeds between Washington-New York, and New York-Boston respectively. The fast and successful Washington-New York *Metroliner* service (see Chapter 15) was introduced as a demonstration project resulting from the HSGT R&D program.

Predictably the CTC (1970) study also concluded that, concerning passenger intercity transportation in the Quebec-Windsor corridor, "in the 1970's the greatest benefit would be derived from improvements in the existing modes, such as on-time reliability (and consequent reduction in waiting times), passenger processing procedures, and rail improvements using existing trackage. . . . The strategy which produces the highest return involves modest improvements to the existing railway system through the introduction of new equipment of the "Turbo" or "Advanced Passenger Train" variety. It appears that more leverage can be obtained from the existing railway system through equipment improvements than through improvements to the track structure and right-of-way." Surprisingly, electrification as a means of improving all railway operations (freight and passenger) was not mentioned in the CTC study. Similar recommendations were made in the Canadair study (McLaren and Myers, 1970), which concluded that intercity services would benefit from application of fast rail rather than introduction of new technologies, such as tracked air cushion vehicles.

Contrary to the CTC's recommendations, the federal government is supporting development of STOL (for Short-Take-Off-and-Landing), with a demonstration service between Montreal and Ottawa initiated on July 24, 1974, at an initial cost of $25 million to the taxpayer.* While it is hoped that this project, if successful, will generate international demand for the new deHavilland of Canada DHC-7 (*Dash Seven*), 48 passenger

---

* During the first year of operations, STOL demonstration project ran up a deficit of about $2 million, or about one dollar for every dollar collected in fares. Coincidentally, this is also the level of subsidy applied to transcontinental trains (see p. 124).

STOL aircraft and Canadian know-how in STOL commercial operations, there is no plan to modernize railway service between Montreal and Ottawa, on a route ideal for all-weather, fast rail operation using such equipment as the *Turbotrain*. Ironically, on the very day the STOL service started, the papers carried a CN announcement that the *Turbotrain*, to go into service on the Ottawa-Montreal run in August, 1974, would not reduce the trip time from 2 hours, due to deficiencies in the track and signalling. In effect, CN would operate a 125 mph train at an average speed of 58 mph. A CN spokesman said the *Turbotrain* isn't intended to compete with STOL, which makes the trip (center to center) in 1½ hours.

It will be noted that the *Turbotrain* running at 77 mph would equal the STOL schedule and would exceed STOL's comfort, convenience and reliability; at 100 mph, or 80% of its top speed, the *Turbotrain* time would be only 1 hr. 10 min., or 20 min. less than the STOL, whose competitive performance margin would be then gone. This was admitted by the Minister of Transport in December, 1974, who stated that the Ottawa-Montreal STOL service could become obsolete with improvements in rail.

As indicated, the STOL demonstration may benefit the troubled aircraft industry in Canada, but it will do little to improve the intercity transportation in general and, in view of the price to the user,* will not even significantly affect the Ottawa-Montreal market. The same is largely true of the other intercity transportation technology that has received support from the government: the LRC (see Chapter 14) train. This improved diesel passenger train will be capable of 120 mph, but – as the *Turbotrain* – it will not be able to realize this performance in Canada, owing to poor track quality and a signalling system geared to lower speeds. As with the STOL project, the LRC – if successful – may augment Canada's exports, but will not improve intercity passenger transportation. To achieve this, a long term policy which would correct the basic deficiencies of the Canadian railway system would be needed. Moreover, although government supports development of the prototype LRC locomotive and coach, the railways – as in the case of the *Turbotrain* – are not committed to its use but have adopted a

---

*When introduced at $20 (one way fare from city-centre to city-centre), STOL cost exceeded by a large factor the rail ($7 or less) and bus ¢($5.25 or less) rates.

"wait-and-see" attitude – another symptom of the lack of an overall policy.

Regarding research, contrary to the above-mentioned CTC recommendations, advanced transportation concepts, such as application of magnetic levitation to surface transportation (recently initiated at Queen's University), are being funded in preference to work on more conventional systems, such as wheel-on-rail. The Canadian maglev effort, at a level of about $200,000 in 1973, is negligibly small compared to the expenditure in Japan of $20 million (Atherton and Eastham, 1973; Hanlon, 1973), and the chances of bringing it to fruition must be judged small. Moreover, as discussed in Chapter 21, the viability of maglev and other exotic surface transportation systems is questionable, and many projects in this area have been already cancelled.

Promises Of a Policy

Since the 1974 "wheat car crisis" and an extraordinarily candid "as non-political as possible" speech by Transport Minister Marchand on March 7, 1974 in the House of Commons, there has been increasing concern with the absence of a transportation policy in Canada and with the lack of authority to manage transportation.

Mr. Marchand condemned the 1967 Act on two counts. First, the Act espoused the principle of competition both between the different modes, and within each one – a principle which "is wrong for Canada," since it is not applicable to all regions of the country. Moreover, sometimes CN and CP "agree not to have any competition." The system suffers from duplication of lines and overcapacity. The railways must agree to consolidate parallel rail-beds and they must not try to dispose of land— which they got "practically free"—at prohibitive prices. Mr. Marchand suggested that the 1967 Act will need major revisions. He indicated that he will recommend to Cabinet that CP be nationalized if this is necessary to develop an integrated national transportation system in Canada. Secondly, the 1967 Act was based on the mistaken premise that passenger transportation will be taken over by airways and highways, whereas in fact this is the area in which "we now see a growing role for railways. High speed railways are being developed in Germany, Britain, France and Japan. Maybe we have to look at the ex-

The Globe and Mail, Toronto, 24 January 1975.

pansion of railways. . . . Trains can now travel at 200 mph, why do we need new airports, one at Mirabel and another at Pickering?"* (Statement to the Canadian Railway Labour Association, Ottawa, March 19, 1974).

Regarding a transportation policy for the future, Mr. Marchand reiterated that Canada had none, that transportation "is a mess," and that there was nobody in Canada who had the authority required to manage the whole transportation field. Mr. Marchand implied that unless he gains such authority he would resign his portfolio.**

While criticising the 1967 Act and deploring the lack of a transportation policy, Mr. Marchand also affirmed pride in the Canadian transportation. He said: "If we compare our system with that of other countries, the United States, France, Ger-

---

*In September, 1975 the Ontario government refused to participate in the construction of Pickering airport near Toronto, and the federal government was compelled to shelve the project. The Mirabel airport was opened in December, 1975.

**The transport portfolio was taken over by Otto Lang in September, 1975; Jean Marchand was appointed Minister without portfolio.

many or Italy, I am sure that we have to conclude that ours is the best." He also stated in April, 1974, that he is not prepared to recommend changes in the 1899 Crowsnest Pass Agreement grain rates. Moreover, Mr. Marchand's suggestion that the 1967 Act should undergo major revisions has met with little enthusiasm from CN and CP. The new CN President, R. Bandeen, felt that the basic elements of the 1967 Act are still valid; the retiring CN's chief N. J. MacMillan considered CN "the biggest and best" railway in the Western world. CP Chairman Ian Sinclair declared that current transportation legislation in Canada is fundamentally sound and "the ultimate sin is to impose political expediency on the problems of a technical and economic nature." The 1967 Act provided a sane balance between, on the one hand, "adequate freedom for our vast transportation system to regulate itself by commercial means," and, on the other, "the freedom for government to ensure adequate transportation in situations where competition is not feasible or transportation cannot be provided profitably."

Mr. Marchand's expressions of concern have been followed, in June, 1974, by election promises. If confirmed in office, the Trudeau government proposed new measures to (i) rehabilitate passenger services, (ii) establish rail freight rates on the principle of equitable pricing rather than free competition, and (iii) provide federal funds for urban transport. The cost was estimated at $1.7 billion over a period of 5 years.

The government would introduce legislation establishing a Canadian Passenger Transport Corporation (CPTC), which would acquire passenger rolling stock and operate passenger services over CN and CP tracks. The CPTC would (a) introduce high speed passenger trains in the Quebec-Windsor corridor, (b) rehabilitate luxury transcontinental trains by introducing specially scheduled excursion trains, (c) develop, buy or lease the most advanced railway technology to build in Canada high speed passenger equipment and systems, (d) set up high quality passenger bus service in areas now poorly served. It was estimated that the program would cost $500 million over the next 5 years, in addition to the subsidies now paid railways, for a total of $1 billion. This proposal amounted to establishment of a Canadian version of AMTRAK (CANTRAK?), which started operations in the U.S. in 1971 (see Chapter 15).

The second item of the 1974 Liberal party package meant abandoning the 1967 Act philosophy "based on the belief that competition would result in lower rates for the consumer of railway service" (Trudeau, speaking in Edmonton on June 13, 1974), and return to regulated rates. This would be implemented gradually; the Crowsnest Pass agreement rates and the Maritime Freight Rate Act would not be affected. Mr. Trudeau also proposed to create a crown corporation that would buy freight cars to be kept in reserve for leasing to the railways when exceptional need arose. The new freight car agency was apparently to be created to take care of the freight cars already owned by the government.

The third item of the election proposals promised federal aid to urban transport.* Ottawa would pay 100% of the cost of new commuter vehicles made in Canada, 50% of the cost of new stations and platforms in commuter train systems, and 25% of the capital expenses for Canadian-made public transit vehicles (buses and subway cars).

The June 1974 election package, obviously and hurriedly designed to get votes rather than better transportation, was abandoned three months later, in the September, 1974 Throne Speech, in favour of a comprehensive examination of all transportation modes by a special task force. The first results of its labors were announced by the Transport Minister on June 16, 1975. Disappointingly, but also – in the light of the past record – predictably, they did not contain proposals of major specific policies or measures, but only yet another enunciation of goals and principles. The following is a typical sample of the objectives beyond reproach listed by the Transport Minister:

– The use of transportation as an instrument of national policy, rather than as a passive support service.
– The transportation system should be accessible, equitable and efficient, rather than economic, efficient and adequate. The notion of efficiency is not lost but the emphasis is on service to Canadians.
– A total transportation system for Canada, providing accessibility and equity of treatment for users is an essential instrument of support for the achievement of national, economic and social objectives.
– Intermodal and intramodal competition should be en-

---

*In February, 1974, the government proposed establishment of a national Urban Transportation Development Corporation "to coordinate and market the development of required new technology in this field."

couraged where economic and technical characteristics permit.
– There should be a combination of public and private ownership of carriers . . . , and of national and regional carriers . . . in the event of conflict, the public interest must prevail . . .
– There should be an objective of commercial viability . . . in the operation of transportation services.
– . . . where a particular . . . national policy requires, the costs . . . should be assumed by the government.
– Where effective competition exists, transportation rates should be established through the working of the market mechanism; where such conditions are absent, prices should be regulated . . .
– Subsidies for the mature services should be reduced, while government support of uneconomic services – where in the national interest – should be increased.

These admirable but hardly innovative objectives reflect what one editorial termed the "monumental vagueness" of the "new transportation policy." If such ideal goals have not been attained before, it is not likely that they could be realized without fundamental changes in the organizational structure and ownership of transportation modes, and in the subsidization and pricing of transportation services, to mention only the most basic aspects. Such changes are not envisaged by the "new policy," which does not reject the 1967 National Transportation Act, and does not propose to interfere with the duality of the railway organization and with the statutory grain rates. Several fundamental issues, as, for example, the restructuring of transportation to attain a better balance between various modes, or the scarcity of oil, are not even addressed. Only in matters of limited significance does the "new policy" verge on specifics, an approach which resembles the recent ad hoc measures reviewed before. Regarding railway transportation, it proposes:

– An intensified effort to upgrade rail passenger services through joint use of terminals and reservation systems of CN and CP.*
– A high speed rail demonstration service in the Quebec-Windsor corridor.

* Proposal reminiscent of the 1933 CN-CP Act, discussed in Chapter 5; "Plus ça change, plus c'est la même chose."

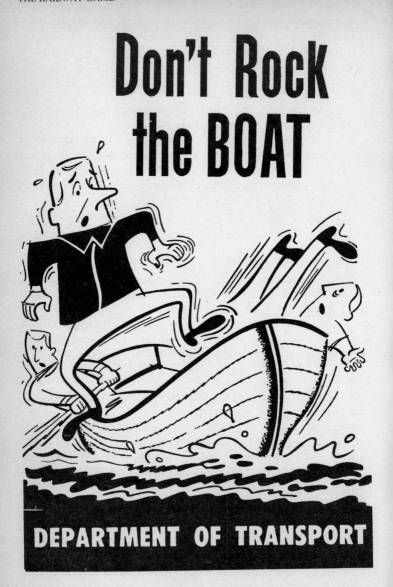

This water safety poster aptly sums up the fundamental theme of transportation policy in Canada.

– A separate (from CN) corporate identity for Air Canada.

– Investigation of a new basis for the freight rate structure, including the possibility of having freight rates based on a combination of variable and fixed costs, rather than on long-run variable costs alone.

– Legislation to end so-called "long-haul short-haul" freight rate discrimination (see p. 120).

– Negotiation of freight rate groupings (i.e. groupings of communities for rate-making purposes, see p. 120).

– Study of freight rates on raw versus finished products (as an interim measure, rates on rapeseed products will be established at minimum compensatory level).

Thus the government proposes mostly more intensified efforts, studies and investigations. The 1974 election promises of a Canadian Passenger Transport Corporation and of federal aid to urban transport have been once again abandoned. Instead of a $500 million passenger rail program, a $28 million Quebec-Windsor demonstration project is to be completed by 1977-78. This is a level of expenditure which, in the light of unit costs quoted in Chapter 21 and estimated by the CTC (1970), cannot possibly result in a major improvement of service quality. Anyway, with modern passenger rail operating routinely in many countries for several years, a demonstration in 1977-78 will be hardly appropriate or necessary. It is significant to note that, in 1975, Canada alone among industrial nations had no new passenger rail equipment on order.

Not surprisingly, the "new policy" announcement of June, 1975 received a poor press, at home and abroad. "If good intentions moved freight and passengers Canada would have the finest transportation system in the world," editorialized *The Toronto Star* of June 18, 1975. "Considering past failures in the field, one might be thankful for the vagueness and the incompleteness of new policy statement. But that's less a virtue than a cause of apprehension about how the new transportation policy will ultimately affect Canada," said *The Ottawa Journal* on June 18, 1975. "Rubbish. Or, if you prefer, pretentious nonsense, warm air, a non-idea wrapped in verbal mush," said the same paper the next day. In U.K., *Railway Gazette International* (p. 246, July, 1975) listed most of the shortcomings of the "new policy" mentioned above under the heading "Marchand gives birth to a mouse."

Yet, as many commentators agreed, there has been one truly significant statement in the June, 1975 "new policy," a statement which does not bear on the transportation policy per se, but only on the relative roles of the government and regulatory bodies. Transportation, and particularly the railways, have traditionally been hot regional and partisan issues (as often evident in this study). The 1967 NTA attempted to remove transportation issues from the political arena. To this end, it gave the Canadian Transport Commission the task of "coordinating and harmonizing the operations of all carriers," and established the CTC as the principal source of transportation policy advice to the government. Thus policy-making became confused with the regulation and supervision of transportation, and, in the outcome, was abandoned. The CTC—"a court of record"—has limited its activities to interminable hearings, issuing of orders and dispensation of subsidies for uneconomic operations. The au-

" . . . and now, a favorite of mine called "The Government Has No Immediate Plans . . ."

The Vancouver Sun, April 1975

thors of the 1967 NTA apparently did not appreciate that policy-making is a dynamic function which cannot be fulfilled through legislation calling for grand national objectives (reminiscent of the current "new policy"), but failing to specify the means to attain them. It is no wonder that the CTC – a politically unaccountable body – has avoided "rocking the boat" and has been concerned with regulation rather than innovation and long-term planning.

These basic flaws of the 1967 legislation have been recognized by the "new policy," which promises to amend the NTA so that the responsibility for transportation policy advice to the government is transferred from CTC to the Minister of Transport; the latter is to have "a clear and public method of providing policy direction to the CTC."

While the proposed change is an obvious and sensible one, it would be presumptous to assume that it guarantees development of a truly viable, long-range transportation policy. There is a danger that it may only amount "to one of those structural principles that governments delight in changing in the apparent illusion that form is also content" (*The Ottawa Journal*, June 18, 1975). Moreover, experience shows that a skilled politician can work his way around any terms of reference, including those of the CTC: the 1967 NTA could have been more of an excuse than a cause for government's failure to develop a transportation policy.

This is a task which would require the government to change its role from that of a passive regulator and protector of the irrelevant past practices, to that of an innovator and long-term planner. Such change cannot occur without exercise of political leadership – a quality that has been sadly lacking on this Continent in recent years. Too often, the opinion-poll-minded political leaders seem not to educate but to mirror public opinion. As observed by an American writer, the image of the leader of the most powerful country in the world who decides to oppose a 20¢ tax increase on a gallon of gas because 81% of the people were against it, is highly disturbing – particularly at a time when drastic measures must be taken to assure desirable conditions ten or twenty years hence. It has been observed that in Canada, it is the people, not the leaders, who lead.

239

POSTSCRIPT: OBSTACLES TO MODERNIZATION

CHAPTER 24

THE INSTITUTIONALIZATION OF OBSOLESCENCE

The evidence reviewed in Parts Two and Three suggests that Canadian railways are – in many respects – obsolete and that this is mainly the result of traditional government railway policies and regulatory legislation. This is not an orthodox view: most often, the unsatisfactory state of railways in Canada – if at all admitted – is blamed on the superior economy and convenience of other transport modes, rather than on the socio-technological obsolescence of the existing system. Neither is this surprising: exposed to vigorous advertizing of support for research, development and the latest transportation techniques (e.g. a magnetic levitation urban transit system for Ontario, see p. 213; see also footnote, p. 151), the public is not inclined to think that the legislators and the governments may be impeding rather than stimulating technological progress. And yet this is precisely what has frequently occurred in the past, and what is also current with technologies other than railways. Several significant examples have been analyzed in detail by Morison (1966); some of his, as well as other cases, are mentioned here to put the current malaise of Canadian railways in broader perspective.

Not unexpectedly, Morison draws much of his material from the military, a rigidly institutionalized society which often delayed the process of modernization by failing to adopt new technology, and to adapt to it. In 1869, the U.S. Navy laid up *Wampanoag*, a new, highly superior steam-powered ship, because its construction did not conform to the generally accepted engineering practice of the day. No ship was built which could match *Wampanoag*'s performance for the next twenty years.

The adoption of the manifestly superior techniques of continuous aim firing by the U.S. Navy, first developed by the British, required personal intervention by President Theodore Roosevelt in 1902 (as a result of a lieutenant's letter), in defiance of the U.S. Navy brass.

During World War II, two different systems of protecting merchant shipping were being considered by the allies: the convoy, or passive system inherited from World War I, and the active system of search and attack, based on deployment of new technologies (long-range aircraft and radar) to seek and destroy the U-boats. The first system was under complete control of the Navy, the second would have to rely on the Army. After a protracted argument, the convoy system was retained: the traditional technology and tactics, which were familiar to the U.S. Navy, won the day.

Technological stagnation through institutionalization may have grave consequences. In the 1918-1940 period, the French general staff neglected the potential of airplane and tank, and adhered to the concept of the static, World War I vintage trench warfare – a military posture which was responsible for the construction of the Maginot Line and contributed significantly to the 1940 debacle in France. Typically, the French military establishment was not inclined to listen to de Gaulle's (1934) unorthodox ideas on the mobile war of the future.

The slow introduction of modern information handling methods into lending-library operations – which are admirably suited to computerization – is one of the current examples. Library clerks checking, stamping, filing and otherwise manipulating books and chits are still a familiar sight in many libraries. The continuing resistance of the labour unions to technological modernization, as in the construction industry or in railways, is another familiar case. The deterioration of mail services in North America (Life,1969) – in spite of phenomenal developments in transportation and communication technologies – is an instance of institutionalized obsolescence well-appreciated by the general public.

Like railways in North America, the fire department is a public service whose technology is archaic and outmoded. "Next time you happen upon the scene of a fire, fight the impulse to watch the flames. Instead, watch the fire department. What you will see is 19th century technology and techniques fighting an age old menace. Water remains the principal extinguishing agent; the fire department's job is to deliver the pumps, hoses, nozzles, and men needed to get the water onto the fire. Delivery by a truck powered by an internal combustion

The New York Times, 25 February 1974.

engine has replaced delivery by horse-drawn wagon: that is the only obvious change" (Frohman, 1973).

Not only the technique of fire-fighting, but even the design of fire stations has been thoroughly institutionalized (Campbell, 1974). In 1865, when the first paid Fire Department was established in New York City, a red-brick, three-story design for firehouses was adopted. These multi-story firehouses were not built to conserve land space, but because horses were housed on the lower floor, firemen on the second, and hay on the third. Until 1922 a fireman, like a lighthouse keeper, lived in his firehouse, serving around the clock. The houses contained most of the firemen's possessions and required large recreation and storage areas. To speed up the turnout in response to an alarm, a wooden pole was installed in one firehouse in 1873, making possible a rapid descent from the second floor. By 1883, the first brass pole was installed, and brass poles have been used ever since, until recently, when stainless-steel poles were installed in new firehouses.

At long last, it has been now recognized that multi-storied, pole-equipped firehouses are detrimental to the performance of firemen. In New York City, in the first five months of 1973, 22 firemen were hurt sliding down poles and 7 were injured on stairs. This resulted in 739 days lost from work. The fire department projected that 69 firemen would be injured in similar accidents for the whole year. In 1960 and 1962, two sleepy firemen were killed when they accidentally fell 15 to 20 feet through pole holes. It has been found that frequent alarms require excessive walking up high flights of stairs, cause fatigue and increase susceptibility to injury. Faced with such evidence, the Fire Department decided to build the first modern, one-story, poleless firehouse in New York City; construction is to start in 1976.

It is evident that even the most progressive and industrialized society may be expected to retard technological progress through institutional restraint, a social phenomenon which has its roots in man's need for identification with a group, his resistance to change and his desire for security. There exists, therefore, a degree of social inevitability of institutional obsolescence. While experience tells us to be on guard, the very nature of institutionalized obsolescence makes its recognition difficult and therefore corrective action is unlikely. From this perspective, the obsolescence of the North American railways, a technology dating back to the early nineteenth century, may well have been expected to develop.

*   *   *

Another factor which has contributed significantly to the obsolescence of railway technology in some countries concerns the peculiar market environment in which the railway industry has been operating. Unlike most sectors of modern industry, the manufacturers of railway equipment have been usually restricted – except for exports to the less developed countries – to the national, rather than international, markets. In fact, they have often been serving only one client – the nationalized railway system in their own country. This has been the case in Europe, where the nationalized railway systems traditionally rely on domestic suppliers and do not attempt to seek competition outside the national borders.

In North America a similar situation has developed in opposite circumstances. Unlike in Europe, there have been numerous clients – some seventy railroad companies – but, since the switch in 1950s from steam to the more sophisticated diesel-electric technology, only one, and later – only two suppliers*. Instead of the client-monopoly of Europe, the domestic-supplier monopoly has prevented international competition.

The mechanism of domestic monopoly – whether client or supplier oriented – has been effective in preventing transnational flow of railway technology and maintaining parochial character of railway industry. The technical progress in railways being remarkably uneven, a significant "railway gap" has developed between Western Europe and Japan on the one hand, the U.S. and Canada on the other. The constraint of national markets has been also detrimental in economic terms, particularly in Europe. It has been restricting suppliers to small volume production, preventing the clients from taking advantage of the "economies of scale," rendering international standardization of railway equipment more difficult and the whole process of technological modernization more expensive.

The client-supplier situation in the railway industry is thor-

---

*Until 1960, virtually all main-line diesel electric locomotives were supplied in North America by the General Motors Corp.; the General Electric Co. entered the field in 1960. In 1974, General Motors locomotives accounted for 65% of the U.S. locomotive fleet (I. Mech.E., 1975, pp. 73-84).

oughly institutionalized and therefore not easily reformed. Nevertheless, as the "railway gap" widens, one may expect the pressure of competition to augment and to encourage internationalization of railway technology. AMTRAK's purchase of French gas turbine trains and construction of this equipment in the U.S. under license (see p. 154) is a recent example of this trend in North America.

CHAPTER 25

THE INADEQUACY
OF TRADITIONAL POLITICS
AND JOURNALISM

As noted in the preceding chapter, the institutionalization of technological obsolescence is closely related to the political processes through which technology is regulated and controlled. It is becoming increasingly apparent that traditional ideological and partisan approach to the solution of complex problems of industrialized societies is ineffectual and inadequate.

Still today, parliament survives as an oral, rhetorical institution amidst our visual civilization. Hard data in the form of graphs and tables is not shown in the House, and not recorded in the Hansard.* The 1933 debates in the House of Commons on Canadian Pacific's proposal for unification of the two railway systems (Fournier, 1935) provide a good illustration of these aspects of the parliamentary procedure; two typical excerpts are included below. The arguments that were advanced against the principle of amalgamation were thus summarized by a member of the Conservative Party, then in control of the House:

"Mr. Beatty [Canadian Pacific's Chairman of the Board and President] in his representations to the Duff commission stated that a saving of $75,000,000 could be made by unification of the two systems, but . . . that saving of $75,000,000 was predicated on his suggestion that five thousand miles of railway in Canada be torn up. I do not think that the people of Canada, or even a small proportion of them, would stand for five thousand miles of our national lines being torn up and destroyed, no matter how badly off we were financially. . . . I do not think it necessary for me to submit to this house detailed reasons why the people of Canada pretty much as a unit object to amalgamation. In 1930 the present Prime Minister said: 'Amalgamation never; competition ever,' and I think that

---

* See Morrison and Brown (1974) for a more extensive discussion of this topic.

pretty well represents the feeling of the vast majority of taxpayers of Canada. I am satisfied that amalgamation, merger, unification or whatever you wish to call it is politically impossible in Canada. I am convinced it is impossible to sell or lease the national railways on satisfactory terms to the state. In my view it is questionable if any greater saving would be accomplished by amalgamation, and I do not believe consolidation or unification would relieve the state of any portion of its capital debt or of the present annual charges. I am convinced that consolidation into one system would result in a decline in the energy, initiative and enthusiasm of employees, the excellent morale at present existing among them having been developed by competition, competition alone will maintain it. Amalgamation would result in a monopoly of rail transportation which by virtue of that very fact would work to the disadvantage of business and of the public. People generally place a high value upon competitive railway service and would be reluctant to dispense with such competition. Moreover a monopoly would be placed in the hands of a very few, a tremendous power which might be unwisely exercised. I am convinced that amalgamation would result in an unwieldy system which could not be efficiently managed. Amalgamation must necessarily be permanent in effect. . . . It is not necessary to point out to the House the trouble there would be in unscrambling the two systems after their being under one control. I believe that amalgamation must necessarily be permanent in effect and does not envision a brighter future with more business and a greater population, and consequently better times for our railroads. For the reasons I have set out I submit that amalgamation or unification of the systems is not only undesirable but impossible." (Canada, 1933a)

The Liberal Party's view was stated by its leader as follows:

"I believe all honorable members on this side are at one with honorable gentlemen opposite in a desire to effect economies by avoiding wasteful competition, and are also desirous of furthering co-operation along right lines as much as possible. But we on this side have a very decided view on the question of amalgamation. We feel that the

247

National Railways should be maintained in
ity as a publicly-owned and publicly-controlled
d that no legislation should be permitted to
arliament at this time which will have the effect
g the integrity of the national system to be de-
its identity to be lost, or the system itself to be
amalgamated with the Canadian Pacific Railway." (Canada, 1933b)

The speeches quoted refer to personal convictions and beliefs, and contain sweeping statements with no attempt to substantiate them through specific comparisons, or to refute detailed estimates which were contained in the CP's proposal. It is apparent that, as pointed out by Fournier (1935), the speakers had not made more than a cursory study of the proposal they were opposing.

Occasionally, the debate in the House of Commons degenerates into buffoonery, as illustrated by the following report in *The Globe and Mail* of October 25, 1974.

Whatever the reasons, the Commons quite often has bad evenings and Wednesday evening of this week was a very, very bad one indeed. Opposition MPs were questioning Transport Minister Jean Marchand about his department's 1974-75 spending estimates – without much success. The Hansard makes unsettling reading.

The trouble began when Conservative Don Mazankowski (Vegreville) asked for an assurance that the low Crowsnest Pass freight rates (sacred to Western MPs) will be preserved.

Mr. Marchand: "The honorable member is not going to get an answer to that from me."

Some honorable members: "Oh, oh."

Eldon Woolliams (PC, Calgary North): "So that is your attitude to Western Canada."

Mr. Marchand: "What do you want me to say?"

Mr. Woolliams: "You know this is important to the economy of Western Canada. You were out in Calgary (at the 1973 Western Economic Opportunities Conference) and promised us so much."

Mr. Marchand: "I never promised anything."

Mr. Mazankowski: "It is a legitimate question that requires a legitimate answer."

Mr. Marchand: "Do you want to be serious?"

Mr. Mazankowski: "I am being serious."

Mr. Marchand: "You are not being serious . . . "

And so it went. At one point, Opposition Leader Robert Stanfield intervened to protest: "I am trying to control myself but it is pretty difficult. . . . I have been in legislatures for about 25 years and I have never seen a farce such as this."

The shortcomings of traditional parliamentary procedure have been recently criticized in Canada by John Reid, Parliamentary Secretary for the Privy Council. "The House of Commons operates in a way that would be appropriate if society were at the level it was in about 1900. . . . " stated Mr. Reid. "In many respects what makes the House of Commons impotent is nothing more nor less than those of us who make up its membership. We have been unwilling to give up the mythology about this place. . . . " The Commons wastes time on trivia and serious debates rather than monologues are almost impossible to find, said Mr. Reid. "The members don't speak of the contents of the bill under study." Speaking of the work of Commons committees, Mr. Reid observed that "MPs don't have enough information to deal with the witnesses. And the witnesses often say they are disappointed with the level of questioning." (Reid, 1975.)

Today, even more so than 50 or 100 years ago, the elected representatives are not capable of making technological decisions solely on the basis of a party platform or expedient politics – just as technologists must now also consider social and environmental impacts of their professional activities. The legislators and ministers need to obtain and understand expert, multi-valued assessment of a spectrum of alternatives in order to choose one from among the many – and even then their choice might be difficult, as in the recent (February, 1974) case of nuclear energy technology in Britain, when a parliamentary committee, exposed to a multitude of "amazingly contradictory" testimony, was too confused to firmly recommend a specific type of reactor.

The need for technical competence among politicians and civil servants was well-appreciated more than one hundred years ago by that farsighted Canadian engineer and social critic, T. C. Keefer, who made the following observations in a lecture delivered at McGill University in 1855:

The best antidote to this incompetency in politicians and their proteges, with respect to engineering subjects, is to supply each political party with a sufficient amount of engineering ability, so that when they have no higher motive than the credit of their party, they may at least have the means of making a good appointment; in short, to make some knowledge of engineering as essential to the embryo Commissioners of Public Works, Railway Commissioners, Canal Superintendents, &c., as is that of the law to the expectant Solicitor or Attorney General, County Judge, or Queen's Counsel. No man can be considered well-educated without some knowledge of Mathematics and Mechanics, although he may make a considerable figure in public life without them – and as a gentleman may study both without being necessarily a Newton or a Descartes, a Watt or an Arkwright, so a popular knowledge of Civil Engineering may be imparted without the necessity of making Smeatons, Telfords, Brunels, or Stephensons.

It is time, therefore, that Civil Engineering became a branch of popular education in our Seminaries of learning, and when this has borne its fruits we shall not feel the want of it in our Legislature as much as is now done. Had there been even a few Engineers in our Parliament (as is the case in the British) there might have been a little less of folly – and something more than folly – perpetrated there. It may be asked, why do not our Engineers go into Parliament? It is to be presumed that some of them could get there as well as Lawyers, Doctors, etc. Most M.P.P.'s are volunteers; few are dragged like Cincinnatus from retirement; and an Engineer has the same right, as he has the same opportunity, to canvass a constituency, make non-committal speeches, be obsequious to the father, flatter the mother, and kiss the child, as any other man. The probable reason is that, like many other respectable men who keep out of Parliament, they are now better employed; but make them by your colleges as numerous as Lawyers, Doctors, etc., and some of them will be driven there – by necessity. (Keefer, 1972, pp. 94-95)

Keefer's admonitions of 1855 have yet to be heeded. Still today, most Canadian and U.S. legislators are lawyers and businessmen, with no formal education or experience in the physical sciences and engineering. Current Canadian railway legislation has not benefited from well-informed, comprehensive technical and economic evaluation of railways and their operations, but has evolved through gradual revision of old statutes and orders.

Difficulties notwithstanding, the responsibility for making technological decisions on the basis of the best available information cannot be abrogated by legislators and governments, and required mechanisms and resources have to be provided. In Canada, the Lamontagne Special Senate Committee on Science Policy (Lamontagne, 1970, 1972, 1973) has examined these problems and recommended reforms which would facilitate their solution. In the U.S., the Office of Technology Assessment was created in 1973 to assist Congress in the evaluation of technological developments and their consequences. In 1974, a new rule was passed regarding the function of committees in the House. It requires, for the first time, that standing committees engage in "systematic, long-range and integrated study of our [U.S.] principal future national problems." A special staff of the Congressional Research Service will support this new function (Toffler, 1975). These can be viewed as the first significant steps that U.S. Congress has taken to improve its competence and effectiveness in dealing with the complexity of modern problems.

Just as the elected parliamentary bodies, the regulatory agencies are equally ineffectual: they rely largely on the procedures of "public hearings," which – while producing thousands of pages of testimony – contribute little information relevant to the evaluation and solution of problems at hand. In Canada, such hearings often seek the "local inspiration" or the views of an uninformed public which, for example, is necessarily unaware of the services which modern rail can provide. The situation has been aptly summarized by an American commentator who, even in the 1930's noted that "What we need is a new transportation system, not endless hearings on a system that doesn't work" (Mertins, 1972, p. 32).

Evidently, there is need for devising better mechanisms for regulation and development of transportation, and for providing competent advice to legislators, governments and bureaucrats. But what about the man in the street? How can he become better informed in order to exercise his franchise effectively for his and society's benefit? In this area, the responsibility must rest largely with all of the information media, which –

so far – have tended to neglect broader implications of technology (except when technology is seen as an evil influence), and have been only superficially reporting on "newsworthy" items.* There is no reason why the general public should not be given specific information, graphed or tabulated, in daily papers** and on TV screens – information of the kind presented in this study – instead of out-of-context, ad hoc opinions expressed by various individuals during brief interviews, data which usually cannot be meaningfully evaluated. Television – the most modern and powerful information medium – faithfully follows the traditional journalistic approach and makes a minimal use of the visual mode of hard information transfer. Clearly, the media will have to become more information-oriented to fulfill their unique role in a democratic, highly-industrialized society.

Summing-up: to manage a complex, technologically-based society, the public, the legislators and the government have to rely on comprehensive information rather than on a political platform, and need to operate within a system which allows such information to be used effectively.

---

* See Morrison (1973), for an extensive discussion of the technological illiteracy of the media. The need to have a well-informed public was recognized by T.C. Keefer (1972, pp. 4-5) and his famous essay of 1849 was a means to satisfy it. (cf. p. xi).

** Indeed, such presentation would render much of the editorial matter more readable. Today, only some of the more serious newspapers (e.g. *The New York Times*) occasionally graph, map and tabulate data.

MAPS:
RAILWAYS IN CANADA

The chronological railway Maps 1 to 5 show at a glance the location of the main lines, the year in which each was first opened to traffic, and the railway system under whose control it operated (not necessarily when first opened to traffic). Although this is the fundamental information indispensable to the understanding of Canadian railways, and although such information is presented most clearly and concisely as a map, it is not available in the literature. Therefore, Maps 1 to 5 had to be drawn on the basis of information scattered among many sources, often incomplete and inconsistent. While every effort was made to insure accuracy, nevertheless Maps 1 to 5 may contain small errors in the dates shown and thus should not be regarded as definitive chronologies of Canadian railways; rather, their purpose is to show the sequence of development of the main railway lines and their relative location, objectives which are not affected by small chronological inaccuracies. A full listing of sources for Maps 1 to 5 is given below, as well as explanatory notes.

The assistance of Helène Dechief, Librarian, and Christopher Andreae, Researcher, CN System Library, Montreal, in checking the chronological maps is gratefully acknowledged. Traffic density Maps 6 to 8 are based on the information kindly provided by G. T. Fisher (1973) of Canadian Pacific and J. Gratwick (1973) of Canadian National.

Chronological maps of Canadian railways (Maps 1 to 5): Sources of information (see References for bibliographical details): Bladen (1932, 1934), Bonar (1950), Canada (1932, 1973), Currie (1957), Dorman (1938), Fleming (1876), Glazebrook (1938), Hopper and Kearney (1962), Innis (1971), Legget (1973), McDougal (1968), Mika (1972), Skelton (1916), Stevens (1960, 1962, 1973), Thompson and Edgar (1933). Also: *CP Services* (map of CP transportation systems), 1971; *CN System Indexed Map*, 1974; *Railroad Map of Eastern Canada*, and *Railroad Map of Western Canada and Alaska*, Canadian Freight Association.

Explanatory Notes

Maps 1, 2 and 3: Numbers indicate years when the lines were first opened to traffic. 18 omitted before numbers from 50 to 99; 19 omitted before numbers from 00 to 25. Some of the lines shown have been abandoned. When first opened, many of the lines shown did not form part of the major systems indicated.

Map 2: Opening dates of bridges and tunnels, the Great Lakes system: 1855-bridge across Niagara River Gorge, Niagara Falls, Ont. (formerly Elgin), to Niagara Falls, N.Y. (formerly Suspension Bridge and Manchester); 1859-Victoria Bridge, Montreal; 1873 - International Bridge, Fort Erie - Buffalo; 1890 - St. Clair tunnel, Sarnia - Port Huron; 1910 - Detroit River Tunnel, Windsor-Detroit; 1917 – Quebec Bridge, Quebec City – Lévis; 1918 - Mount Royal Tunnel, Montreal.

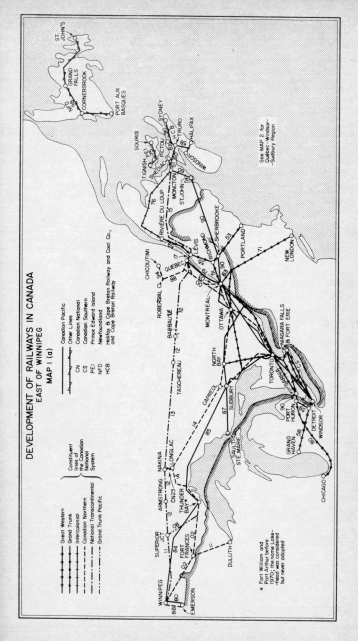

DEVELOPMENT OF RAILWAYS IN CANADA
EAST OF WINNIPEG
MAP I (a)

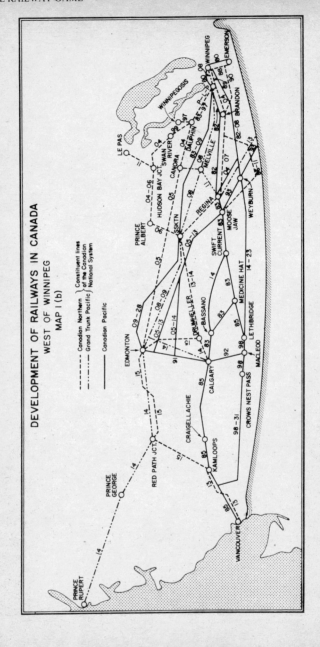

DEVELOPMENT OF RAILWAYS IN CANADA
WEST OF WINNIPEG
MAP I (b)

Canadian Northern } Constituent lines
Grand Trunk Pacific } of the Canadian
National System
Canadian Pacific

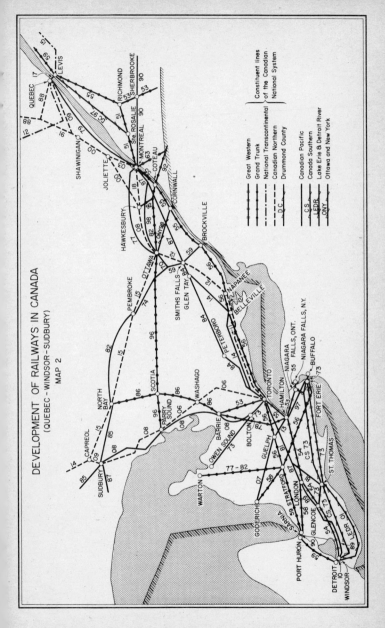

DEVELOPMENT OF RAILWAYS IN CANADA
(QUEBEC - WINDSOR - SUDBURY)
MAP 2

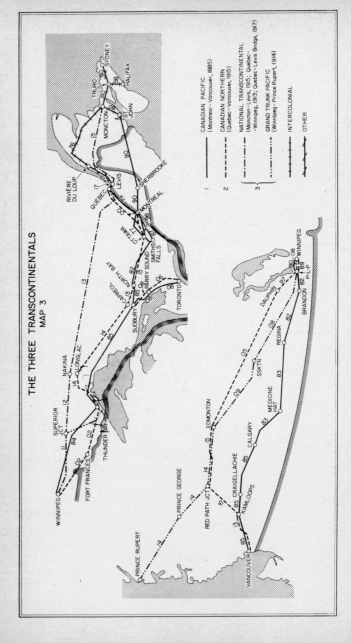

THE THREE TRANSCONTINENTALS
MAP 3

1 —————— CANADIAN PACIFIC
(Montreal – Vancouver, 1885)

2 – – – – – CANADIAN NORTHERN
(Quebec – Vancouver, 1915)

3 NATIONAL TRANSCONTINENTAL
(Moncton – Levis, 1915; Quebec –
Winnipeg, 1913; Quebec – Levis Bridge, 1917)
GRAND TRUNK PACIFIC
(Winnipeg – Prince Rupert, 1914)

INTERCOLONIAL

OTHER

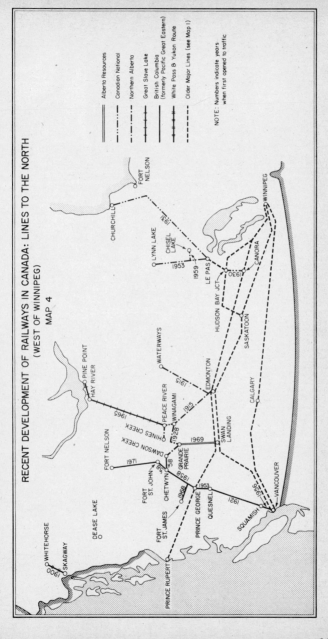

RECENT DEVELOPMENT OF RAILWAYS IN CANADA: LINES TO THE NORTH
(WEST OF WINNIPEG)
MAP 4

Alberta Resources
Canadian National
Northern Alberta
Great Slave Lake
British Columbia (formerly Pacific Great Eastern)
White Pass & Yukon Route
Older Major Lines (see Map 1)

NOTE: Numbers indicate years when first opened to traffic

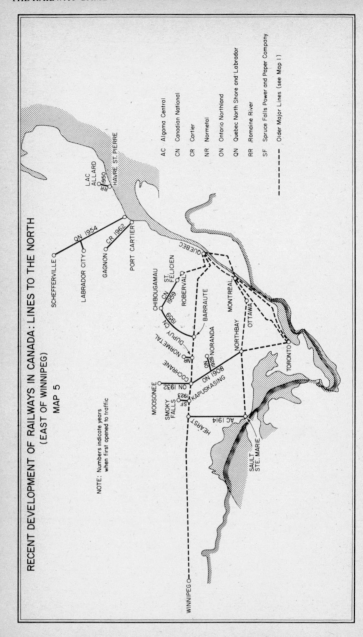

RECENT DEVELOPMENT OF RAILWAYS IN CANADA: LINES TO THE NORTH
(EAST OF WINNIPEG)
MAP 5

NOTE: Numbers indicate years
when first opened to traffic

AC   Algoma Central
CN   Canadian National
CR   Cartier
NR   Normetal
ON   Ontario Northland
QN   Quebec North Shore and Labrador
RR   Romaine River
SF   Spruce Falls Power and Paper Company
---- Older Major Lines (see Map 1)

SCHEFFERVILLE
LABRADOR CITY
QN 1954
GAGNON
CR 1962
PORT CARTIER
LAC ALLARD
RR 1960
HAVRE ST. PIERRE
CHIBOUGAMAU
QN 1959
ST. FELICIEN
ROBERVAL
QN 1959
BARRAUTE
DUPUY
CN NORMETAL
NR NORMETAL
NORANDA
ON 1928
COCHRANE
ON 1908
QUEBEC
MONTREAL
OTTAWA
NORTHBAY
TORONTO
MOOSONEE
ON 1932
SMOKY FALLS
SF 1923
KAPUSKASING
HEARST
AC 1914
SAULT STE. MARIE
WINNIPEG

260

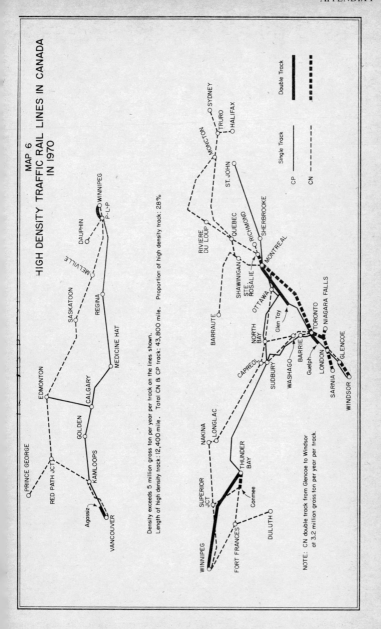

MAP 6

HIGH DENSITY TRAFFIC RAIL LINES IN CANADA
IN 1970

Density exceeds 5 million gross ton per year per track on the lines shown.
Length of high density track: 12,400 mile.   Total CN & CP track: 43,800 mile.   Proportion of high density track: 28%

NOTE: CN double track from Glencoe to Windsor
at 3.2 million gross ton per year per track.

Single Track   Double Track

CP ——————   ████████████

CN - - - - - - - -   ▪ ▪ ▪ ▪ ▪ ▪ ▪

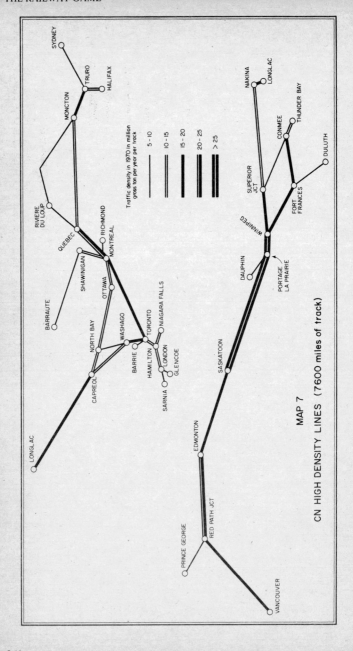

MAP 7

CN HIGH DENSITY LINES (7600 miles of track)

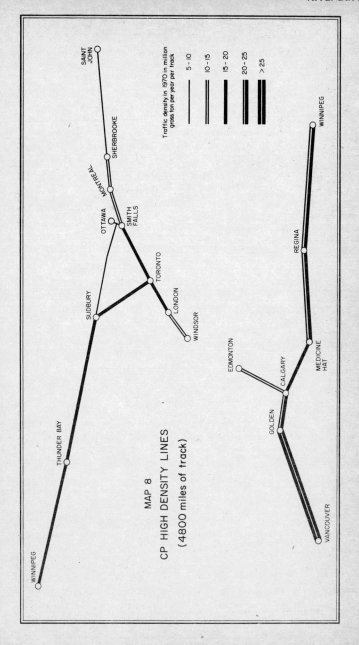

MAP 8

CP HIGH DENSITY LINES
(4800 miles of track)

Traffic density in 1970 in million
gross ton per year per track

5 - 10
10 - 15
15 - 20
20 - 25
> 25

SAINT JOHN
SHERBROOKE
MONTREAL
OTTAWA
SMITH FALLS
TORONTO
LONDON
WINDSOR
SUDBURY
THUNDER BAY
WINNIPEG
WINNIPEG
REGINA
MEDICINE HAT
EDMONTON
CALGARY
GOLDEN
VANCOUVER

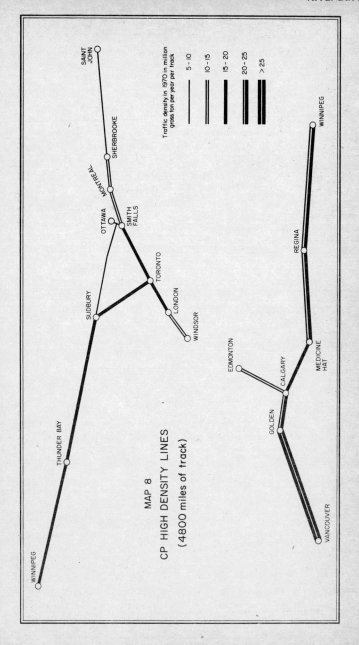

TRAVELLING
BY RAILWAY

On The Canadian National

*Westbound CN passengers
advised to bring own food*

By SUE McNICOLL
Journal Reporter

There is a rumor going around that the Canadian National Railway is trying to discourage passenger service on its trains.

I recently learned the hard way that it's true.

And I wasn't the only one. Passenger comments of "never again" and "I've learned my lesson" were overheard while alighting from the train in Edmonton after a recent trip from Ottawa.

There has always been a certain aura of romanticism about the idea of long-distance train travel. But the old days are over and the lamentable fact, I found, is that CN would rather deal in cargo than people.

The strongest word of advice I can give to anyone taking the train out west is to take as much of your own food as possible. Train prices were atrocious.

The last time I travelled out west, in 1968, food was included in the cost of the ticket – but no more.

After paying $2.50 for juice, one egg, three fatty pieces of bacon and tea the first morning I should have realized what it was going to be like. But I didn't and went back for lunch. I paid $5.50 for a steak and kidney pie and a soft drink.

Food complaints

At least it was edible. Many travellers, though, complained about the quality of the food.

Service in both the canteen and dining car was terrible although there did not appear to be a lack of staff or an overflow of customers. Twice my bills were added incorrectly.

A friend and I took Dayniter accommodations from Edmon-

A unique travel idea for people who don't give a hoot about the rat race.

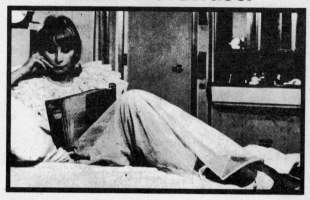

CN train travel.

It's the way where everything is leisurely, relaxed and just that much nicer.

Travel on our Super Continental from Vancouver to Toronto or Montreal. Or on our trains between Montreal, the Gaspé, Sydney and Halifax.

There's all that roomy comfort. And big picture windows for viewing one of the most beautiful sights in the world. The Canadian countryside.

There's the friendly atmosphere. CN's good food, good service. And a variety of accommodations, including economical coaches and Dayniters, in addition to berths, roomettes and bedrooms.

Of course, CN offers a range of fare plans so everyone can get the best possible value for his travel dollar. There are Red, White & Blue fares, as well as Family, 65-Plus, Youth and Group discounts.

This time, take it nice and easy and relaxed. Take the train.

For more information, contact your Travel Agent or CN Passenger Sales Office.

CN Advertisement, October 1974

265

ton to Vancouver for $35 return and found the food was infinitely better – we took our own.

Dayniter accommodation is slightly more comfortable than coach. Seats recline and there is a leg rest and a fair amount of room. However, your body must still get used to sleeping in strange positions. It took about 26 hours to travel from Edmonton to Vancouver.

We met two young men going from Vancouver to Montreal in the Dayniter car. This I would recommend for only the hardy – 24 hours is about the limit.

On our trip to Vancouver the toilet in our carriage broke down, along with the air conditioning.

Facilities broke down

On the return trip to Ottawa from Edmonton all the pipes in our washroom quit functioning and the air conditioning in my sleeping car also stopped working. The temperature climbed to 32 degrees C.

We were without water and fresh air for almost 24 hours. Most of us escaped to other cars for breathers although the train was full at the time and we could not be moved on a permanent basis.

We finally arrived at a station where something could be done to rectify the problem. It was here that they discovered there was actually nothing wrong with the air conditioning but that some joker had turned our air conditioning off and our heat on.

No apologies were offered although one porter suggested we write to CN about our problems.

Which brings me to the porters. Very friendly. For women travelling alone I honestly have to say too friendly. I was not the only woman to experience problems – a mother with two children was also propositioned. Many of them though were genuinely helpful.

A CN ticket from Ottawa to Edmonton with upper bunk accommodation was $197 return. Add to that the cost of food on the train and the total is close to a return air fare between the two cities. (The same accommodation on a CP Rail train was about $35 more.).

Anyone wanting to check luggage to his destination should be sure to arrive at the station at least a half hour before departure time. I arrived 25 minutes before departure and was told it was too late to check my suitcase. It was a bother to have to keep it with me for the three-night, two-day trip.

There were, however, some positive aspects to the trip.

First, the four different trains I took all arrived on time.

Secondly, it did provide an alternative form of travel for myself, and others like me, who do not relish flying.

Lastly – my main enjoyment generally from train travel – were the people I met. As one traveller said, you get to know your fellow travellers better than on a plane where you might only see them for a couple of hours.

One conductor I spoke to said CN is trying to discourage train travel and all those working on the trains know it. He convinced me.

Next time I travel a long distance I may, just may, overcome my fear of planes.

The Ottawa Journal, 14 June 1975

Aussie's luxury train
travel in Canada turns out
to be a nightmare

The following is a letter to the editor of The Globe and Mail.

For many years, my ambition had been to view the Rocky Mountains and to travel in the CNR Super Continental (Right Track, Wrong Train – June 20). This ambition was fulfilled after my wife and I reached Vancouver in S.S. Oronsay from Sydney, Australia, on June 17. We had bookings for CNR from Vancouver to Winnipeg June 18; and for Air Canada Winnipeg-Toronto-New York June 20. My appetite for the Canadian train had been whetted by a CNR folder showing wonderful "vista dome" carriages on the train and stating "Travelling is fun . . . comfort . . . relaxation," etc.

My tickets were for first-class travel and a double bedroom in the train, Train 2, Car 252, Room (A) – $219.70 for two of us. Air, Winnipeg to New York – $292.65, for two. Both tickets covered meals en route, but obviously there were more meals during the train journey and these proved to be excellent. The map of North America shows Winnipeg to be about mid-point between Vancouver and New York, so that the rail fare seems relatively reasonable.

I was handed your newspaper on the Air Canada aircraft upon joining it at Winnipeg, and a portion of the leading article, which I quote, hit home hard in view of my own experience of the so-called "Super" train.

"The railways . . . have made what service remains as inconvenient and uncomfortable as possible; they have made it inordinately expensive . . ."

My wife and I had the following experiences on the CNR train:

(1) There were *no* vista-dome cars on the train. On inquiry, we were told they were being refurbished and would be in service on June 24.

(2) The bedroom allotted us ("A" in Car 252) was in an antiquated carriage which I would estimate to be due for a "vintage" classification. The antique metal washbasin and toilet were of a type in use on Australian trains 40 years ago.

(3) I was informed that there were no showers on the train. This is incredible, on a journey across the entire width of a continent. Even on the one-night trip from Sydney to Melbourne, Australia, the Southern Aurora express has showers in first-class compartments.

(4) The "iced"-water faucet (so labelled) in our bedroom ran warmish water for a short time, then rusty drips only.

(5) The antique toilet ceased to flush after the first two hours, although a strong stream of mist-laden air, at pressure, issued from the water flush outlet.

(6) All water in the bedroom ceased by 10 p.m. on June 18. (Next morning we were told it was leaking out the bottom of the car.)

(7) The car porter supplied us (on request) with a pail of water (Jack and Jill style) for washing and toilet-flushing; and, on further request, with a paper cup of water for my wife to take essential heart tablets. This water was obtained from another car on the train.

(8) It was a heat-wave period; 90 degrees was forecast for Kamloops that afternoon, for example. The car was sealed off from fresh air. The air-conditioning appeared ineffective, and the car became unbearably stuffy by about 10 p.m. My wife and I lay on top of our bunks and both were affected by stinging eyes and sneezing, with nasal congestion. The only relief was to walk into another car and stand for a while.

(9) We were transferred into a more modern car after we left

Edmonton, and the conductor advised us that the broken-down car's water and air-conditioning could not be repaired en route.

In short, I must say I wholeheartedly concur with the comments in your editorial. I feel I was sold a pup in believing the advertising material regarding "luxury train travel" in Canada. If I knew how to obtain reimbursement of fare in compensation for a nightmare trip, I would act in that way.

But at least the mountains were kind, in that they were clear and wonderful to view; the scenery lived up to all our expectations. I would suggest CNR send responsible officials to Australia to see how our modern trans-continental Indian-Pacific Sydney-Perth express operates, or our Sydney-Melbourne Southern Aurora. AND they'll be able to have a shower!

Oh, yes the CNR train was 1½ hours late at Winnipeg, and we almost missed our connection to the Air Canada flights (for which airline I give full marks).

Roland H. Sheldon
Beecroft, N.S.W.
Australia

The Globe and Mail, July 4, 1974

Tale of a rail

"Any travel agency," said the snarly CNR voice at the other end of the telephone, even before the question could be finished. The question was whether a train ticket to Montreal early next morning could be purchased downtown at a civilized time that afternoon. This person had an aversion to lining up for anything before 7.30 a.m.

Any travel agency soon boiled itself down to one particular agency, where the caller was told the tickets were indeed sold. Well, drat the luck! By the time the hopeful traveller arrived, it turned out the one person in the office who knows how to sell a train ticket to Montreal had gone away on holidays.

The bus ride to Montreal was just fine.

Returning the following night, the tourist did the natural thing – took the train that so conveniently departed from next door to the hotel. Sure, it was the "milk run" that stopped what seemed like 15 times, but it didn't seem to add more than 20 minutes to the journey.

That, after all, was less than the additional 25 minutes it took to get a taxi at the Ottawa Station. This traveller had committed the error of living too close to the station, something that makes one's bargaining power practically nil in a seller's taxi market. A man with the misfortune to live in Sandy Hill was last seen standing alone on the curb. He may still be there.

Some railway officials argue that inter-city trains are really not feasible between cities as far apart as Toronto and Montreal. The Ottawa-Montreal distance, we are told, is where trains are best suited to compete with other forms of transportation.

It must be the people who decide how to run them who aren't suited to it.

The Ottawa Journal, May 25, 1974

Shocking service by CN
in Northern Ontario

Train travel left a lot to be desired for passenger who called it disgraceful.

The following is a letter to the editor of the Globe and Mail.

This past August while travelling in Northern Ontario I had occasion to use what must be the poorest railway service anywhere in North America. I refer to Canadian National Railways' mixed train between Hearst and Nakina. The so-called service is a disgrace to CN and to Canada.

The published timetable bears no relation at all to fact. The train supposedly leaves Hearst three times a week at 9 a.m. and arrives at Nakina at 3.30 p.m. On the day I travelled the latter was our *departure* time; we arrived at the destination a mere seven hours and 50 minutes late! The brakeman told me that, in his 23 years of duty, it has never been less than three hours late, and on one occasion was 30 hours behind schedule. The time table allowed us eight hours to make a leisurely connection at Nakina for the Super Continental to Toronto, but the crewmen considered us lucky to have a bare half-hour.

My most serious quarrel, however, is not with the timetable, it is with the revolting condition of the coach, a monstrosity built in 1911 and hardly cleaned since. We were greeted on boarding by a shower of foul-smelling water from above. It seems the tank has been leaking for two years and has not been repaired. It was soon remedied by an employee who drained the water, and thus we enjoyed the novelty of flush toilets modified to use the gravity principle. One can well imagine the state of the toilet. A yellowing poster informed me that the Railway Act prohibited spitting and gambling, but did not mention the railways' obligation to provide adequate service. The unscheduled shower had soaked the toilet paper, there were no paper towels and of course no soap. Mercifully, CN had removed the light bulb, thus sparing passengers the nauseating sight when daylight failed.

The rest of the coach also reflected the long years of neglect of even the simplest maintenance – floors unwashed, windows caked in filth, light fixtures filled with insect corpses, window panes missing in places, seats streaked with dirt and grime. And when nightfall came and still we were jostled and jolted along the ill-repaired track, four miserable yellow bulbs began to emit a faint glow that became dimmer still when the train slowed, and failed entirely when the brakeman turned on the lights in the baggage section.

I would be far less critical of these conditions if they were the standard throughout Canada, to be borne by all. However, it is obvious to me that this unacceptable service is allowed to continue only on a route that is patronized largely by the most downtrodden and unfortunate Canadians, our native people. Since the Indian people of the area have little alternative, and since their voice is heard by so few, they must put up with facilities that would be unthinkable anywhere else in this country. That CN uses 60-year-old equipment, undoubtedly long since written off by its accountants, with even the most minimal of maintenance neglected, on a service heavily subsidized by public funds and in an area served by few other forms of transportation, is a shocking breach of its obligations to provide a decent standard of service.

Oscar Mullerbeck
Don Mills

(*The Globe and Mail*, 11 September 1974)

On the Canadian Pacific

60 passengers travel
Buffalo-Toronto run
in train's baggage car

A Sarnia man says he and almost 60 other people travelled in a baggage car Sunday night on a CP Rail train from Buffalo to Toronto.

Carl Grant was returning from New York City, but says when he switched trains at Buffalo he was told a passenger car had broken down and he would have to stand or ride in the baggage car.

Mr. Grant says he counted 43 people in the baggage car when it left Buffalo. By the time it reached Toronto, about two hours later, the number was closer to 60.

"The car was filthy, absolutely filthy," he said yesterday, still angry over the incident.

"Some passengers looked like they had been through a war; others looked like tramps before they had completed their journey."

Mr. Grant says there were no windows in the car so the side door was kept wide open to keep the temperature down. The car had not been wiped clean, but five benches, which weren't fastened to the floor, were provided for passengers. Other people stood or sat on the floor, he said.

"If they had ever had an accident a lot of people would have been hurt pretty badly," he said.

"If they were thinking at all they would have chartered some buses when they realized they were going to be overloaded."

Another passenger, Harry Price, 70 said he and his wife travelled in the baggage car as far as their home at Hamilton. Two weeks ago on a trip to Buffalo, he had to sit in a baggage car for one hour when the train was overloaded, he said.

The two-car CP Rail train runs once daily at 5:30 p.m. from Buffalo and normally seats 118 passengers.

Allan Hill, general manager of operations and maintenance for CP Rail, said the problem was partly due to the Toronto Transit Commission strike which curtailed bus service between Buffalo and Toronto. Greyhound buses from Buffalo are driven by Gray Coach drivers, who are on strike.

Mr. Hill said the baggage car had to be used when one of the passenger cars broke down and couldn't be repaired in time for Sunday's run.

He said CP has tried to get extra cars from Montreal, but has obtained only one because the subway strike there has increased the demand for CP's commuter service.

E. C. Johnston, superintendent of passenger services for CP, said the company didn't like to put people in the baggage cars but couldn't turn them away if it was the only means of travel available to them.

"We put the baggage car on Sunday night, not so much for the passengers, but because at least two cars are needed to operate the signals along the track." Mr. Johnson said he hadn't looked into the idea of chartering buses instead for the extra passengers. He said there was almost no way of knowing in advance how many people would be travelling a particular route any one day.

"What's it going to be like if this happens next week when it's a holiday?" Mr. Grant asked.

(*The Globe and Mail*, 27 August, 1974)

On AMTRAK (USA)

As noted in some detail in Chapter 15, AMTRAK has been making significant progress in improving standards of service and modernizing train equipment. The reports reproduced below indicate that this hasn't been an easy task (J.L.).

"In Los Angeles . . . I went to the downtown Santa Fe ticket office to pick up a reservation which had been made for me on the City of San Francisco Amtrak service east to Iowa. The clerk couldn't have been more helpful in phoning around for details. But when he got it sorted out, it still took him 20 minutes to type up an accordion of ticket stubs involving a Pullman roomette and Amtrak conveyance east via Southern Pacific, Union Pacific and the Burlington. In Europe you buy one little piece of paper for a trip from Paris to Istanbul across seven countries – two of them Communist. Your ticket is then duly inspected, punched and returned to you all along the way."

– Reporter Don Cook, *Los Angeles Times*, February 22, 1972 (Southerland and McCleery, 1973, p. 47).

C-Plus for
13 Hours
On Amtrak
By Tom Wicker

It is a sound if sometimes trying rule for newspaper evangelists to practice what they preach. Therefore, as one who frequently urges the revival of train travel, on Jan. 27 I boarded Amtrak's Silver Star at Hamlet, N.C., for a return trip to New York City. Here is a report on this pioneering experience:

Ticketing and reservations: Lousy. In New York, at least, Amtrak's lines seem perpetually busy, and when a caller finally gets through, it is usually to a recording that urges patience and fortitude. Then, in the case under study, the call was disconnected anyway. Several other tries finally produced a live ticket agent at the other end of the line, together with adequate schedule information and a reservation. Tickets were supposed to be billed to a credit card and mailed, under an "urgent" designation. Four days later, no tickets having arrived, another call elicited the information that the tickets would have to be picked up. Ultimately, they were. Right after that, a duplicate set arrived in the mail.

Stations: Interesting. The magnificent old mansard-roofed station at Hamlet, a relic out of my boyhood, is a far cry from the beehive of activity it used to be. It's still adequate for the purpose and a new coat of paint is making it more presentable; as at many other Amtrak stops, the past is being rather nicely preserved for present uses. Station personnel were courteous and helpful but there were no auxiliary services – food, newspapers, bookstands – available early on a Sunday morning. Penn Station in New York, recently rebuilt, rivals most airports in convenience, except for its sketchy information services.

On-time Performance: Not bad. The Silver Star (Train No. 82) rolled into Hamlet almost precisely on time at 7:35 A.M., which spoke well for a long overnight journey that had started in Miami at 3 P.M. the day before. But the train stayed in Hamlet for a half-hour, ran consistently about twenty minutes behind schedule on the rest of the trip north, sat in Washington's Union Station for an hour, and finally pulled into Penn Station at 8:25 P.M., fifteen minutes late. On many an air trip I've done worse, and at least there was no circling about in one of those endless and sometimes scary "holding patterns."

Equipment: Mediocre. The cars seemed relatively modern but carpeting and upholstery were worn and dingy. The club car was overheated. So was Bedroom D, Car 8230, which offered no way to turn down the heat. This bedroom was not very different from those familiar to travelers during World War II and before; with its own bathroom, its privacy and a small work table set up by an obliging porter, it nevertheless provided reasonably comfortable travel circumstances – decidedly superior to the middle seat in the airlines' coach class. Also available were roomettes, something borrowed from the Northern Pacific called a Slumbercoach, and what appeared to be modern reclining-seat day coaches. The latter were well filled.

Food: Good. To judge from an excellent breakfast, this may be one service in which Amtrak, with its old-fashioned dining cars, can surpass the airlines. There were two dining cars on the Silver Star, complimentary orange juice and morning coffee in the sleeping car lounge, complimentary champagne cocktails in the afternoon, bar service all day, and sandwiches were advertised as available all night.

Service: Excellent. Waiters and porters were courteous, friendly and willing. So were the conductor and the dining car steward. Passenger service agents were available and conducting games and entertainment in the lounge cars for those who wanted to participate. An "early bird dinner" was advertised for those who wanted to eat between four and six P.M., and pillows were provided to coach passengers. The Silver Star did not have a movie, but its companion – and somewhat more luxurious – train on the New York-to-Florida run, the Silver Meteor, offers a feature film as well as something called "mini-flicks."

Roadbed: Varied. Riding comfort and quiet suggested that the roadbed was mostly excellent between Hamlet and Washington; some substantial speeds were obtained on the longer runs, without sacrifice of comfort. From Washington to New York, as Metroliner passengers know, and particularly between Washington and Baltimore, it's best to stay seated and hang on to something when you get up.

Scenery: Different. There was nothing like the magnificence of some airline vistas, of course. Still, taking the train is a good way to see the American countryside close-up; the tracks are a lot closer to woods, fields, streams and the main streets of small towns than are the interstate highways.

Over-all: C-plus. The trip consumed thirteen daytime hours, the last two or three of which seemed interminable. Had it been an overnight journey, however, it wouldn't have seemed so long; and on a trip of up to five or six hours, even the equipment now available can get you there comfortably, pleasantly and more or less on time. Given a few more years and resources, the evidence of Train No. 82 is that Amtrak ought to be able to do considerably better than that.

The New York Times, 29 January, 1974.

Amtrak Story

To the Editor:

A footnote to Tom Wicker's Jan. 29 column on Amtrak:

After three days of busy signals from the Amtrak phone, I reached a clerk at 11:15 P.M. Feb. 13.

Me: Is there a train to Philadelphia about 5 P.M. Saturday?

He: (after a long pause) Yes.

Me: At 5 exactly?

He: Yes.

Me: What time does it arrive?

He: 5:30.

Me: That's impossible.

He: What do you mean by that?

Me: You can't get there from here in half an hour.

He: (in an irritated tone) 6:30.

Me: Does it also stop in North Philadelphia?

He: Yes.

Me: What time?

He: 6:30

Me: Huh?

He: Ten minutes later.

Me: Huh?

He: That's a Penn Central train. You have to call them.

Me: Which is a Penn Central train?

He: The 5 o'clock.

Me: But you told me about your train that stops in Philadelphia.

He: Yes.

Me: You mean there are two different trains at 5 o'clock?

He: Within a couple a minutes.

Me: Can we start over again?

He: You have to call Penn Central.

I called Penn Central today to be told to call Amtrak. The line is still busy.

Natalie Jaffe
New York, Feb. 14, 1974

The New York Times, 25 February, 1974.

On SNCF (France)

Luxurious Dining
On Paris to Lyon Express

By CRAIG CLAIBORNE
Special to The New York Times

PARIS—Until we took the train from Paris to Lyon a few months ago, we had forgotten that dining on a train can be pleasure enough to be an end in itself. Our greatest frames of reference had previously been a cafeteria-type disaster on an Amtrak train between Boston and New York; a ham and cheese special between New York and Philadelphia, and a bag of peanuts en route from Jamaica to East Hampton.

On the Paris-Lyon express we found ourselves speeding along at 100 and more kilometers per hour in immaculate, bright and airy surroundings that were, to quote ourselves, an invitation to the senses.

The table was done up in dazzling napery, the silver was polished and the menu light-years removed from anything we had ever encountered. It included a first course of soupe des pecheurs (fish soup) or quenelles de brochet Dieppoise (poached forcemeat of fish with a white wine and seafood sauce). We chose the soup and found it uncommonly good, although a trifle salty.

We noted that had we been served the same soup on an American train, we would have become positively gluttonous and sent our compliments to the chef. Instead the waiter offered us the quenelles, which were excellent. We proceeded then to roast guinea hen (there had been a choice of the guinea hen or beef and lamb kidney en brochette), admirably cooked, and a fantastic Brazilian bombe with candy coffee beans and whipped cream.

On this present trip we found an occasion to take Le Mistral, which travels to the south of France. We boarded it in Paris at 1:40 P.M., a decent hour to begin a meal for a four-hour ride to Lyon. It is possible on the TEE, or Trans-European-Express, to reserve a seat in the dining car from which you need not move during the course of the trip. After a meal the dinner accoutrements are simply removed and you are left to dawdle over coffee and Cognac or whatever other amusements you may have at hand.

The setting was comfortably familiar. The same comparable starched white linen, polished silver and crystal. And a menu to appeal to the senses. To one American it was impressive in its imagination. As a first course there was a choice of sweetbreads Dijonnaise in a puff pastry shell or snails en brochette. As a main course there was a choice of stuffed chicken or braised beef with a red wine sauce. There was salad, cheese and a choice of sherbet or fresh strawberries in red wine.

The meal which we shared began auspiciously with the sweetbread course. Cubes of the braised delicacy were in a light, well-seasoned sauce along with sliced mushrooms and pieces of well-cooked salt pork. The snails were large and tender and served with a smooth, professionally made velouté of chicken.

The chicken was very well roasted and served with a flavorful pâté-like ground pork filling. The steak – coeur du Charolais – was rare, but we had the assurance of one of our dinner companions that while it was quite tender and edible, the flavor, even with a Burgundy wine sauce, was on the bland side. The salad was simple, the cheese well varied and at the proper stage of ripeness. The strawberries were a bit overripe, but the sherbet, made with Cassis, the dark currant cordial of Dijon, was brought nearer perfection with spoonfuls of sweetened raspberries.

Negative notes: The coffee was equally as weak as you would find on American trains . . . and a half bottle of Beaujolais tasted just a bit of the cork, although a second was in sound and admirable condition.

Our first-class ticket from Paris to Lyon cost about $23. The cost of the reserved seat in the dining car cost about $5. The cost of the meal was about $7.60. Half bottles of white Burgundy cost about $2; red Beaujolais, $2.60.

In France we applied for our tickets at the French Government Tourist office. They may also be purchased at train stations, and it is best to reserve in advance.

The New York Times, June 27, 1974

Travelling nightclub

Canadian tourists coming to France take note: the French railroad has hitched a nightclub to overnight trains between Paris and the sunny Riviera.

The bar-dancing car is attached to a new cinema coach at weekends on the overnight Paris-Nice run until September.

The Ottawa Journal, 16 July 1975.

GLOSSARY OF
RAILWAY TERMS
AND ABBREVIATIONS

Categories of railway tracks and track length measures:

Line, or *route*, or *first main track* length: length of single track extending the entire distance between terminals; length of the railroad.

Second main track: the second track running parallel to the first main track on the same road bed.

Other main track includes 3rd, 4th, etc. tracks, where more than two tracks are laid on the same road bed.

Main running track, or *running track* length includes length of all tracks used for working trains between terminals (the sum of the three categories listed above).

Other tracks include all tracks branching off from main running tracks at stations; tracks in marshalling yards; cross-over switch tracks; industrial tracks; tracks inside buildings.

Transportation output:

Ton-miles: a measure of transportation output, the product of distance (in miles) over which a weight (in tons) has been moved.

Gross tons, and *gross ton-miles* include the weight of railway cars and of the payload (freight and/or passengers)

Net tons, and *net ton-miles*, or *freight ton-miles* include only the weight of the freight payload.

Passenger-miles equal the product of the number of passengers times the distance (in miles) over which they have been moved.

Traffic density (gross or net) equals *ton-miles* (gross or net) per year divided into the length (route miles or track miles) of the corresponding lines or tracks.

Units of traffic are defined as the sum of *net ton-miles* (*freight ton-miles*) and *passenger-miles*.

Operating ratio is defined as the ratio of *operating expenditures* to *revenues*; the smaller the *operating ratio*, the more profitable a railway (other things being equal).

Railway operations:

ATC — automatic train control

ATO — automatic train operations

CL — carload

COFC — container on flat car

CTC — centralized traffic control

LCL — less than carload

TOFC — trailer on flat car

piggy-back — TOFC system (transportation by rail of trailers which are moved on highways by truck tractors)

containerization — handling of freight (within a continent, or in transoceanic shipments) in standard size containers (e.g. 20 x 8 x 8.5 ft, or 40 x 8 x 8.5 ft)

unit train — train which carries a large quantity of one cargo (e.g. coal) from one origin to a single, final destination

line-haul — (short-haul, long-haul) – movement of trains between terminals (stations) on the main or branch lines of the railway, exclusive of switching operations

intermodal — between different transportation modes, e.g. intermodal competition as between railways and trucks

intramodal — within a transportation mode, e.g. intramodal competition as between CN rail and CP rail

rationalization — reorganization of railway operations aimed at elimination of duplication of railway lines and services, integration of facilities and operations, and maintenance of only those services which are truly competitive vis-á-vis the other modes.

Other terms:

STOL — short take off and landing (aircraft or type of air transportation)

maglev — magnetic levitation: system of transportation which uses electro-magnetically suspended vehicles

281

TACV   – tracked air cushion vehicle, or system of transportation which uses vehicles supported on a layer ("cushion") of air on a guideway (track)

infrastructure   – facilities and services associated with the way or access part of transportation; in the case of railways, the infrastructure includes roadbeds and tracks, stations, freightyards, maintenance shops, communications, traffic control, etc.

train-set or self-propelled-car train or multi-unit train   – a train composed of (usually) a fixed number of cars, some or all of which are self-propelled

REFERENCES

References are listed alphabetically according to the senior author, and in chronological sequence for each author. The following abbreviations are used in the listing of references:

ASME   American Society of Mechanical Engineers, New York
CTC   Canadian Transport Commission, Ottawa
FRA   U.S. Federal Railroad Administration, Washington
IEEE   Institute of Electrical and Electronic Engineers, Inc., New York
IUR   International Union of Railways, Paris
RGI   Railway Gazette International, London
RSMA   Railway Systems and Management Association, Chicago
RTC   Railway Transport Committee, CTC, Ottawa
SBB   Schweizerische Bundesbahnen, Bern
TDA   Transportation Development Agency, Ministry of Transport, Montreal
TRF   Transportation Research Forum, U.S.A.

Aldcroft, D. H. (1968), *British Railways in Transition*, MacMillan, London.

AMTRAK (1974), *1974 Annual Report*, National Railroad Passenger Corporation, Washington, D.C.

APEC (1973), "From Out of the West, a New Approach to Rail Transit," *APEC Newsletter*, 17 (8), Atlantic Provinces Economic Council, Halifax, August, 1973.

Atherton, D. L., and Eastham, T. R. (1973), *The Canadian Magnetic Levitation Program*, Annual Conference, Roads and Transportation Association of Canada, Halifax, N.S., October 9-12, 1973.

Bandeen, R. A. (1974), "CN: Buying Cars and Locomotives is no longer Enough," *Railway Age*, pp. 36, 40, November 24, 1974.

Berry, R. S. and Fels, M. F. (1973), "The Energy Cost of Automobiles", *Science and Public Affairs*, pp. 11-17, 58-60, December, 1973.

283

Berton, P. (1970), *The National Dream*, McClelland and Stewart Ltd.

Berton, P. (1971a), *The Last Spike*, McClelland and Stewart Ltd.

Berton, P. (1971b), "What We Once Did We Can Do Again," *Maclean's*, September 1971, p. 79.

Berton, P. (1974), *The National Dream* and *The Last Spike*, McClelland and Stewart Ltd.

Bezdek, R. and Hannon, B. (1974), "Energy, Manpower, and the Highway Trust Fund," *Science*, *185*, 669-675, 23 August, 1974.

Bladen, M. L. (1932), "Construction of Railways in Canada to the Year 1885," *Contributions to Canadian Economics*, *5* (2), 43-60, University of Toronto Press.

Bladen, M. L. (1934), *Contributions to Canadian Economics*, *7* (4), 61-107, University of Toronto Press.

Bonar, J. C. (1950), "Chronological History of Canadian Pacific Railway Company and Antecedent Companies," 37 pp., Vol. 7, *Canadian Pacific Railway Company and its contributions towards the early development and to the continued progress of Canada*.

Campbell, B. (1974), "Era of Poleless Firehouse due in '76," *The New York Times*, 25 February, 1974.

Canada (1917), *Report of the Royal Commission to Inquire into Railways and Transportation in Canada* [Drayton-Acworth Report], King's Printer, Ottawa, 1917, 86 pp.

Canada (1932), *Report of the Royal Commission to inquire into railways and transportation in Canada*, 1931-2 [Duff Report], King's Printer, Ottawa, 115 pp.

Canada (1933a), *House of Commons Debate*, March 7, 1933, pp. 3000-1.

Canada (1933b), *House of Commons Debate*, March 9, 1933, p. 3052

Canada (1951), *Report of the Royal Commission on Transportation* [Turgeon Report], King's Printer, Ottawa, 9 February 1951, 307 pp.

Canada (1961), *Royal Commission on Transportation*, [MacPherson report], Vol. 1, 49 pp.; Vol. 2, 155 pp., Ottawa

Canada (1967), "An Act to Define and Implement a National Transportation Policy for Canada, to Amend the Railway Act and other Acts in Consequence Thereof and to Enact other Consequential Provisions [The National Transportation

Act]," *Statutes of Canada 1966-67*, 14-15-16 Elizabeth II, Chapter 69, pp. 595-670, Ottawa, 1967.

Canada (1970a), "An Act to Define and Implement a National Transportation Policy for Canada [The National Transportation Act]," *Revised Statutes of Canada*, Vol. V, Chapter N-17, pp. 5473-5521, Ottawa, 1970.

Canada (1970b), "An Act Respecting Railways [The Railway Act]," *Revised Statutes of Canada*, Vol. VI, Chapter R-2, pp. 6299-6542, Ottawa, 1970.

Canada (1973), *The National Atlas of Canada*, Department of Energy, Mines and Resources, Ottawa, pp. 203-208.

Canada Grains Council (1972), *Summary of Grains Group Reports on Transportation and Handling of Western Canadian Grain*, Winnipeg, July 1972, 30 pp.

Canada Grains Council (1973), *Fact Sheet No. 1: Grain Handling and Transportation*, Winnipeg, March 1973, 30 pp.

Cann, J. L., and Wilson, J. T. (1968), *Development of a high performance train system for the Montreal-Toronto corridor*, IRCA-UIC "High Speeds" Symposium, Vienna, 17 pp.

Cockshutt, E. P., (1973), *Energy in Transportation*, National Research Council Report No. DME/NAE 1973(3), pp. 25-32, Ottawa.

Chodos, R. (1971), *Right-of-Way*, United Transportation Union, Ottawa, 99 pp.

Chodos,R. (1973), *The CPR: A century of Corporate welfare*, James Lewis & Samuel, Toronto, 178 pp.

Collins, C. G. (1973), "Auto-Train: An Intermodal Breakthrough," *Transportation Research Forum, Proceedings*, 14th Annual Meeting, pp. 81-94, 1973.

Commoner, B. (1973), "Trains into Flowers", *Harper's Magazine*, December 1973, pp. 78-86.

Cottrell, W. F. (1951), "Death by Dieselization: A Case Study in the Reaction to Technological Change," *American Sociological Review, 16* (3), 358-365.

CTC (1967R-74R), *Annual Report* (1st to 8th), Ottawa.

CTC (1970), *Intercity Passenger Transport Study*, Information Canada, 103 pp.

CTC (1971), *An Interim Report by the Railway Transport Committee on the Rationalization of Montreal/Toronto-Vancouver Passenger Train Services*, 4 November, 1971.

CTC (1972a), *Initial Report of the Railway Safety Inquiry*, RTC, CTC, 27 pp., April 19, 1972, Ottawa.

CTC (1972b), *Decisions and Orders*, RTC, CTC, 20 November, 1972.

CTC (1972c), *Waybill Analysis*, "Carload All-Rail Traffic," RTC, CTC, 44 pp., Ottawa, 1972.

CTC (1973), *Third Report of the Railway Safety Inquiry*, RTC, CTC, 7 pp. and 3 appendices, December 28, 1973, Ottawa.

CTC (1974), *Order No. R-18073*, February 12, 1974.

Currie, A. W. (1957), *The Grand Trunk Railway of Canada*, University of Toronto Press, 556 pp.

Currie, A. W. (1967), *Canadian Transportation Economics*, University of Toronto Press, 719 pp.

Darling, H. J. (1974), *The Structure of Railroad Subsidies in Canada*, York University Transport Centre, Toronto, October, 1974.

De Gaulle, C. (1934) *Vers L'armée de métier*, Berger-Levrault, Paris, 211 pp. Also in English, *The Army of the Future*, Lippincott Co., Philadelphia and New York, 179 pp., 1941.

Dorman, R., (1938) *A Statutory History of the Steam and Electric Railways in Canada, 1836-1937*, and *Appendix to* [of maps], Canada Department of Transport, Ottawa.

Emerson, A. H. (1968), "Main Line 25 kV 50 Hz A. C. Electrification of London Midland Region of British Rail," pp. 119-162A, *Performance of Electrified Railways* [Conference on], 14-18 Oct., 1968, IEE Conference Publication No. 50, London.

Fisher, G. T. (1971), 50kV Through the Rockies, *Railway Gazette International*, October 1971, pp. 380-383.

Fisher, G. T. (1972), *Testing of High Performance Electric Locomotives*, IEEE Conference Paper No. C72-941-8-IA, 6 pp.

Fisher, G. T. (1973), Private communication.

Fleming, S. (1876), *The Intercolonial*, Dawson Bros., Montreal, 268 pp.

Fletcher Prouty, L. (1974), "Running the Railroads," *Harvard Business Review*, p. 174, Sept.-Oct. 1974.

Flood, M. (1968), *Payment Systems and their Development in the Railway Running Trades*, Economics and Research Branch, Canada Department of Labour, 106 pp., Queen's Printer, Ottawa.

Fontgalland, B. de (1972), "Europe's Railway of Tomorrow," *Railway Gazette International*, 128 (6), 211-212, June 1972.

Forrester, J., (1971), "Counterintuitive Behaviour of Social Systems," *Technology Review*, January 1971.

Fournier, L. T. (1935), *Railway Nationalization in Canada*, Macmillan Co. of Canada, Ltd., Toronto, 358 pp.

FRA, (1974), *A Review of Factors Influencing Railroad Electrification*, A Report by the Government-Industry Task Force on Railroad Electrification, Federal Railroad Administration, Washington, D.C.

Frech, E. (1974), "Grain Farmers Want a New Rail Deal," *The Globe and Mail*, February 23, 1974, p. 8.

Freedman, S. (1965), *Report of the Industrial Inquiry Commission on Canadian National Railways "Run throughs"*, 163 pp.

Friedlander, G. D. (1968), "Railroad Electrification: Past, Present and Future, *IEEE Spectrum*, pp. 50-65, July 1968; pp. 56-66, August 1968; pp. 77-90, September 1968.

Friedlander, G. D., (1972), "Railroad Revival – On the Right Track," *IEEE Spectrum*, pp. 63-66, August 1972.

Friedlander, G. D., (1974a), "Progress in Rail Transportation," *IEEE Spectrum*, pp. 66-70, January 1974.

Friedlander, G. D. (1974b), "Riding Sweden's Slick Rail System," *IEEE Spectrum*, pp. 53-64, March 1974.

Friedlander, G. D. (1974c), "West Germany - the Phoenix Rises," *IEEE Spectrum*, pp. 62-70, April 1974.

Friedlander, G. D. (1974d), "Germany Automates its Rails," *IEEE Spectrum*, pp. 73-77, July 1974.

Friedlander, G. D. (1974e), "Riding Swiss Rails - an Electrifying Saga," *IEEE Spectrum*, pp. 44-54, August 1974.

Friedlander, G. D. (1974f), "Electronics and Swiss Railways," *IEEE Spectrum*, pp. 68-75, September 1974.

Friedlander, G. D. (1975a), "Transportation Progress," *IEEE Spectrum*, pp. 80-83, January 1975.

Friedlander, G. D. (1975b), "The French (train) Connection," *IEEE Spectrum*, pp. 45-52, March 1975.

Froham, A. L. (1973), "Fighting Fires: Only the Truck is New," *Technology Review*, 75 (6), 36-41.

Glazebrook, G. P. de T. (1938), *A History of Transportation in Canada*, The Ryerson Press, Toronto, 475 pp.

Gratwick, J. (1973), Private communication; *Schematic Listing, Traffic Densities per Subdivision on CNR System*, CNR, Montreal, 1970.

Gunston, B. (1972), "The Aerospace Train," *Flight International*, pp. 536-540, October 19, 1972.

Hammond, R. (1964), *Railways in the New Air Age*, Oxford Univ. Press, 154 pp.

Hanchet, W. H. D. (1972), *Transportation R & D in Canada*. 1972, TDA, Montreal, 1972.

Hanlon, J. (1973), "Magnets Boost High Speed Trains," *New Scientist, 15*, February 1973, pp. 360-362.

Haritos, Z. (1973a), *Rational Road Pricing Policies in Canada*, Cat. No. TT72-3/1973, 182 pp., Information Canada, Ottawa.

Haritos, Z. (1973b), *Transport Costs and Revenues in Canada*, CTC., Ottawa, December 1973, 28 pp.; also *Journal of Transport Economics and Policy, 9* (1), January, 1975.

Harries, H. (1971), *A Review and Summary of Western Canadian Freight Rate Inequities*, Hu Harries & Associates, Ltd., Edmonton, November 10, 1971.

Hirst, E. (1973), "Transportation Energy Use and Conservation Potential," *Science and Public Affairs*, pp. 36-42, November, 1973.

Hoel, L. A. (1973), "What's New in Transit in Europe," *Technology Review, 75*, (8), 54-63, July/August 1973.

Hope, R. (1972), "Three Faces of Japan's State Railway," *RGI*, 128 (10), 372-374, October 1972.

Hopper, A. B., and Kearney, T. (1962), *Canadian National Railways synoptical history of organization, capital stock, funded debt and other general information as of December 31, 1960*, CNR, Montreal, October 15, 1962.

Hubbert, M. K. (1956), "Nuclear Energy and the Fossil Fuels," *American Petroleum Institute*, Drilling and Production Practice, pp. 7-25.

Hubbert, M. K. (1962), *Energy Resources*, National Academy of Sciences, Washington, D.C., Pub. No. 1000-D, 141 pp.

Hubbert, M. K. (1969), "Energy Resources," in *Resources and Man*, National Academy of Sciences, W. H. Freeman, San Francisco, pp. 157-242.

Hunt, J. (1973), "Peyton Chides Labour for Believing Rail Cut Rumours," *Financial Times*, Nov. 29, 1973.

I. Mech. E. (1975), *International Engineering Conference: 150th Anniversary of Passenger Railways, 22-26 September 1975*, The Institution of Mechanical Engineers, London, 1975, 311 pp.

Innis, H. A. (1971), *A History of the Canadian Pacific Railway*, University of Toronto Press, 365 pp.

IUR (1968, 1971, 1972, 1973), *International Railway Statistics*,

Year 1968, 1971, 1972, 1973, International Union of Railways, Paris.

Jenkins, J. O. (1972), "Evaluating Management Information Systems," *Chartered Mechanical Engineer*, pp. 55-56, December 1972.

Jones, D. H. (1973), *Decision, in the Matter of the General Railway Safety Inquiry, and in the Matter of the Public Disclosure of Railway Accident Investigation Reports*, RTC, CTC, May 10, 1973, Ottawa, 56 pp.

Katoaka, H. (1969), "The New Tokaido and New San Yo Lines," pp. 104-109, *Aluminum Cars for Rapid Transit*, Symposium, Aluminum – Verlag GmbH, Dusseldorf, 1969.

Keefer, T. C. (1899), "Presidential Address," Appendix to Proceedings, *Proceedings and Transactions of the Royal Society of Canada*, 2nd series 5, Meeting of May, 1899, pp. 14-15.

Keefer, T. C. (1972), *Philosophy of Railroads and other Essays*, edited, with an Introduction by H. V. Nelles, University of Toronto Press.

Khan, A. M. ed. (1975) *The Surface Transportation Problem in Canada*, Proceedings of panel discussions, 1, 2, 3, Faculty of Engineering, Carleton University, Ottawa, 1975.

Kizzia, T. (1974), "Look What's Happening to AMTRAK," *Railway Age*, pp. 18-21, May 13, 1974.

Klein, R. (1974) *Railroad Electrification*, ASCE/EIC/RTAC Joint Transportation Meeting, Montreal, July 15-19, 1974, American Society of Civil Engineers Meeting Preprint, MTL-66.

Lamontagne, M. (1970, 1972, 1973), *A science policy for Canada*, 902 pp. Vol. 1: "A Critical Review: Past and Present," 1970; Vol. 2: "Targets and Strategies for the Seventies." 1972; Vol. 3; "A Government Organization for the Seventies," 1973; Information Canada, Ottawa.

Legget, R. F. (1973), *Railroads of Canada*, Douglas, David & Charles, Vancouver, 255 pp.

Lewis, C. B. (1971), *A Survey of Canadian Activity in Transportation R & D*, Special Study No. 17, Science Council of Canada, Ottawa, May 1971.

Life (1969), "What Oils the U.S. Mails? Just listen," *Life*, 67 (22), 24-29, 28 November, 1969.

Little, A. D., Inc. (1974), "For the Long Haul," *The Bulletin of*

Arthur D. Little, Inc., No. 509, Cambridge, Mass., September-October, 1974.

Loving, R. (1974), "AMTRAK is About to Miss the Train," *Fortune, 84* (5), 272-275, 278-290, May 1974.

Lukasiewicz, J. (1972), "The Ignorance Explosion: A Contribution to the Study of Confrontation of Man with the Complexity of Science – Based Society and Environment," *Transactions of the New York Academy of Sciences,* Series II, *34*(5), 373-391, May 1972. Also "The ignorance explosion," *Leonardo, 7* (2), 159-163, Spring 1974.

Lukasiewicz, J. (1973a), *Modernization of Railways in Canada*, Faculty of Engineering, Carleton University, Ottawa, 132 pp.

Lukasiewicz, J. (1973b), *The Institutionalization of Canadian Rails's Obsolescence*, Faculty of Engineering, Carleton University, Ottawa, 55 pp.

Lukasiewicz, J. (1975), *Oil and Transportation in Canada and the United States*, Energy Research Group Report ERG 75-1, Carleton University, Ottawa, February, 1975; also *High Speed Ground Transportation Journal*, Fall 1975 (in press). Also, *Energy-Based Rationalization of Transportation in North America*, ASCE/EIC/RTAC Joint Transportation Engineering Meeting, Montreal, July 15-19, 1974; American Society of Civil Engineers Meeting Preprint, MTL-18, 27 pp.

Mackintosh, W. A. (1934), "Railways and Settlement," *Canadian Frontiers of Settlement*, vol. 1, *Prairie Settlements*, Toronto.

Machefert-Tassin, Y. (1975) "Z 7001 Tests Pave the Way for Electric TGVs", *RGI*, June 1975, pp. 213-216.

Marrens, R., and D. Thomas (1975), "STOL Dream Plane a Risk?" *The Globe and Mail*, p. 7, 24 June 1975.

McDougal, J. L. (1968), *Canadian Pacific: a Brief History*, McGill University Press, Montreal.

McLaren, W. S. and Myers, B. B. (1971), *Guided Ground Transportation Study*, Transport Canada, Ottawa, Nov. 1971.

Meadows, D. H., Meadows, D. L., Randers, J., Behrens, W. W. (1972), *The Limits to Growth*, Universe Books, 205 pp.

Mendelsohn, M. (1972), *Productivity Trends in the Canadian Railways, 1956-1968*, CTC Economics Branch, Report 27, 77 pp., Ottawa, January 1972.

Mertins, H. (1972) *National Transportation Policy in Transition*,

Lexington Books, C. D. Heath & Co. Lexington, Mass., 224 pp.

Meyer, J. R. and Morton, A. L. (1974), "A Better Way to Run the Railroads." *Harvard Business Review*, pp. 141-148, July-August, 1974.

Middleton, W. D. (1975), "Electrification: Is it Going to happen?" *Railway Age*, pp. 28-37, March 10, 1975.

Mika, N. and H. (1972), *Railways of Canada*, McGraw-Hill Ryerson Ltd., Toronto-Montreal, 176 pp.

Morison, E. E. (1966), *Men, Machines and Modern Times*, MIT Press, 235 pp.

Morris, R. B. (1972), "Current Collection at High Speeds," RGI, 128 (5), 176-178, May 1972.

Morrison, R. W. (1973), "Responsibility Evaded: Reporting on Technology in the Mass Media," *Science Forum*, 6 (3), 3-6, June 1973.

Morrison, R. W., and Brown, D. (1974), *Technology and Politics: Inside the Black Box*, unpublished manuscript, Carleton University, Ottawa.

Munro, J. M., and Constable, G. A. (1974), "Energy Use in Canadian Transportation: the Patterns of Future Adjustment," *Proceedings, 15th Annual Meeting, TRF*, pp. 589-602.

Muratov, P., and Feldman, E. D. (1972), "Electrification criteria on Soviet Railways," *RGI*, pp. 21-24, January, 1972.

North, F. K. (1975), "Canada Faces an Inevitable Energy Crisis Before the End of this Decade," *Science Forum*, 8(4), August 1975.

Nouvion, F. F. (1971), "Electric or Diesel Traction – The Right Basis for Comparison," *RGI*, October 1971, pp. 377-380.

Nouvion, F. F. (1972), *Diesel and Electric Operation in France*, IEEE Conference Paper No. C-72-936-8-IA, 43 pp.

Nouvion, F. F. (1974), "Electric or Diesel Traction – How The Balance has Shifted," *RGI*, 130 (8), 300-303, August 1974.

NRC (1971-72), *Report of the President 1971-72*, National Research Council, Ottawa.

NEB (1969), *Energy Supply and Demand in Canada and Export Demand for Canadian Energy*, National Energy Board, Information Canada, pp. 175, Ottawa.

O'Hanlon, T. (1974), "The Mess that Made Beggars of Pan Am and T.W.A.," *Fortune*, October 1974.

Pratt, E. J. (1972), *Towards the Last Spike*, Macmillan, Toronto.

Prud'homme, A. (1975) "Evolution of Permanent Way for 300 km/h Lines," *RGI*, pp. 144-148, April, 1975.

Purdy, H. L. (1972), *Transport Competition and Public Policy in Canada*, University of British Columbia Press, Vancouver, 327 pp.

Reid, J. (1975), *House of Commons Debates, 119* (144) 6359-6362, also The Canadian Press, "House Archaic Privy Council Secretary Says," *The Ottawa Journal*, June 3, 1975.

RGI (1972a), "The Right Size of Train Crew," *RGI, 128* (3), 102-102, March 1972.

RGI (1972b), "Japan Prepares for the Next 100 Years," *RGI, 128* (10), 369-382, October 1972.

RGI (1972c), "UIC Working Party Looks at High-Speed Rail Links." *RGI, 128* (3), 105-106, March 1972.

RGI (1973a), "Black Mesa Line," *RGI*, pp. 16-18, January 1973.

RGI (1973b), "UIC Drafts its Master Plan for Europe," *RGI*, p. 429, November 1973.

RGI (1974a), "Cheaper Under the Wires," *RGI*, pp. 172-182, May 1974.

RGI (1974b), "Giant St. Louis Yard May Pioneer Consolidation in US Cities," *RGI*, pp. 486-7, December 1974.

RGI (1975a), "Ten Members in the 120 km/h Club," *RGI*, p. 269, July, 1975.

RGI (1975b), "Waterloo Wins Again," *RGI*, p. 41, February 1975.

Rice, R. A. (1970), *System Energy as a Factor in Considering Future Transportation*, ASME, 70-WA/Ener-8, 19 pp., New York, 1970.

Rice, R. A. (1972), "System Energy and Future Transportation," *Technology Review, 74*(3), 31-37.

Roseman, E. (1973), "Why Provinces Battle for Lower Freight Rates?" *The Financial Post*, 30 June 1973, pp. MI-M2.

RSMA (1974), "Railroad Electrification", *The Railway Management Review, 74*(2), A1-A106, Chicago, 1974.

SBB (1971a) "Zeitliche Ubersichten 1903-1971," *Statistischen Jahrbuch der SBB*, 1971.

SBB (1971b), "Internationale Ubersichten 1970," *Statistischen Jahrbuch der SBB*, 1971.

Shaw, G. B. (1928), *The Intelligent Woman's Guide to Socialism and Capitalism.* Brentano's, New York.

Skelton, D. D. (1916), *The Railway Builders*, "The Chronicles of Canada," P. 9, Vol. 32, Glasgow, Brook & Co., 254 pp.

Southerland, T. C. and McCleery, W. (1973), *The Way to Go: The Coming Revival of U.S. Rail Passenger Service,* Simon and Schuster, New York, 256 pp.

Statistics Canada (1969), *Transportation Service Bulletin*, Issue 1, Cat. No. 50-001, Ottawa, November 1969.

Statistics Canada (1970, 1973), *Railway transport*; Pt. I: "Comparative Summary Statistics, 52-207;" Pt. II: "Financial Statistics, 52-208;" Pt. III: "Equipment, Track and Fuel Statistics, 52-209;" Pt. IV: "Operating and Traffic Statistics, 52-210;" Pt. V: "Freight carried by Principal Commodity classes, 52-211;" Pt. VI: "Employment Statistics, 52-212;" Statistics Canada, Ottawa.

Statistics Canada (1970a), *Transportation Service Bulletin*, Issue 2, Cat. No. 50-001, Ottawa, March 1970.

Statistics Canada (1972), *Electric Power Statistics*, Cat. No. 57-204 Annual, 6503-516, September, 1972.

Stevens, G. R. (1960), *Canadian National Railways*, Vol. 1, "Sixty Years of Trial and Error (1836-1896)," Clarke, Irwin & Co., Ltd., 514 pp.

Stevens, G. R. (1962), *Canadian National Railways*, Vol. 2, "Towards the Inevitable (1896-1922)," Clarke, Irwin & Co., 547 pp.

Stevens, G. R. (1973), *History of the Canadian National Railways*, Macmillan Co., 538 pp.

Summers, C. M. (1971), "The Conversion of Energy," *Scientific American*, Sept. 1971.

Sylvester, R. (1974), "Laughter, the Best Medicine," p. 109, March 1974, *Reader's Digest* (quoted from *Chicago Tribune-New York News Syndicate).*

Takiyama, M. (1974), "Shinkansen in a Changing World," *RGI*, pp. 463-466, December 1974.

Tessier, M. (1973), *The Most Recent Developments in the Field of Very High Speeds in France – Electric Traction and Turbotrains*, International Automotive Engineering Congress, Detroit, Michigan, January 8-12, 1973, SAE Paper No. 730061, 20 pp.

Thompson, N., and Edgar, J. H. (1933), *Canadian Railway Development*, Macmillan, Toronto, 1933, 402 pp.

Toffler, A. (1975), "A Future for Parliaments," *Futures*, pp. 182-183, June 1975.

Transport Canada (1975), *New Transportation Policy and Initiatives*, Directorate of Public Affairs, Transport Canada, Ottawa, June 1975.

Transport Canada (1975a), *Transportation Policy: a Framework for Transport in Canada, Summary Report*, 37 pp., Information Canada, June 1975.

Transport Canada (1975b), *An Interim Report on Inter-City Passenger Movement in Canada*, 150 pp. Information Canada, June 1975.

Transport Canada (1975c), *An Interim Report on Freight Transportation in Canada*, 53 pp., Information Canada, June 1975.

TRF (1972), *Proceedings, 13th Annual Meeting*, 623 pp.

TRF (1973), *Proceedings, 14th Annual Meeting.*, 839 pp.

TRF (1974), *Proceedings, 15th Annual Meeting*, 623 pp.

TRF (1975), *Proceedings, 16th Annual Meeting*, 358 pp.

USA (1974), *Statistical Abstract of the United States*, G.P.O., Washington, D.C.

Watt, K. E. F. (1974), *The Titanic Effect*, Freeman, 268 pp.

Williams, E. W. (1971), *The Future of American Transportation*, Prentice-Hall, Inc.

Winter, C. R. and MacNabb, G. M. (1974), *Energy Supply and Demand in Canada, 1970-2000*, paper 1.3-3, Ninth World Energy Conference, Detroit.

Witkin, R. (1973), "Intercity Trains Ordered to Improve their Quality," *The New York Times*, 28 December 1973.

Index

In this Index 37f means pp. 37 and 38; 37ff means pp. 37, 38 and 39; 37n means footnote on p. 37; plate nos. are shown in bold type; authors of references (see p. 283 *et seq.*) are not listed in this Index except where extensively quoted in the text.

CARLETON CONTEMPORARIES

A series of books designed to stimulate informed discussion of current and controversial issues in Canada and to improve the two-way flow of ideas between people and governments.
Issued under the editorial supervision of *The Institute of Canadian Studies, Carleton University, Ottawa*

THE RAILWAY GAME

J. Lukasiewicz

As world oil is depleted, railways are becoming increasingly important in answering ever-growing transportation needs. Despite the vigorous railway renaissance in Japan and Western Europe, however, North America lags dangerously in technological development and public support for an ailing industry. *The Railway Game* is a constructive study that demonstrates present deficiencies of railway transportation in Canada and the United States, seeking to arouse public concern and to promote a move towards necessary reforms. The book presents a comprehensive history of railway development, stresses present technological and economic realities, and offers sensible proposals for the future. Extensively illustrated with maps, charts and photographs.

McClelland and Stewart Limited
The Canadian Publishers

0-7710-9905-3